Video Editing Basics with Media Composer | First

For Media Composer | First 2020.x Software

Avid Technology, Inc.

Copyright and Disclaimer

Published by Rowman & Littlefield
An imprint of The Rowman & Littlefield Publishing Group, Inc.
4501 Forbes Boulevard, Suite 200, Lanham, Maryland 20706
www.rowman.com

6 Tinworth Street, London SE11 5AL, United Kingdom

Copyright © 2021 by Avid Technology, Inc. and its licensors.

All rights reserved. No part of this book may be reproduced in any form or by any electronic or mechanical means, including information storage and retrieval systems, without written permission from the publisher, except by a reviewer who may quote passages in a review.

Library of Congress Cataloging-in-Publication Data available

ISBN 978-1-5381-4382-7 (paperback)
ISBN 978-1-5381-4383-4 (e-book)

♾️™ The paper used in this publication meets the minimum requirements of American National Standard for Information Sciences—Permanence of Paper for Printed Library Materials, ANSI/NISO Z39.48-1992.

The media provided with this book, and any accompanying course material, is to be used only to complete the exercises and projects contained herein. Rights are not granted to use the footage/sound materials in any commercial or non-commercial production or video.

Product features, specifications, system requirements, and availability are subject to change without notice.

Trademarks

Avid, the Avid logo, Avid Everywhere, Media Composer, Pro Tools, Avid NEXIS, MediaCentral, iNEWS, AirSpeed®, Sibelius, Avid VENUE, FastServe, and Maestro, and all related product names and logos, are registered or unregistered trademarks of Avid Technology, Inc. in the United States and/or other countries. The Interplay name is used with the permission of the Interplay Entertainment Corp., which bears no responsibility for Avid products. All other trademarks are the property of their respective owners. For a full list of Avid trademarks, see: http://www.avid.com/US/about-avid/legal-notices/trademarks

PremiumBeat License Statement

The PremiumBeat music and sound effects included are licensed for use in the context of this Avid training only. If you wish to use the music or sound effects in other projects or applications, additional licensing must be purchased on PremiumBeat.com. Unlicensed use is unlawful and prohibited.

The sale or distribution of this book without its cover is unauthorized. If you purchase this book without a cover, you should be aware that it was reported to the publisher as "unsold and destroyed." Neither the author nor the publisher has received payment for the sale of this "stripped" book.

About Avid

Avid delivers the most open and efficient media platform, connecting content creation with collaboration, asset protection, distribution, and consumption. Avid's preeminent customer community uses Avid's comprehensive tools and workflow solutions to create, distribute and monetize the most watched, loved and listened to media in the world—from prestigious and award-winning feature films to popular television shows, news programs and televised sporting events, and celebrated music recordings and live concerts. With the most flexible deployment and pricing options, Avid's industry-leading solutions include For more information about Avid solutions and services, visit www.avid.com, connect with Avid on Facebook, Instagram, Twitter, YouTube, LinkedIn, or subscribe to Avid Blogs.

ACKNOWLEDGMENTS

Avid Learning Services would like to recognize the following contributors for the development of this book:

Brad McCrystal, Bryan Castle, Jr., and Andy Hagerman.

We would also like to recognize the immeasurable contributions of the worldwide community of Avid Certified Instructors for their ongoing suggestions and comments, based on their experience in the classroom and their professional expertise, which have resulted in the continued improvement of Avid's curriculum.

About the Author

Brad McCrystal began his television career in 1975 as an Operator Trainee with the Australian Broadcasting Corporation. Color had just been introduced and the first-generation B&W quad format videotape machines were replaced by new colour VTR's. While color was an obvious improvement, the new machines were equipped with perhaps a more revolutionary innovation. They introduced electronic control and editing to the videotape department.

For a 3-year period in the early 1980's, Brad moved to a production house where he learned the craft of electronic offline/online editing, a skill that equipped him for the television industry's rapid transition from film to electronic postproduction.

Back at the ABC, Brad began cutting documentaries on the DVision, an early non-linear system. By the late 1990's Brad had trained on Avid's Media Composer and became an Avid Certified Instructor. As the ABC transitioned completely away from linear tape-to-tape editing, he travelled to various ABC centers around the country training News and Production editors in Media Composer. Brad continued as a Senior Editor at the ABC, working on many of the broadcaster's major documentary series.

In 2009 he took up an appointment as Adjunct Teaching Fellow at Bond University on Queensland's Gold Coast. Within the University's Faculty of Society and Design he teaches film students the craft of editing using Avid's Media Composer. Brad also continues as a freelance editor and instructor.

ABOUT THE MEDIA

Avid Learning Services would like to thank our partners for generously providing the media, music, and sound effects used in this course.

EditStock

In proud partnership with Avid, EditStock.com provided much of the footage in this course. Schools have the option to upgrade their footage packages, gaining the following features:

- Un-watermarked footage
- Usage rights for student demo reels
- Additional footage for every project
- Lined scripts and music
- Higher resolutions such as ProRes and RED

EditStock, footage worth Editing. For more information, visit http://www.editstock.com.

PremiumBeat.com

PremiumBeat.com is a curated royalty-free music website that provides high-quality tracks and sound effects for use in new and traditional media projects. The PremiumBeat.com library is sourced from the world's leading producers with exclusive, pre-cleared music. This allows for a smooth licensing experience on popular video-sharing sites like YouTube and Vimeo.

With thousands of handpicked tracks in more than 30 styles, PremiumBeat.com music is ideal for online videos, mobile apps, television, radio, feature films, and other professional applications. Be sure to also check out the PremiumBeat.com blog for the latest news and tutorials on production and post-production. For more information, visit http://www.premiumbeat.com.

CONTENTS

Lesson 1: Introduction to Media Composer | First 1
    About the Media Composer | First software 1
    About This Book 1
    System Requirements 1
    Accessing and Installing the Media Composer | First Software 2
    Course Media 3
    Creating a YouTube Account 4
    Becoming Avid Certified 5
    Avid Certified. Real skills. Proven. 6
  Exercise 1 7

Lesson 2: A Quick Start Guide 9
    Launching Media Composer| First 10
    Opening a Project 11
    The Interface 12
    Playing Media 18
    Review/Discussion Questions 22
  Exercise 2 23

Lesson 3: Getting Organized 25
    Creating a new project 26
    The Bins 26
    Inputting Media 32
    Saving a Project 35
    Review/Discussion Questions 36
  Exercise 3 37

Lesson 4: Ingest 39

    Getting Started 40
    How to Ingest Video Clips 40
    Ingesting Audio Media 49
    Ingesting from Camera Cards 54
    Media Management 56
    Review/Discussion Questions 59

  Exercise 4 60

Lesson 5: Drag and Drop Editing 63

    Deciding Which Part of a Clip to Use 64
    Getting Started 64
    Performing the First Edit 66
    Overwriting a Clip Onto the Timeline 68
    Splicing a Shot Onto the Timeline 69
    Replacing a Shot in the Timeline 70
    Adding Voice Over 72
    Review/Discussion Questions 73

  Exercise 5 74

Lesson 6: Refining the Sequence 77

    Moving Segments in the Timeline 78
    Deleting Segments From the Timeline Using Extract/Splice-in .. 84
    Automatic Selection of Segment Modes 86
    Review/Discussion Questions 87

  Exercise 6 88

Lesson 7: Music and Audio 91

    Locating Audio Cues 92
    Adjusting Audio in the Sequence 95
    Review/Discussion Questions 100

  Exercise 7 101

Lesson 8: Introduction to Transition Effects 105
Creating Visual Transition Effects 106
Accessing effects from the Effects Palette 113
Modifying Effects in the Effect Editor 114
Review/Discussion Questions 119

Exercise 8 120

Lesson 9: Using 3-Point Editing 121
Building Your Sequence with Splice-In 122
Editing with Overwrite 125
Removing Material From a Sequence 126
Review/Discussion Questions 129

Exercise 9 130

Lesson 10: Using Multiple Tracks 133
Overview 134
Working with Tracks 135
Review/Discussion Questions 144

Exercise 10 145

Lesson 11: Assembling a Dialogue Scene 147
The Unscripted Documentary 148
The Scripted Drama 148
Review/Discussion Questions 158

Exercise 11 159

Lesson 12: Trimming Dialogue Scenes 161
Understanding Trim 162
Using Overwrite Trim to Clean up Audio 169
Using Ripple Trim to Adjust Pacing 170
Creating Split Edits 172
Maintaining Sync 173

Review/Discussion Questions 176

Exercise 12 177

Lesson 13: Introduction to Segment Effects 179

Adding Segment Effects 180
Stabilizing Shaky Footage 183
Using Color Correction to Improve the Footage 185
Hiding Jump Cuts with FluidMorph 194
Resizing a Shot 196
Using Standard Keyframes 198
Review/Discussion Questions 200

Exercise 13 201

Lesson 14: Combining Multiple Effects 203

Nesting Effects 204
Review/Discussion Questions 212

Exercise 14 213

Lesson 15: Freeze Frames and Motion Effects 215

Types of Motion Effects 216
Creating Freeze Frames 217
Creating Motion Effects 220
Review/Discussion Questions 226

Exercise 15 227

Lesson 16: Combining Layers and Creating Titles 231

Vertical Effects 232
Creating Titles Using Avid Titler+ 233
Review/Discussion Questions 239

Exercise 16 240

Lesson 17: Exporting Your Video 243

    Exporting Your Video 244

    Review/Discussion Questions 249

Exercise 17... 250

LESSON 1

Introduction to Media Composer | First

Welcome to Media Composer | First and the Avid Learning Series. This book will introduce you to the power of Media Composer software and marks your first step toward developing core skills. The material in this book covers the basic principles you'll need to complete a Media Composer | First project, from initial setup to final output.

This course is designed for those who are new to professional video editing, and also for experienced editors who are unfamiliar with Media Composer software. this book will focus on how Media Composer | First works, making it a perfect introduction to the software for novices and skilled professionals alike. Although this book is not aimed at teaching the theory behind film and television production, the content of this course does provide some background on the craft of editing, making it appropriate for students and others new to the art.

For those interested in gaining official Avid certification, this book is also a valuable introduction for further learning and through the Avid Learning Series curriculum.

About the Media Composer | First software

Media Composer | First is a limited yet feature-rich version of the industry-standard Media Composer family of applications. This version is freely available to anyone interested in learning the craft of film editing and becoming proficient at using non-linear editing software. By learning how to use Media Composer | First, you will be able to transition to the more fully featured versions with ease, making it a great start on the road to a career in Film, Television or video production.

About This Book

This book has been designed to familiarize you with techniques you will use to complete a Media Composer | First project. Each Lesson and exercise will focus on a phase of the editing process, starting with organizing media, assembling a sequence, refining a sequence, creating titles and effects, and outputting your program so that others can view it.

System Requirements

This book assumes that you have a system configuration suitable to run the Media Composer | First software. To verify the most current system requirements, visit:

http://avid.secure.force.com/pkb/articles/en_US/Compatibility/Media-Composer-First-System-Requirements

Your Editing System

Whether you are editing on a laptop or a desktop computer, your hardware requirements are the same.

A Windows or Macintosh system with an internal Hard Drive or Solid-State Drive for running the Operating System and the Media Composer | First application.

An optional external Hard Drive for storing media files. A project can often use large amounts of media, so it is important to have enough storage. In particular, an internal Solid-State Drive may not have enough capacity or throughput for running the computer OS and Applications plus storing and playing back your media files.

One or more computer monitors. While Media Composer | First is designed for use with a single monitor, a second screen is always useful.

Internal or external loudspeakers, or good quality headphones. The ideal setup is a stereo pair of external loudspeakers, but if you are working in a noisy environment, headphones may be a more practical solution.

A mouse or tablet (e.g. Wacom) is generally preferable to using a trackpad on a laptop.

An internal or external Card Reader compatible with the type of media storage in your camera. Alternately, an appropriate input port on the computer to which you can connect your camera for media file transfers.

Accessing and Installing the Media Composer | First Software

To access your free copy of Media Composer | First, go to the Avid web page below and follow the 3-step process outlined on the site.

https://my.avid.com/get/media-composer-first

This process will involve creating a user account with Avid. This account will provide a number of services including keeping track of your downloads and software licenses.

When you have successfully downloaded the Media Composer | First software, open the installation package and follow the prompts. In addition to the Media Composer | First, the Avid Link app is also installed on your computer. Finally, the installation process will add a Media Composer | First taskbar icon (Windows) or Dock icon (Mac OS X), and a shortcut to the application in the Start menu (Windows).

If you experience difficulties with the installation (or operation) of Media Composer | First, there are a couple of immediate things you can do to resolve the issues.

- Go to the Avid Learn and Support web page: **https://www.avid.com/media-composer-first/learn-and-support**
- Search the Lounges or post a question via the Avid Link app.

What is Avid Link?

Avid Link is a free application that gives you direct online access for managing your Avid account and software licenses. Additionally, it provides a convenient way to find, connect, and collaborate with other creative people, promote your work, get discovered, and purchase and manage products—all in the one interface.

You can open Avid Link from the taskbar icon (Windows) or Dock icon (Mac OS X), or from the Start menu (Windows). The Avid Link tray icon is always available, so even if you close Avid Link with the window close button, it is minimized to the tray, and can be open again by clicking the tray icon.

There is also a mobile version of Avid Link that you can download from the Apple App Store or from Google Play. It will keep you connected with your editing community even when you are not sitting at your desktop computer.

Course Media

The course media designed to accompany this book can be downloaded from EditStock.com (see "Downloading Media" in this lesson). Once the media is downloaded, you will then need to place the media files in the correct locations on your system (these steps are covered in "Installation Instructions", also in this lesson).

Downloading Media

The link below allows you to download the media you will need for this book. Optionally, you can also enter your name and email, sign up with EditStock, and browse their library.

1. Go to **https://editstock.com/products/media-composer-first** for instructions.
2. Click on the Download Project Files image to download a ZIP file containing the media.

Installation Instructions

After you download a media zip file, unzip the file and you will see a folder called Media Composer | First Course Materials. There are five sub folders:

- Avid MediaFiles
- Avid Projects_Student
- Music
- Rock Climber QTs
- Ski Field_Footage

These files need to be located in specific locations on your system. Please follow the instructions (below) exactly, or you may not have access to all the project files and media that you will need for this book.

1. Make sure Media Composer software is installed and that you have opened the application at least once. Opening the application creates important folders that you will use during this process (to learn more about launching Media Composer | First, please refer to the "Launching Media Composer | First section of the second lesson). After launching the application, you can safely click the "quit" button in the Project Selection Dialog box you just opened).

2. Copy the contents of the "Avid Projects_Student" folder to the following location:
   - Windows: **Library\Public Documents\Shared Avid Project**
   - Mac: **Users\Shared\AvidMediaComposer\Shared Avid Projects**

3. Copy the contents of the **Avid MediaFiles** folder to the following location:
   - If you have a locally attached external hard drive you have designated for use with Media Composer, navigate to the root level of that drive and copy the folder to that location.
   - Windows: **drive:\Users\Public\Documents\Avid Media Composer**
   - Mac: **Users\Shared\AvidMediaComposer**
     Note that if an Avid MediaFiles folder already exists at this location, double-click it to reveal the MXF folder within, and drag the folder or folders from the downloaded content (for example, Avid MediaFiles/MXF/10) into the MXF folder on your hard drive.
4. Drag the following folders to a convenient location for easy access, such as the Desktop, or your Documents folder:
   - Rock Climber QTs
   - Ski Field_Footage
   - Music

 Do not rename or move the Avid MediaFiles folder located on the media drive. Media Composer | First uses these folders, with these specific folder names, to locate media files.

Creating a YouTube Account

Media Composer | First provides a number of ways to create a final product, including direct methods of publishing a finished video to YouTube, Vimeo or Facebook.

For the purposes of this course, if you do not already have an account with YouTube, it is recommended that you create one before starting this course:

1. Go to the YouTube web site (**https://www.youtube.com**).
2. Click the **Sign In** button in the upper right-hand corner.
3. When the sign in page loads, select **Create Account**.
4. After you have created an account, click your account icon in the upper right-hand corner.
5. From the menu that appears, choose **Settings>Account**.
6. In your account page, click the **Create a New Channel** link.
7. Finally, you will be prompted to name the channel. When you're done, click the **Create** button.

In the following lessons, when you publish your first video to YouTube from Media Composer | First, you will log in to your YouTube account via the Media Composer | First interface.

Becoming Avid Certified

Avid certification is a tangible, industry-recognized credential that can help you advance your career and provide measurable benefits to your employer. When you're Avid certified, you not only help to accelerate and validate your professional development, but you can also improve your productivity and project success. Avid offers programs supporting certification in dedicated focus areas including Media Composer, Sibelius, Pro Tools, Worksurface Operation, and Live Sound. To become certified in Media Composer, you must enroll in a program at an Avid Learning Partner, where you can complete additional Media Composer coursework if needed and take your certification exam. To locate an Avid Learning Partner, visit **https://www.avid.com/education**.

Media Composer Certification

Avid offers two levels of Media Composer certification:

- Avid Media Composer User Certification
- Avid Media Composer Professional Certification

User Certification

The Avid Certified User program offers an established and recognized credential, valuable to both academic users and industry professionals alike, to distinguish you from your peers and accelerate your career. Certification requires you to display a firm grasp of the core operational skills, workflows, and concepts of non-linear editing on a Media Composer system. To achieve certification, you must take and pass both the MC101 and MC110 courses and corresponding exams.

Courses and books associated with Avid Media Composer User Certification include:

- Media Composer Fundamentals I (MC101)
- Media Composer Fundamentals II (MC110)

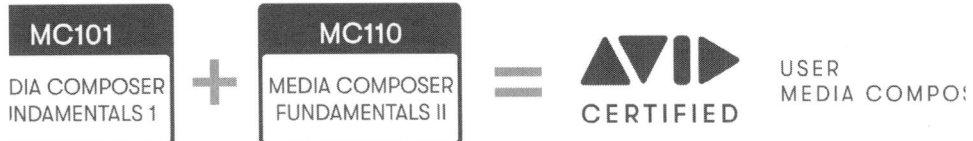

These Avid Media Composer User Certification courses can be complemented with MC239, *Color Grading with Media Composer and Symphony*.

Media Composer | First courses develop similar skills and competencies as those taught in the *Fundamentals I* course. First-certified users can achieve Avid Certified User status by going on to take the *Fundamentals II* course at an Avid Learning Partner location.

Professional Certification

The Avid Media Composer Professional Certification builds on Avid Media Composer User Certification and prepares editors to competently operate a Media Composer system in a professional production environment. Professional certification requires a more advanced understanding of Media Composer, including advanced tools and workflows involved in creating professional programs.

Courses and books associated with Avid Media Composer Professional Certification include:

- Media Composer Professional Editing I (MC201)
- Media Composer Professional Editing II (MC210)

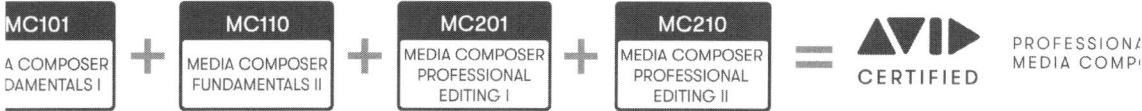

These Avid Media Composer Professional Certification courses can be complemented with MC239, *Color Grading with Media Composer and Symphony*.

For more information about Avid's certification programs, please visit **http://www.avid.com/en/education/certification**.

Avid Certified. Real skills. Proven.

Avid User and Professional Certifications help professionals attain and demonstrate the skills and credentials they need to increase their value, competency, and efficiency in the highly competitive media industry.

Avid certification programs cover the broad range of Avid products, as well as other professional roles, including Avid Certified Instructor, Avid Certified Support Representative, and Avid Certified Administrator.

If you want to learn more about Avid training, please check out our official online resource by going to **www.avid.com/education**. There you will find information about our training partners, specifics on the various certification options available, and detailed course descriptions for each course offered through our programs.

EXERCISE 1

 Exercise Break 1.1
Put what you have learned into practice.

GOALS

- Create an Avid account
- Download and Install the Media Composer | First application
- Download and Install the Media Composer Course Materials
- Create a YouTube account

In preparation for this course (refer to lesson one for details):

1. Set up an account with Avid and download and install Media Composer | First.
   a. Media Composer Installation page: **https://my.avid.com/get/media-composer-first**
2. Download and install the Course Materials.
   a. **https://editstock.com/products/media-composer-first**
3. If necessary, set up a YouTube account and create a channel.
   a. Go to the YouTube web site **(https://www.youtube.com)**.
   b. Click the Sign In button in the upper right-hand corner.
   c. When the sign in page loads, select Create Account.
   d. After you have created an account, click your account icon in the upper right-hand corner.
   e. From the menu that appears, choose Settings>Account.
   f. In your account page, click the Create a New Channel link.
   g. Finally, you will be prompted to name the channel. When you're done, click the Create button.

LESSON 2

A Quick Start Guide

In this lesson you, will learn the quickest way to open and play a project, and publish it when you're finished. You don't need a lot of knowledge to begin with – this lesson will just give you a taste of how Media Composer | First works. Later lessons will help fill in the blanks.

At the end of this Lesson you will find review questions and an exercise to help consolidate what you've learned, and let you try a few things for yourself.

Media: Rock Climber

Duration: 40 Minutes

GOALS

- **Launch Media Composer | First**
- **Create a project**
- **Recognize the basic components of the Media Composer | First interface**
- **View clips and sequences in bins**
- **Navigate through clips and sequences**
- **Start a sequence**
- **Play a sequence**
- **Publish a sequence**
- **Exit Media Composer | First**

Launching Media Composer| First

Launching Media Composer | First is like launching any other application on your computer. The Media Composer | First icon appears as shown in Figure 2.1.

Figure 2.1 The Media Composer | First application icon looks identical in Windows and Mac OS.

To launch Media Composer | First in Windows:

- Double-click the **Media Composer** icon on the desktop, or select **Start > All Programs > Avid > Avid Media Composer**.

To launch Media Composer | First in Mac OS X:

- Click the **AvidMediaComposer** icon in the Dock to launch the application, or double-click the **AvidMediaComposer.app** found in the **Applications > Avid Media Composer** folder.

While launching, the Media Composer | First splash screen appears as your computer loads the application. (See Figure 2.2.)

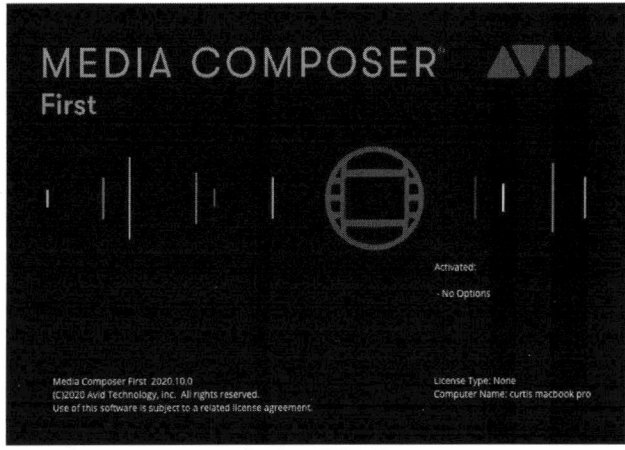

Figure 2.2 The Media Composer | First splash screen.

 The Media Composer I First splash screen shows you the specific version of Media Composer IFirst that you are running and identifies various components as they are loaded. If you ever encounter a problem, this information will be helpful to the Avid Customer Support representative assisting you.

After Media Composer | First has loaded, you will see the dialog box shown in Figure 2.3. The window consists of a number of useful areas.

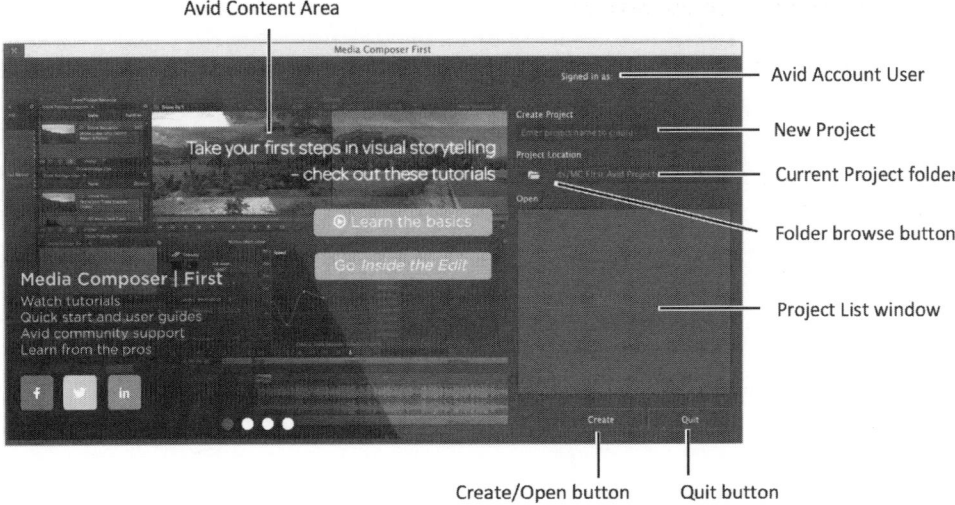

Figure 2.3 The Project Selection dialog box is used to locate and open existing projects, and to create new ones.

- **Avid Account User**: The name you use to log in to your Avid account appears here.
- **Current project folder**: This field indicates the location where Media Composer | First will save a new project or is currently looking for opening existing projects.
- **Folder browse button**: Use this button to set a custom location for accessing or saving your projects (Media Composer | First creates a default folder for saving projects when you launch the application for the first time).
- **New Project**: Click in this field and type a name to create a new project.
- **Project list**: This section lists projects located in the Current Project Folder directory. Click the name of an existing project to select it.
- **Create/Open button**: This button changes its name and function depending on whether you have clicked in the Create Project window or selected an existing project in the Project List.
- **Quit Button**: This button allows the user to exit Media Composer | First.
- **Avid Content Window**: When connected to the internet, this section of the dialog box provides direct access to additional content and/or tools available from Avid. For example, you can access Quick Start videos if you want to learn more about using the application.

Opening a Project

Opening an existing project in Media Composer | First is fairly straightforward. Projects are displayed in the Project Selection Dialog Box according to the **Current Project Folder** setting:

1. If your desired project is in the folder indicated in the **Current Project Folder** field, it will appear in the **Project List Window** (if it is not, click the folder icon to the left of the field to choose the location for your projects). For the purposes of this book, your projects should be in one of the following locations:

- Windows: **Library/Public Documents/Shared Avid Projects/Avid Projects_Student**
- Mac: **Users/Shared/AvidMediaComposer/Shared Avid Projects/ Avid Projects_Student**

2. Double-click the desired project in the **Project List Window**. The project will open. For the purposes of this lesson, choose **Rock Climber Demo**.

The Interface

The Media Composer | First interface has three primary sections, shown in Figure 2.4. When a new project opens these sections (called panels) are set up and ready to start. They are:

- **Bins** – where you save clips and sequences (you'll learn more about clips and sequences in the next section). The term 'bin' comes from the physical container used by film editors to hang strips of celluloid film in an editing room.
- **Composer** – where you watch and listen to your clips and sequences.
- **Timeline** – where you see graphical representations of sequences.

Figure 2.4 The Media Composer | First interface

The Bins Window

You will spend most of your time using the Bins window to access your source material from open bins.

To open the bins from the **Bins Container** pane:

1. Double-click the icon to the left of the bin named **Clips**.
2. Double-click the icon to the left of the bin named **Sequences**.

Both bins' contents will appear as tabs in the Bins pane. To see the contents of an open bin, click the tab for that bin at the top of the Bins pane.

There are two types of clips in the Clips bin of the **Rock Climber Demo** project. Each type can be identified by the clip icon to the left of the clip name:

This icon represents a video clip. A **video** clip will contain images with or without audio. For the purposes of this lesson, double-click any video clip. The clip will appear in the left side of the Composer window.

This icon represents an **audio** only clip. It does not contain any images.

The Sequences bin contains a single sequence, identified by this **sequence** icon. For the purposes of this lesson, double-click the **Rock Climbing** sequence. The sequence's elements will appear in the Timeline window and in the right ride of the Composer window.

The Composer Window

By default, the Composer window, shown in Figure 3.9, displays two monitors. The left one, called the Source monitor, is used to preview and select the parts of source clips that you will edit into the timeline. The right window, the **Record** monitor, displays the resultant sequence as you edit clips together.

Across the top of the Composer window are displays that show you the names and other information relating to your clips and sequences. (Each info window contains a menu with additional info and options.) The numeric windows display Timecode values for both the source clip and sequence.

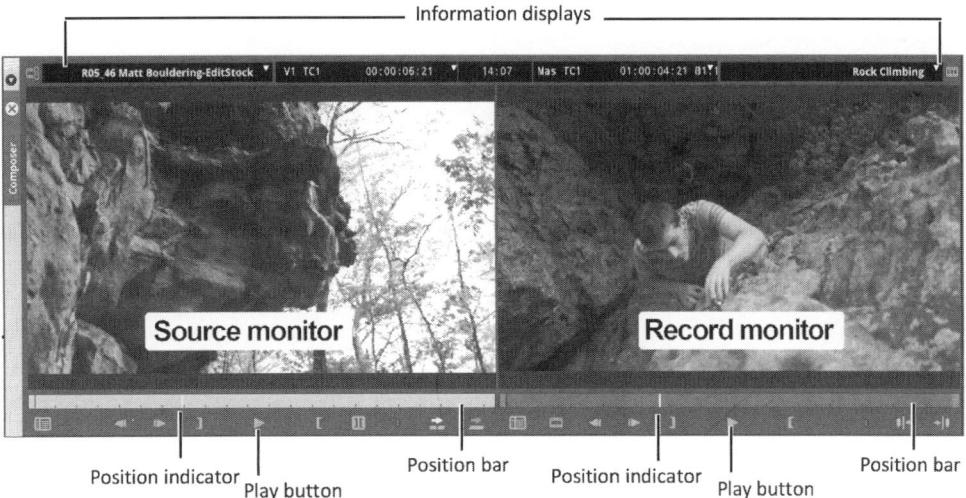

Figure 2.5 The Composer Window

Transport Buttons and Editing Tools

Buttons and tools are arranged in a single row across the bottom of the Composer window.

Some buttons appear under both monitors, and each set corresponds to its respective monitor—e.g. the Play button under the Source monitor plays the source clip, while the play button under the Record monitor will play the sequence.

To play a clip in the Source monitor, or a sequence in the Record monitor, do one of the following:

- Click the **Play** button under Source or or Record monitor, depending upon what you want to view.
- Select the monitor you want to view and press the **space bar** on your computer keyboard.
- Select the monitor you want to view and press the **5 key** on the QWERTY section your computer keyboard (not the numeric keypad, if your computer has one).

To stop a clip or sequence from playing, do one of the following:

- Click the **Play** button again under either monitor.
- Press the **space bar** on your computer keyboard.
- Press the **5 key** on the QWERTY section your computer keyboard (not the numeric keypad, if your computer has one).

You can quickly scrub through a clip by clicking and dragging the green **Position indicator** in the green Position bar under the Source monitor. You can similarly scrub through a sequence by clicking and dragging the blue **Position indicator** in the blue Position bar under the Record monitor, or by clicking and dragging the blue **Position indicator** in the Time Bar or Timecode track in the Timeline panel as shown in Figure 3.10.

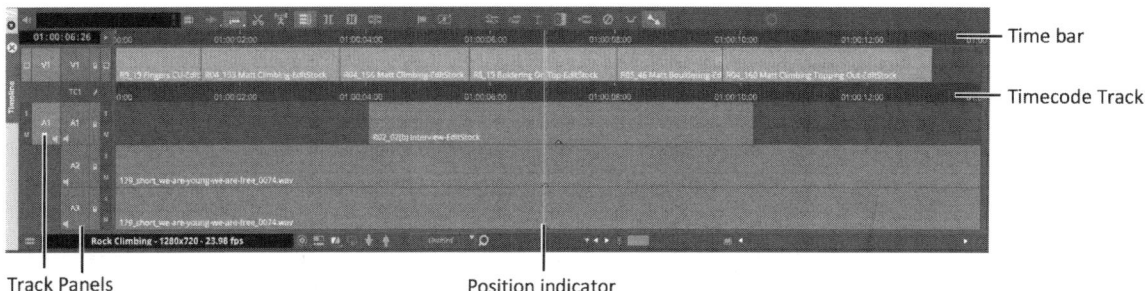

Figure 2.6 The Timeline window

The Timeline

The timeline window displays a graphical representation of your sequence, organized into tracks. Figure 3.10 shows a fairly basic sequence is displayed which is watchable when you play the timeline. It contains one video track and three audio tracks. Sequences can have more tracks depending on the need. Media Composer | First supports up to 4 video tracks and 8 audio tracks. The Timeline panel will be empty until a sequence is loaded into the Record monitor.

 A sequence is a series of video and audio segments that comprise your film or your program. It is the thing you're creating. The Timeline is the panel you build it in.

In the Timeline panel, a sequence is played from left to right. The Position indicator is the vertical blue line that marks the current frame of video and audio being shown in the Record monitor. The blue Position indicator is commonly referred to as the "playhead" and is can also be viewed as the Position indicator in the Record monitor.

To play or navigate through a sequence in the Timeline, select the Timeline panel and use any of the interface buttons under the Record monitor or shortcut keys on the keyboard. You can also scrub through the sequence by clicking and dragging the blue Position indicator in the timeline panel from within either the Time bar or the Timecode track.

The Track Panel, shown in Figure 3.10, displays two columns of Track buttons. The left green column (in the image V1 and A1) refers to the tracks available in the clip loaded in the Source monitor.

The right blue column (in the image V1, A1, A2 and A3) refers to the tracks available in your sequence. The Track selector buttons allow you to control the source and record tracks when editing. You will use the Track selector buttons extensively while editing in Media Composer | First.

Working with Windows

As you learned so far in this chapter, when you open up a Media Composer | First project, you'll see a basic workspace containing a **Bin Container**, a **Composer** window, and a **Timeline** window. These windows initially open as connected panels. You can also see that these connected windows have a vertical title bar on the left side of each window which includes a tab with the name of the window.

Each of these windows can exist in one of two states:

- A **Docked Window** is a window that is connected within the paneled user interface. When you open up a new sequence, windows will appear in this state.

- A **Floating Window** is a window that is undocked.

Armed with this information, you have a great deal of flexibility in arranging your windows to suit your workflow, for example:

- Any window (docked or floating) can be docked into a section of the paneled user interface. Figure 2.7 shows the Effect Editor window (which you'll learn about in a later lesson), a floating window, being dragged (by clicking on the vertical title bar fo the window) into the paneled user interface. The green tabs indicate all of the locations that the window *could* be dragged to, with a highlighted section indicating where the window would be dropped when the mouse is released. A docked window can be similarly moved simply by clicking on the window's title bar and dragging it to a new location within the paneled user interface.

Figure 2.7 Docking a floating window

A docked window can be made into a floating window in one of two ways: Either click on the window's title bar and drag it out of the paneled user interface, or click the pop-up menu button at the top of the title bar and choose **Float This Panel**, as shown in figure 2.8.

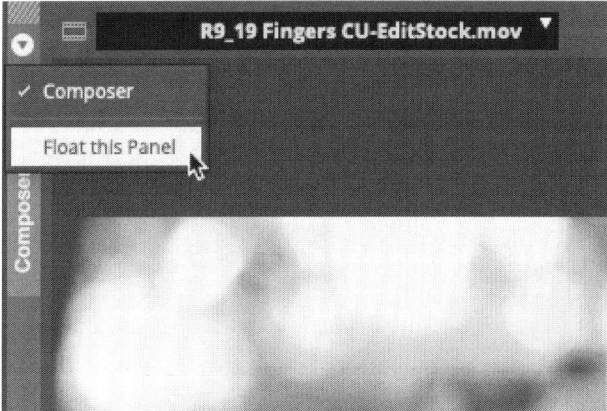

Figure 2.8 Un-docking the Composer window

A window (either docked or floating) can be vertically tabbed in order to function in multiple ways, but occupy the same space. For example, you might decide that you rarely need the Source Browser (a window you'll learn more about in the next lesson) and the Timeline window at the same time. You can have both windows occupy the same space by tabbing them. In order to tab the window, hold the **Option** key (mac), or **Alt** key (windows), and drag the window to the window with which you want to share space. A green bar will indicate the destination window, as shown in figure 2.9. When you're done, you'll see both names indicated in the vertical title bar (see figure 2.10) – just click the name of the window that you want to view.

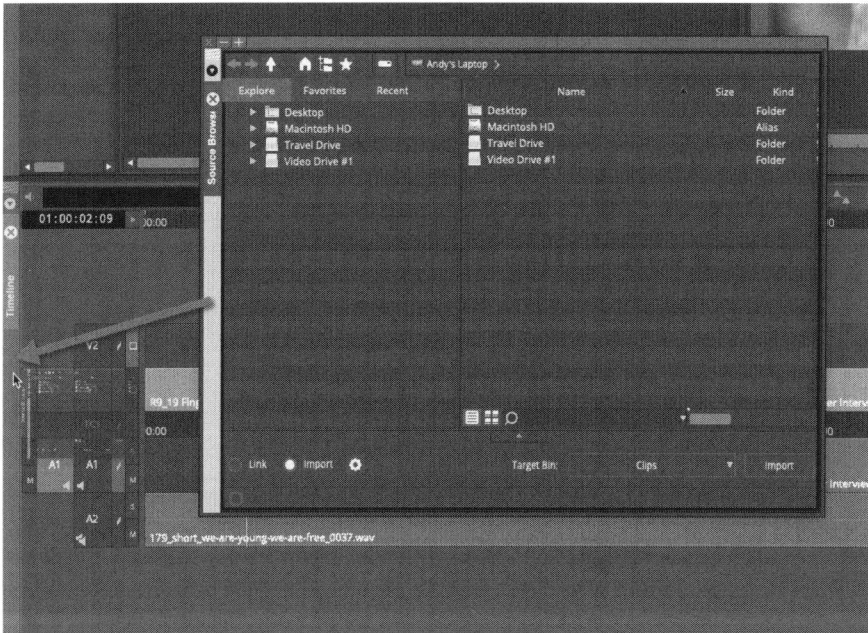

Figure 2.9 Creating a tabbed window

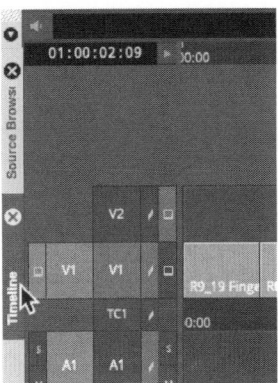

Figure 2.10 Choosing the desired window, from a tabbed window

Managing your Workspace

Different phases of production might call for different window layouts (or *Workpaces*), and you might want to save one of your customized layouts as well. Media Composer makes this easy in two different places – the **Windows>Workspaces** drop-down menu, and the **Workspace Bar**.

Figure 2.11 shows the **Windows>Workspaces** drop-down menu. The top segment includes some standard layouts, some of which you'll use during the course of this book. If you want to customize one of these top four workspaces, make whatever changes you want, and then click the **Save Current** menu item. To restore any of these to their default layout, click the **Restore Current to Default** menu item.

To create a brand-new workspace, click the **New Workspace** menu item. You'll be prompted to name your new workspace (in this case, I named mind "This Works"), and it will appear below the default workspaces.

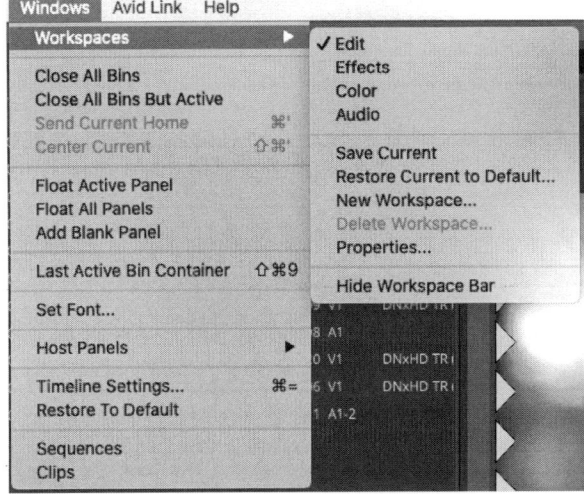

Figure 2.11 The Windows>Workspaces menu

The **Workspace Bar** mirrors much of the functionality of the Workspaces menu and is easily accessible from the rightmost side of the user interface. As you can see in figure 2.12, the default and new workspaces are displayed, with the active workspace indicated by a small triangle.

Figure 2.12 The Workspace Bar

At the bottom of the Workspace Bar, you'll see a small pop-up menu button. Clicking this button will reveal menu items similar to the Windows>Workspaces menu.

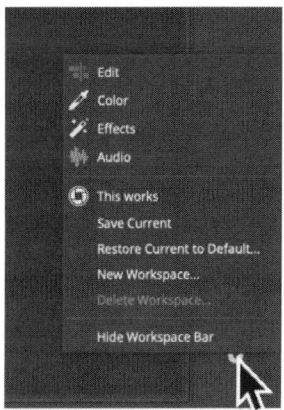

Figure 2.13 The Workspace Bar pop-up menu

Playing Media

If you've been following the steps so far in this lesson, you've opened up a project named **Rock Climber Demo**, double clicked on a clip in the **Bins** section (putting the clip into the Source Monitor) and opened (again by double-clicking) a Sequence named **Rock Climbing**. Now let's look at the different ways that you can play your media.

All created bins are displayed as a list on the left side of the **Bins Panel**, in an area called the **Bins Container**. Figure 2.14. All open bins are displayed as tabs on the right side in the area called the **Bins Pane**. By default, Media Composer | First opens the Clips bin and the Sequences bin in the Bins Pane. You can view the contents of each bin by selecting the corresponding tab at the top of the Bins Pane.

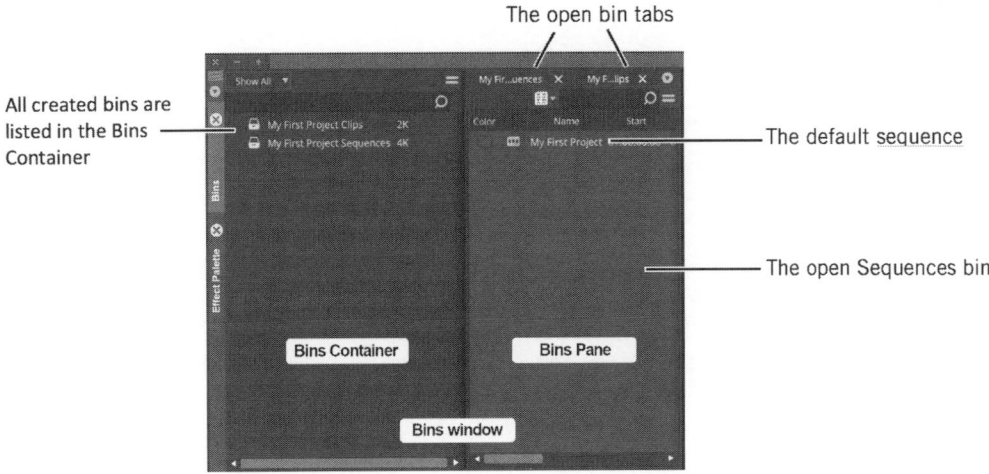

Figure 2.14 All bins are listed in the Bins Container while open bins are displayed in the Bins Pane.

Playing a Clip in the Bin

To play a clip in the clip bin, select **Frame View** from the **Bin Display** options. Select the **thumbnail** for the clip that you want to play and either:

- Press the **Space Bar** on your computer keyboard, or
- Press the **number 5** key on QWERTY section your computer keyboard (not the numeric keypad, if your computer has one)

Playing a Clip in the Composer Window

To play the clip in the Composer window, depending on the bin view, do either:

- In the bin, double click the **thumbnail** in Frame View or the **clip icon** in Text View
- **Click and drag** the thumbnail or clip icon onto the left-hand screen in the Composer panel of the Media Composer | First window

The left-hand screen is called the **Source Monitor** and is shown in Figure 2.15. You cannot open a clip in the right-hand screen of the monitor section. To play the clip, select the Source Monitor and do one of the following:

- Click the **Play** button under the Source Monitor
- Press the **Space Bar** on your computer keyboard
- Press the **number 5** key on the QWERTY section your computer keyboard (not the numeric keypad, if your computer has one)

Figure 2.15 The clip is displayed in the Source Monitor of the Composer window.

Playing a Sequence

In Figure 2.5, you will see that both the source monitor and record monitors have Position Indicators, shown as green and blue lines respectively. In Figure 2.6 you will also see that in the timeline area, there is a blue Position Indicator located at the end of the sequence. The blue Position Indicators show the location of the current frame being displayed in the Record Monitor.

To go to the beginning of the sequence, do one of the following:

- Press the **Home** key on your computer's keyboard (if your computer has a **Home** key). The blue Position Indicator will jump to the beginning of the sequence.

- Click and drag the blue **Position Indicator** under the Record Monitor to the left, back to the start of the sequence. The Position Indicator in the timeline section will move similarly.

- In the Timeline section click and drag the blue **Position Indicator** in either the Time Bar (at the top of the timeline section) or the TC1 timecode track (adjacent to the A1 and V1 tracks) to the left, back to the start of the sequence. The Position Indicator in the Record Monitor will move similarly.

As you drag a Position Indicator, you navigate through time, or scrub through the video and audio in the sequence. (The Source Monitor also has a Position Indicator that allows you to scrub through a clip.)

To play from the beginning of the sequence, click either the Record monitor or Timeline panel, then do one of the following:

- Click the **Play** button under the Record Monitor

- Press the **Space Bar** on your computer keyboard

- Press the **number 5** key on the QWERTY section your computer keyboard (not the numeric keypad, if your computer has one)

The J-K-L Keys

A very useful set of transport controls on the keyboard are the J-K-L keys. They can help you to quickly navigate backwards and forwards through a source clip or sequence. Many editors use these keys because they are grouped together in a convenient location on the keyboard, and with practice they make searching through clips and sequences very efficient. The J-K-L keys work as follows:

- Depending on what you want to navigate through, select the Source monitor, Record monitor or timeline window.
- To play a clip or sequence forward at real-time speed, press the **L** key once.
- To stop, press the **K** key.
- To play backward at normal speed, press the **J** key once.
- To play forward faster than real-time, press the **L** key repeatedly. Every time you press the **L** key, the system will play faster, at 1×, 2×, 3×, 5×, and 8× normal speed, respectively.
- To play backward faster than real-time, press the **J** key repeatedly. The system will in reverse by the same increments: 1×, 2×, 3×, 5×, and 8× normal speed.
- To play backward at 1/4 speed, press and hold the **K+J** keys.
- To play forward at 1/4 speed, press and hold the **K+L** keys.
- Hold down the **K** key, and then quickly tap either **J** or **L** to move just one frame at a time.

Saving and Closing the Project

Media Composer | First automatically saves a project at regular intervals as you work and when you close the project.

To close a project:

1. From the menu bar, select **File > Close Project**. Media Composer | First will display the Project Selection dialogue box.
2. To exit Media Composer | First, Click the **Quit** button.
3. A small window opens, asking you to confirm that you want to leave the application, as shown in Figure 2.16. Click the **Leave** button to exit Media Composer | First.

Figure 2.16 The confirmation window

Review/Discussion Questions

1. When Media Composer | First launches, what is the name of the window that allows you to create a project or open an existing project?

2. What are the names of the 3 primary windows in the Media Composer | First interface?

3. Where are clips and sequences saved?

4. What does the Source monitor in the Composer window display?

5. What does the Record monitor in the Composer window display?

6. From what two places can you view and play a clip?

7. What does the Timeline window display?

8. How can you scrub through a sequence?

9. What are the buttons you can press to play a clip or sequence?

10. How does the function of the L key differ from the Space Bar when playing a clip or sequence?

EXERCISE 2

Exercise Break 2.1
Put what you have learned into practice.

GOALS

- Open a Project
- Manage Workspaces
- Play Media
- Save the project

1. If not already launched, launch Media Composer | First, and open the **Mountain Climber Demo** project.

2. If not already visible in the Bins Pane, open the Clips and Sequences bins by double-clicking on the bin icons to the left of the bin names in the Bins Container panel.

3. From the **Clips** Bin, double-click the **R04_156 Matt Climbing-Editstock** clip to open the clip in the source monitor.

4. Play the clip in the source monitor.

5. From the **Sequences** bin, double-click the **Rock Climbing** sequence.

6. Play the sequence in the record monitor.

7. From the **Tools** menu, open the **Source Browser** window. The window will appear initially as a floating window. Bring the window into the paneled user interface, by tabbing it with the **Timeline** window.

8. From the Tools menu, open the **Audio Mixer**. This window will also open as a floating window. Dock the window in the paneled user interface, placing it between the Bins window and the Composer window.

9. Save the window arrangement as a **New Workspace**, named Lesson 2.

10. Recall the default **Edit** workspace.

11. Save your project, and close Media Composer | First.

LESSON 3

Getting Organized

In Lesson 2 you learned how to quickly open and play a project. In this lesson you will become more familiar with the Media Composer | First interface and learn how to create a new project, import media, and better organize and manage the assets you work with in a project.

Your exercise at the end of the lesson will be to create a new project in preparation for the following lessons.

Media: Rock Climber

Duration: 45 minutes

GOALS

- Creating a new Project
- Organize project assets using bins and folders
- Input media
- Save a project and close the application

Creating a new project

As you learned in lesson 2, after Media Composer | First has launched, you will see the Project Selection dialog box shown in Figure 3.1. This is where you can create a new project.

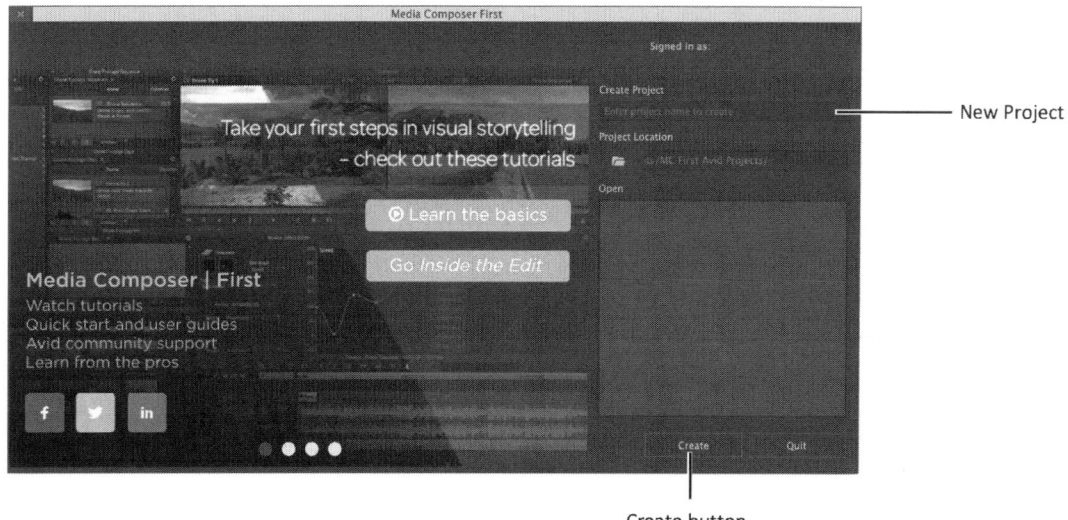

Figure 3.1 The Project Selection dialog box is used to locate and open existing projects, and create new ones.

To create a new project:

1. In the Project Location dialogue area click on the **folder icon** and navigate to the destination in which you want to save your project. If you don't already have one, create an **Avid Projects** folder on your destination drive. It is important to take a note of the file path so you can easily locate your project the next time you launch Media Composer | First.

2. Click in the **Create Project** field of the Media Composer First window and type a name for your project.

3. Click the **Create** button at the bottom of the window.

4. The initial Media Composer First window will close, and the Media Composer | First interface will open with a default workspace.

The Bins

The **Bins panel** is the central hub of Media Composer | First. The Bins panel consists of two panes. The left pane is the **Bins Container pane** which allows you to organize a project's resources into Bins and Folders while the right pane shows open bins in the **Bins pane**. Open bins appear as a series of tabs across the top of the Bins pane.

Lesson 3 ■ Getting Organized

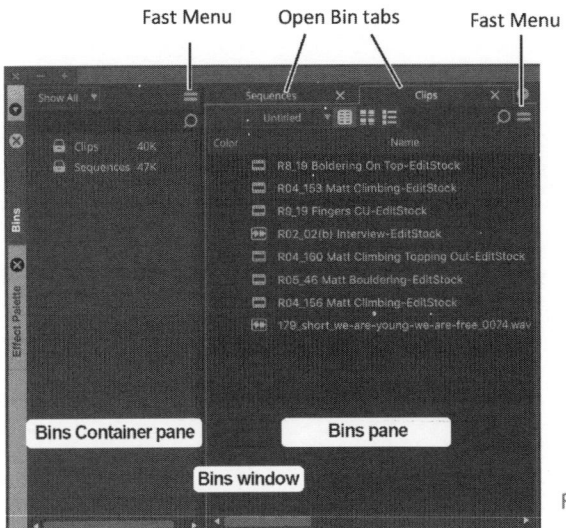

Figure 3.2 The Bins Window is the central hub of your project.

You can change the relative areas of the Bins Container pane and the Bins pane within the Bins panel. To change the relative sizes of the panes:

1. Position the mouse over the border between the Bins Container and the Bins pane. The mouse pointer changes to a left/right arrow.

2. **Click + drag** the border to change the relative sizes of the two panes.

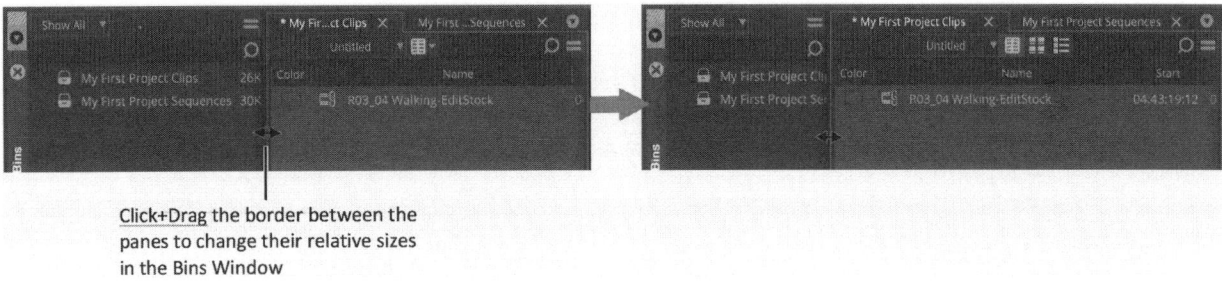

Figure 3.3 Changing sizes of panes in the Bins Window

The Bins Container pane

When a new project is created, Media Composer | First automatically populates the Bins Container with two bins. They are both named after the project, with one having the word 'Sequences' appended to the end of the name while the other has 'Clips' appended to the end.

The Sequences bin is one of the most important bins needed in a project. When you save all your sequences into the Sequences bin, you will never struggle to find where you have saved your work.

No footage can be saved directly within the Bins Container pane itself. All 'assets' you use in a project must be saved in bins. Bins hold audio and video master clips, subclips, sequences, titles, effects, graphics . . . everything! You can also put bins into folders to further organize a project.

- Media Composer | First is limited to a maximum of 5 bins per project.
- You can rename a bin by clicking on the text in the Bin Container pane and typing the new name. (Both bins in Figure 3.2 have been renamed from the default names.)

Essential Tool: The Fast Menu

At the top of the Bins Container pane, as well as in each Bin and in the Timeline window there is a button called the Fast menu. The menu in each location provides different options, but the icon is always the same (see Figure 3.4).

Figure 3.4 The Fast menu button

As the name suggests, the Fast Menu allows quick access to features and controls that you often need in managing each pane or window.

Bin views

A bin is far more than just a container. It also functions as a database, a light table, and a log sheet. There is a special layout that goes with each of these functions. As mentioned in Lesson 2, there are three different options for viewing a clip in the clip bin – **Text View, Frame View** and **Script View**. Each can be selected by clicking on their respective Bin Display button. Depending upon how wide the Bins Pane is, the Bin Display buttons can be selected from a row of buttons or a drop menu at the top of the pane, as shown in Figure 3.5.

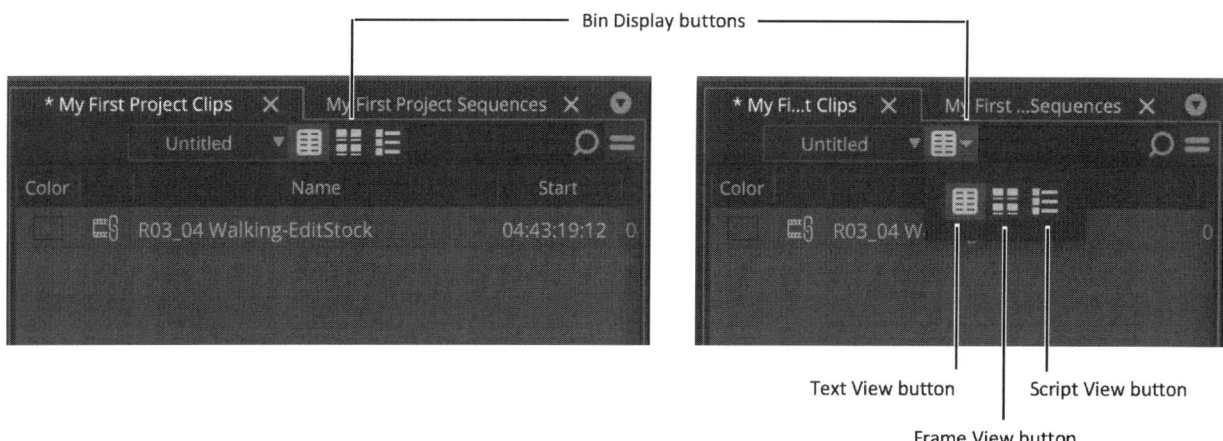

Figure 3.5 Bin Display buttons

Figure 3.6 shows a clip displayed as either a row of text in columns of information or as a representative thumbnail image.

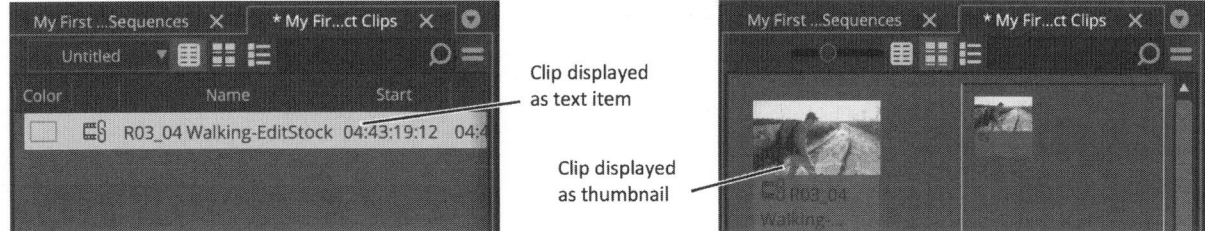

Figure 3.6 A clip displayed as either text or a thumbnail image in the bin

Text View

Text view displays all the contents of the selected bin in a list. Think of it as the "database" mode. This is the default view.

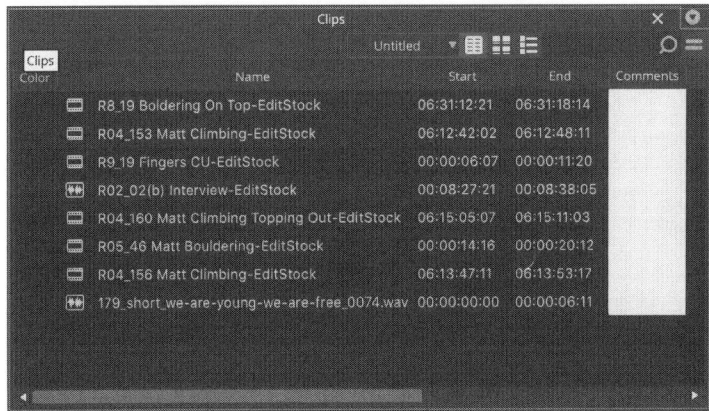

Figure 3.7 The Bin in Text View

In Text view, you can choose to display additional columns of information associated with each clip.

To select the columns of information to display, do the following:

1. Open the **Fast Menu** at the top of the Bins pane.
2. Click **Choose Columns...**
3. The Bin Column Selection window will open, as shown in Figure 3.8.
4. Click the columns of information you want to display in the bin. Selected columns are highlighted.
5. Click the **OK** button. The Bin Column Selection window will close, and the selected columns of information will be displayed in the bin. You may need to use the scroll bar at the bottom of the bin to see the various columns of information.

When in Text view, you open a clip in the Source monitor by double-clicking a clip icon or dragging the icon to the Source monitor.

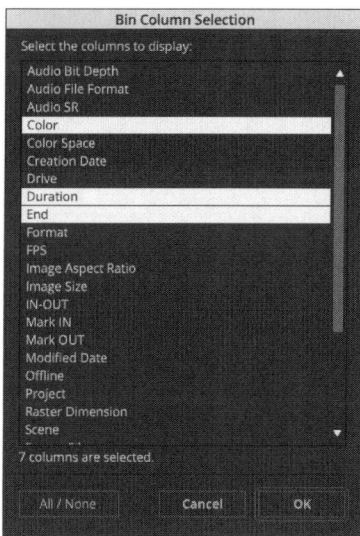

Figure 3.8 The Bin Column Selection window

Frame View

Frame view shows you a representative frame or 'thumbnail' for each item in the bin, as shown in Figure 3.9. It's like looking at your shots on a virtual light table. This can be a convenient way to work if you prefer a thumbnail view of a clip rather than only a textual description.

Figure 3.9 Frame view is like a light table, letting you see a thumbnail image for each asset rather than just a name.

Frame view enables you to easily rearrange your shots just by clicking and dragging them to a new location. You are free to arrange the thumbnails in any way you like. Perhaps you want to group shots together based on what they look like rather than their text descriptions? Or perhaps you might want to arrange a series of shots in an order that could effectively tell a story when edited together in the timeline? Frame view gives you the ability to organize your clips in any way that suits your workflow.

When in Frame view, you open a clip in the Source monitor by double-clicking a thumbnail or dragging it to the Source monitor.

Script View

The third way of viewing bin contents is Script view. It is a combination of Text view and Frame view with an added Comments field. You can type anything you like in the Comments field, but it is typically used for logging notes and keywords to help you manage your footage and easily search for clips.

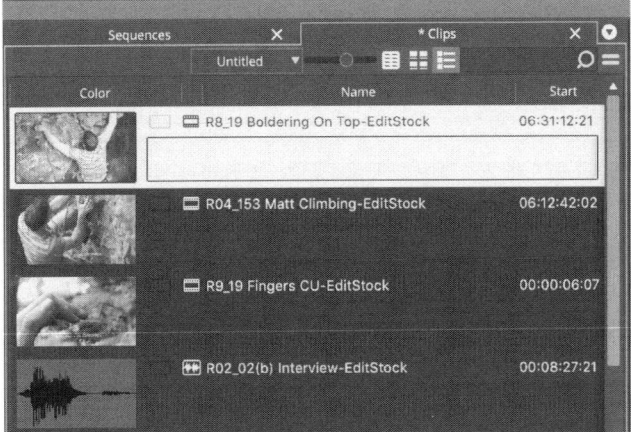

Figure 3.10 Script view combines the visual thumbnail of Frame view and the statistical info of Text view with a handy area to type in Comments.

The comments you enter into Script view also automatically appear in the Comments column of Text view.

The columns in the last Text view you displayed prior to switching to Script view also determines the columns of information shown in Script view.

When in Script view, you open a clip in the Source monitor by either double-clicking a thumbnail or the clip icon or by dragging the thumbnail or icon to the Source monitor.

Creating Bins and Folders

To create a bin, do one of the following:

- Click the **Fast Menu** at the top of the Bins Container pane and select **New Bin**.
- Right-mouse click in the Bins Container pane and select **New Bin**.
- From the menus at the top of the user interface, select **File > New > New Bin**.

When a new bin appears in the Bins Container, the text is highlighted ready for you to type an appropriate name.

1. For the purposes of this lesson, the new bin has been named **Music**. See Figure 3.11.
2. A second bin has also been created and named, **Sound effects**.

To create a folder, do one of the following:

1. From the **Fast Menu**, select **New Folder**.
2. Right-mouse click in the Bins Container pane and select **New Folder**.

A new folder will appear in the Bins Container with the text highlighted. In this case, the folder has been renamed **Audio**.

To move bins into a folder:

1. Click and drag the bins into the folder. To view the bins in the folder, click the **disclosure triangle** to the left of the folder icon as shown in Figure 3.11.

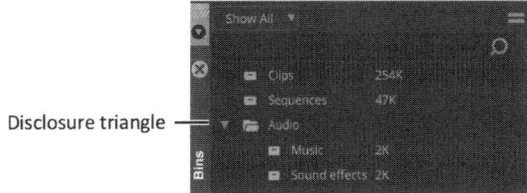

Figure 3.11 Folder with bins inside

2. To delete the folder and the bins contained in it, select the **folder** in the Bins Container window and reopen the **Fast Menu**. Click **Delete Selected Items**. A red Trash Can will appear in the Bins Container with the folder inside it. Figure 3.12.

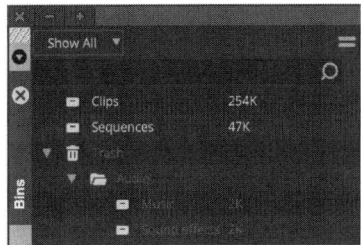

Figure 3.12 The Trash can and contents

3. To empty the Trash can, from the **Fast Menu**, click **Empty Trash**. A window will appear asking you to confirm that you do in fact wish to permanently delete the bins from your drive. Click the **Empty Trash** button to delete the bins.

Inputting Media

Before you can begin editing, you will need to access media files for your project.

- **Media files** are the video and audio files you will work with.
- You can access your video and audio media by creating **clips** in your project that link to those media files. **Clips** are the graphic representation of media in the Media Composer | First application and include information about the corresponding media files and where they are located.
- Sequences are the result of editing clips together to create a story.
- Clips and sequences are saved in 'container' files called bins.

Adding a clip to a bin

At the top of the Bins pane select the **tab** for the open bin in which you want to save clips. As shown in Figure 3.7 the Clips bin has clips in it already but any newly created bin will be empty.

1. Using your computer's operating system, navigate to the media that you want to add to your bin. (In the case of this lesson, the media you need to do the exercise resides in the folder in which you've downloaded the media that accompanies this book. You will need to locate and open the folder named **Rock Climber QTs**. It contains media files as movies. You will be working extensively with these files in later lessons.)

2. Align the size and position of the media folder in your operating system's browser, so you can see both it and the open bin in the Bin pane of Media Composer | First. From the folder, select one of the files and do one the following:

   - In a Windows computer, hold the **Alt** key and click and drag the file into the open bin in the Bins Pane.

   - In a Macintosh computer, hold the **Option** key and click and drag the file into the open bin.

You create a direct link between a clip and its corresponding media file by holding down the Alt/Option key as you drag the file into a bin. An alternative method is to import the media file. This makes a copy of the media file and creates a clip in a bin that references the copy. You'll learn more about the difference between importing and linking to media in lesson 4.

What is Timecode?

Each frame in a video or audio file is assigned a discrete number to help you and the computer locate specific frames as you edit. The numbering system, called 'timecode' adds a time stamp to each frame with an 8-digit number registering hours, minutes, seconds and frames. For instance, when you start recording in your camera the first frame might be assigned the number 00:00:00:01. Each successive frame will have a number that increments over time. The second frame in the recording would therefore be numbered 00:00:00:02 and so on. Depending upon the frame rate of your video, the last 2 digits will count frames up to the maximum number of frames per second. Let's say you are shooting at 30 frames per second. The last two digits in the timecode display will increment from 01 to 29 then reset to 00 at which point the seconds column will increment by 1. As you play a clip in the Source monitor or a sequence in the Record monitor, the corresponding timecode display will rapidly show you the changing time stamps. In our example, for the first second of the clip, this is how the timecode window display would change:

Frame 01 - 00:00:00:01
Frame 02 - 00:00:00:02

Frame 29 - 00:00:00:29
Frame 30 - 00:00:01:00

Adding a clip into the Timeline

The empty Timeline window displays the message, '**Drag clips here to start editing**'. You can add an entire clip into the Timeline, by either:

- Clicking and dragging the **thumbnail** or **clip icon** from the clips bin into the **Timeline** window.
- Clicking and dragging a **clip** shown in the **Source Monitor** into the **Timeline** window.

The first time you drag a clip to the timeline, the **Project Properties** dialog box will open, as shown in Figure 3.13. This dialog box give you the option of either matching the project's **Raster** (frame size) and **Edit Rate** (frame rate) to those of the clip, or allowing you to select another combination of settings from the drop lists in the window. Unless you have a good reason to change from the default settings, press the **OK** button.

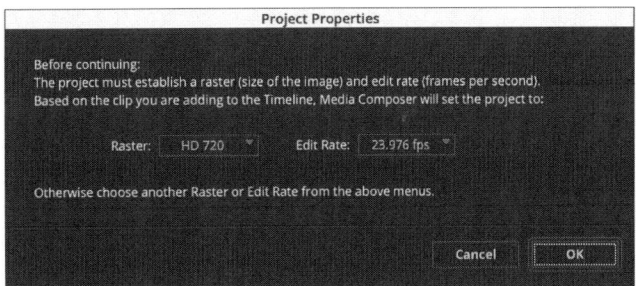

Figure 3.13 The Project Properties window

The clip will be added into the Timeline. If you have used any other video editing software in the past, you will be familiar with the concept of a timeline. The Timeline is a graphical representation of the video and audio contained in a sequence. In the example shown in Figure 3.14 the sequence comprises two horizontal tracks – **V1** for the video and **A1** for the audio.

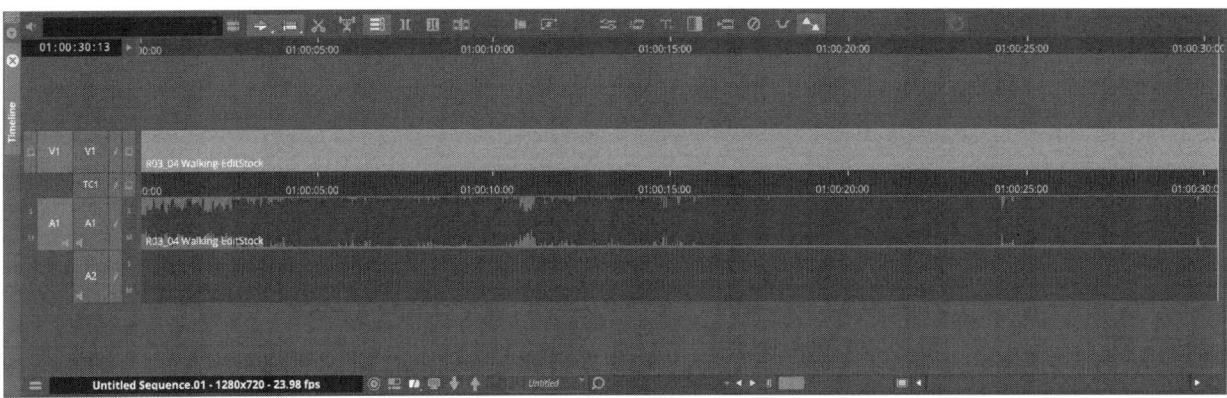

Figure 3.14 The clip edited into the Timeline

The sequence also appears in the right-hand screen of the Composer section (this area of the composer section is called the **Record Monitor**).

Figure 3.15 The sequence is displayed in the Record Monitor of the Composer window

Saving a Project

Media Composer | First automatically saves an open project at predetermined intervals as you work.

You can also do a manual save at any time. From the menu bar at the top of the interface select the displayed option: **File > Save Bin** or **File > Save All Bins** or **File > Save All**. The save option that appears will depend on what needs to be saved to update the project.

When you close a bin, Media Composer | First will automatically save any changes that you have made to the contents of that bin.

When you close a project, Media Composer | First will also do a final save of the entire project.

To close a project:

1. From the menu bar at the top of the application choose **File>Close Project**.
2. A progress bar will be shown as the project file saves any final changes. This process usually happens very quickly.
3. When the project has been saved, you are returned to the Project Selection dialog box.
4. If you need to keep working, you can open another project or create a new project.
5. To close the application, click the **Quit** button in the Project Selection dialog box. A confirmation window will open. Click the **Leave** button to close Media Composer | First or click the **Cancel** button to return to the Project Selection dialog box.

Review/Discussion Questions

1. Which window serves as the central hub of your project?

2. What is a bin?

3. Where are open bins displayed?

4. What are the 3 different ways in which you can display the contents of a bin?

5. What is the difference between a clip and a media file?

6. How can you easily create a clip from a media file?

7. How can you easily add a clip into the Timeline?

8. What do the tracks in the Timeline show you?

EXERCISE 3

Exercise Break 3.1
Put what you have learned into practice.

GOALS

- Create a new project
- Create and name bins
- Save the project

1. Launch Media Composer | First and from the Project Selection dialogue box create a new project named **My First Project_(Student ID)** and click the Create button.

2. The Media Composer | First interface will open with 2 default bins in the Bins Container pane. The two bins will also be open and tabbed in the Bins pane. Notice that the default Sequences bin will already have a sequence saved in it.

3. You will need 3 bins for this project. In the Bins Container pane create an extra bin. Click on the text for each bin and rename them: **Sequences, Clips, Music**.

4. (If this exercise is being used to assess what you have learned in this lesson, you may need to take a screen capture of the Bins panel so that it clearly shows the 3 bins you have created and renamed in the project. You may also need to take screen captures upon completion of the following steps in this exercise.)

5. Create clips from different media files in the folder **Rock Climber QTs** by **Alt/Option** dragging them into the Clips bin. Input a minimum of three clips into the bin.

6. From the clips bin, drag and drop one of the new clips into the default sequence that is already open in the Timeline window. The Project Properties window will open. Click **OK**. The clip will snap to the **head** (beginning) of the sequence.

7. From the bin, drag and drop another of the new clips into the timeline. Depending on where you position the clip, it will automatically snap to either the head or tail of the clip that is already in the sequence or it will snap to where you have parked the blue Position Indicator. Move the new clip so it snaps to the head of the sequence. When you drop the new clip, notice what happens to the original clip in the timeline. Some of it, if not all of it, has been replaced by the new clip.

8. Undo that edit by going to the menu bar at the top of the screen and selecting **Edit > Undo Overwrite,** or by using keyboard shortcuts (**Control+Z** (Windows) or **Command+Z** (Mac)). The second clip will be removed from the timeline and the first clip should be restored to its original position in the timeline.

9. This time, drag and drop the same clip so it snaps to the end of the timeline. If you play the sequence, you will see you have edited the two shots together. This is a very easy way to start assembling a sequence, producing an unrefined result commonly called a **rough cut**. You will learn how to take more control of the editing process in later lessons - this is just to give you a feel for it.

10. Drag and drop the third clip so it snaps to the end of the timeline.

11. If required, take a screen capture of the timeline, clearly showing the three clips in the sequence.

12. Close the project and exit Media Composer | First.

LESSON 4

Ingest

In Lesson 3 you created a new project containing three bins named Clips, Sequences and Music.

You will start this lesson by creating another project and then learning more about how to locate media files and make them available to use in that project. , a process that is commonly referred to as "ingest".

At the end of Lesson 4 your exercise will be to ingest media files into your project.

Media: Ski Field and Rock Climber QTs

Duration: 40 minutes

GOALS

- Identify the difference between importing and linking media files
- Use the Source Browser to locate media files
- Import & Link to video files
- Import & Link to audio files
- Input from camera cards
- Deleting media & master clips
- Understand Project & Media management

Getting Started

To follow along with the steps of this lesson, you'll need to create a new project and organize your bins, which you learned to do in Lesson 3:

1. Launch Media Composer | First and create a new project named **Ski Field_(Student ID)**.

2. You will need three bins in this project, so you'll need to create one new bin in addition to the two preexisting bins. Name the three bins: **Clips, Sequences and Music**.

How to Ingest Video Clips

In video production workflows, the process of bringing media into a project is commonly called "ingest". There are two ways to ingest media into a Media Composer | First project:

Link: Linking connects original media files directly to the project in Media Composer | First. Unlike importing, it does not copy the media files or move them to a specific location. Media Composer | First will access the files from their current location and in their current formats.

Import: Importing makes copies of the original media files. The copies are different in two ways to the original files; Firstly, the copying process produces files that are of a different type to the original files. Secondly, those copies are saved in a specific location determined by Media Composer | First.

Using the Source Browser

In Lesson 3, you ingested media into a project by dragging the files from their original location. The Source Browser provides a better way of ingesting media, giving you more control over how the files are handled. The Source Browser has options to either Link or Import media and is the main tool for getting media files into Media Composer | First, and is shown in Figure 4.1.

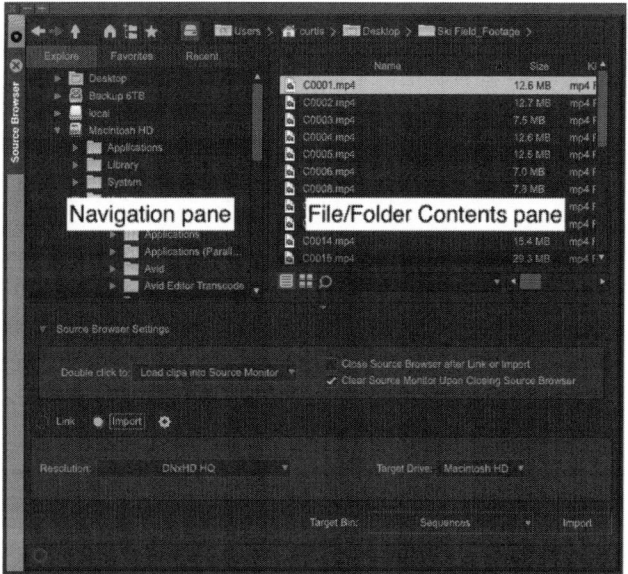

Figure 4.1 Use the Source Browser to Link or Import clips into your project

Before using the Source Browser, open the **Clips** or **Music** bins in your **Ski Field_(Student ID)** project, then do one of the following:

- Select **File > Input > Source Browser**.
- Click the **Fast Menu** in an open bin and select **Input > Source Browser**.
- Right-click in an open bin and select **Input > Source Browser**.

Linking to a Media File

In the Source Browser, the Navigation pane allows you to search all the drives and folders attached to your computer.

1. In the Navigation pane, navigate through the drives and folders until you find the folder **Ski Field_Footage**. Double-click the folder.

2. The File/Folder Contents pane will show you the files contained in that folder. Like a bin, the File/Folder Contents pane allows you to view its contents in either Text or Frame view. You can change the view by clicking the appropriate icon in the lower left of the folder contents pane.

3. Select all the files by doing one of the following:
    - Click the first file, then **Shift+click** the last one you want to select. All files in between are selected.
    - **Ctrl+click**(Windows) or **Command+click** (Mac) each file you want.
    - **Ctrl+A** (Windows) or **Command+A** (Mac) to select all files.

4. At the bottom left corner of the Source Browser, select the **Link** radio button.

5. At the bottom right corner of the Source Browser, use the **Target Bin** selection menu to choose the **Clips** bin from the list, as shown in Figure 4.2. Because you had already opened the **Clips** and **Music** bins, they should both appear in the Target Bin drop-down list. You also have the choice of creating a new bin. The choice you make in this menu will determine into which bin your media will be added.

Figure 4.2 Target Bin selection

 If you did not open any bins in your project, the Target Bin selection window will only display New Bin... You will need to open the bin you are interested in before you see it in the Target Bin selection menu.

To link to the selected media files, do one of the following:

- At the bottom right corner of the Source Browser click the **Link** button.
- **Drag and drop** the media files from the File/Folder Contents pane to the open Clips bin.

The Clips bin now contains Master Clips linked to the media files you had selected. Each clip icon displays 2 links of a chain on the right side, telling you that the project has linked to the media files, and not imported them.

Notice in Figure 4.3 that the clips have adopted the names of the media files.

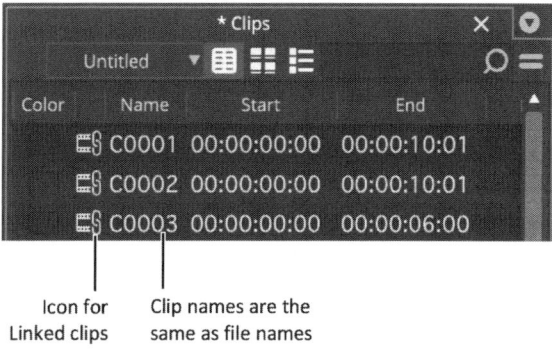

Figure 4.3 The linked Master Clips

Close the Source Browser by clicking the **red X** in its top corner or clicking the **purple X** in the white circle in the side bar, shown in Figure 4.4.

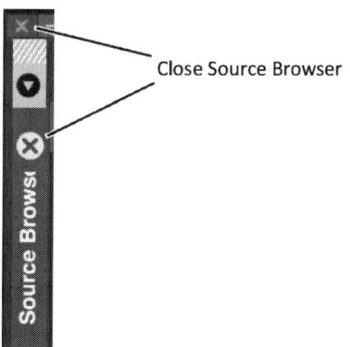

Figure 4.4 Closing the Source Browser

Importing a Media File – Preparing for Import

Because the process of importing (as opposed to linking) makes a new copy of a media file and saves it in a folder determined by Media Composer | First, it is important that you specify what type of file you want to create and on what drive you want to save it. For consistency, you typically only need to do this once at the beginning of a project, and then leave it alone. Set it and forget it.

To specify the type of file you want to create and where to save it, do the following:

1. From the Menu Bar at the top select **Avid Media Composer > Preferences...** . The Settings window opens as shown in Figure 4.5.

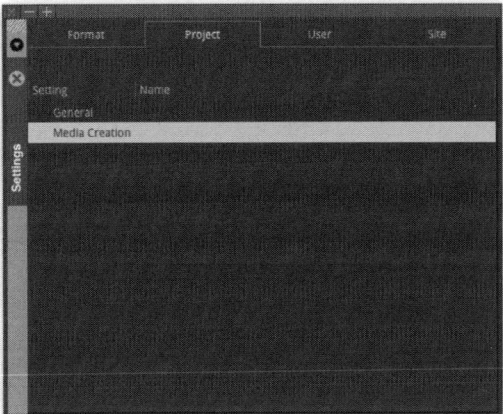

Figure 4.5 The Settings window

2. From the top of the Settings window, select the **Project** tab.
3. Double click the **Media Creation** option. The Media Creation window opens as shown in Figure 4.6

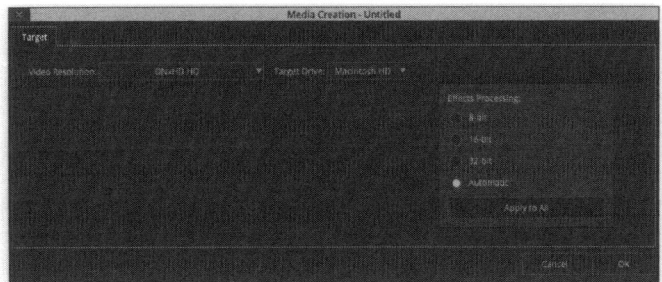

Figure 4.6 The Media Creation window

4. Click in the **Video Resolution** drop list to reveal all the available resolutions that you can use to create the copy of a media file. In Media Composer | First, the **Video Resolution** setting determines which **codec** will be used to create the media.

    Codecs are designed to reduce the file size of video media while preserving as much of the image quality as possible. The process of reducing the file size is called **compression** or **encoding** and the process of recovering the video image from the compressed file is called **decompression** or **decoding**. The term 'codec' is actually a contraction of the two words **enCOde** and **DECode**.

    As you can see from the list shown in Figure 4.7, there are a lot of codecs to choose from.

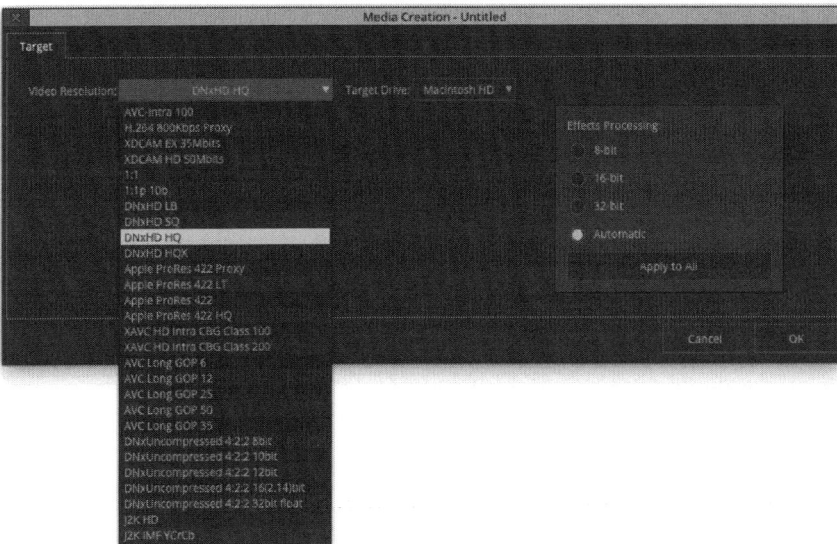

Figure 4.7 The Video Resolution drop list

Choosing a video resolution (codec) can be a daunting task. For an editing application, the need to constantly decompress and recompress heavily compressed video files can take up a lot of computer resources and this can significantly impact on performance. Avid DNxHD or Apple ProRes are both codecs that produce excellent quality copies of video media files without taking up too much drive space. Because they are not heavily compressed, they are also easy for editing applications to process, especially when you are creating visual effects that combine multiple video files.

5. To select the drive in which you want to save the copy of the media file, click the **Target Drive** drop list.

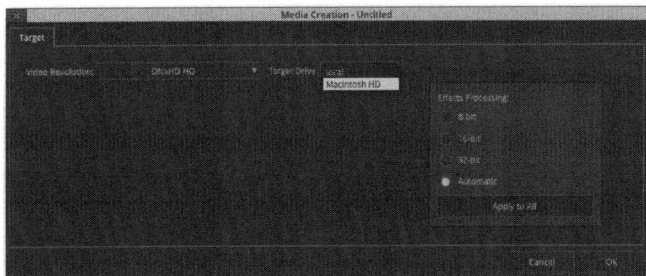

Figure 4.8 The Target Drive drop list

6. The drives listed here will be dependent on your computer system. Media Composer | First will list all drives that it determines are suitable for saving media files. Select the drive that best suits your working environment. It is always preferable to store media files on a drive other than the drive in which the operating system and applications reside.

7. When you have finished choosing a Video Resolution and Target Drive, click the **OK** button and the Media Creation dialogue box will close.

8. Close the Settings window by clicking on the **red X** at the top of the window.

Frame Size and Frame Rate

Modern video cameras often allow you to change settings so you can record your video at different frame **sizes** and frame **rates**. The frame size is the physical dimension of each video frame, and usually expresses the width x height of the frame in '*pixels*' (a contraction of the term *picture elements*). The frame rate refers to how many video frames have been recorded each second and is expressed as 'frames per second'. It is generally the best idea to import media files so the media copies are created with the same frame size and frame rate as the original footage.

When you are working with material that you have shot yourself, you will probably already know what the frame size and frame rate settings of your camera were at the time of filming. However, that is not always the case, especially when you are working with footage shot by someone else.

Before importing media files, it is advisable to check to see what those settings were. Fortunately, that information is imbedded in the media files themselves.

To check the settings of the **Ski Field** footage:

1. Using your computer's operating system, open the **Ski Field_Footage** folder.

2. Select any one of the media files and open it in a media player (such as Quicktime Player*)*.

3. Quicktime Player can display information about the media file in a window called the **Inspector**, as shown in Figure 4.9.

   In the case of the **Ski Field** footage, the frame size is shown to be 1920 x 1080 and the frame rate is 25 frames per second. It also tells you the original files were encoded using the H.264 codec.

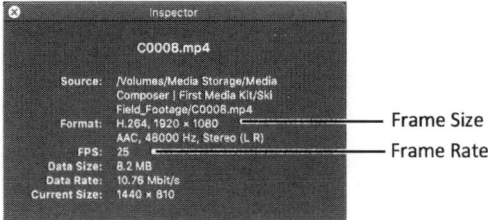

Figure 4.9 The Inspector in Quicktime Player

Importing a Media File – Importing

Armed with this information, you are now ready to import media into your Media Composer | First project. To import some of the same media files you linked to earlier, do the following:

1. In Media Composer | First, reopen the Source Browser and, in the Navigation pane, select the **Ski Field_Footage** folder.

2. From the File/Folder Contents pane, select one or more of the media files. Don't select too many as the importing process can take a while. This example is just to show you how the process works.

3. At the bottom left of the Source Browser, select the **Import** radio button. If this is the first time you have imported video media into a project, Media Composer | First will ask you what frame size and frame rate you want to apply to the media files it will create., and the Project Properties dialogue box will open.

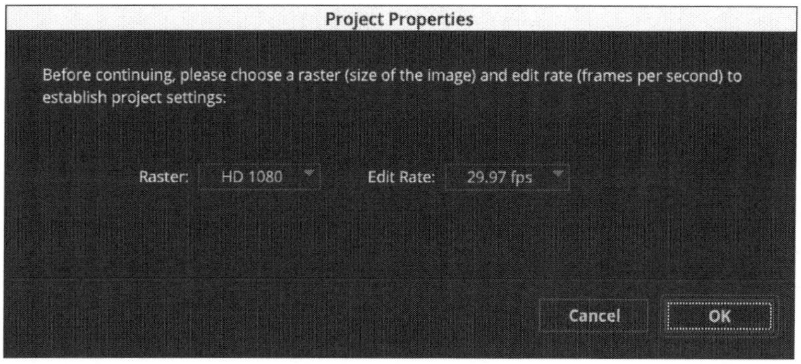

Figure 4.10 The Project Properties dialogue box

4. The Project Properties dialogue box allows you to select the frame size, called **Raster** in Media Composer | First, and the frame rate, called **Edit Rate**, for the project.

5. Open the Raster drop list and choose the Raster that matches the frame size of the footage. In this case, the designation **HD 1080** is the appropriate choice. 1080 refers to the pixel height of the video frame.

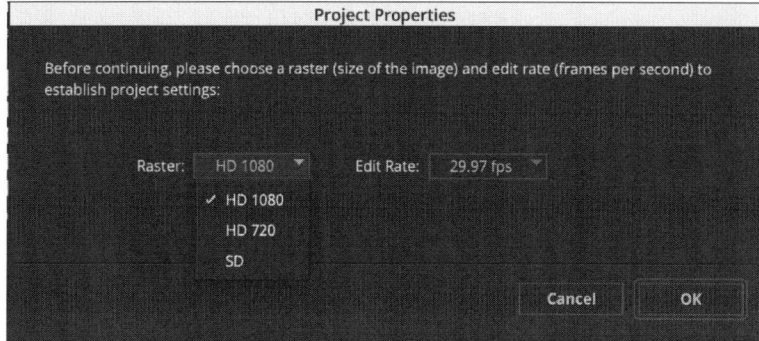

Figure 4.11 The Raster drop list

6. Open the Edit Rate drop list and choose the frame rate of the footage. In this case the Ski Field footage has a frame rate 25 fps.

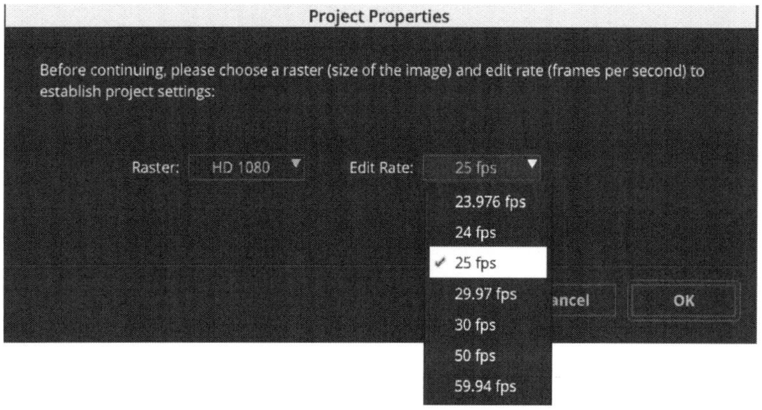

Figure 4.12 The Edit Rate drop list

7. Click the **OK** button and the Project Properties window will close.

8. At the bottom right corner of the Source Browser, use the **Target Bin** selection menu to choose the destination bin for your clip(s). For the purposes of this demonstration, choose the Clips bin as the destination for the clip.

9. To import the selected media file, do one of the following:

    - At the bottom right corner of the Source Browser click the **Import** button.

    - **Drag and drop** the media file from the File/Folder Contents pane to the desired bin (in this case, the Clips bin).

If Media Composer | First detects that there is a difference between the video resolution of the original media file and the video resolution you set earlier in **Preparing to Import a Media File**, an alert appears as shown in Figure 4.13.

This window only opens if the resolution of the original file is also listed in the Media Creation drop list.

If the resolution of the original file is not listed in the Media Creation setting then the window will not open and the import will continue uninterrupted, using the resolution you set in Media Creation.

Figure 4.13 The Import Resolution Conflict window

When you click OK, the system offers you the option to link and consolidate/transcode the media (using the Media Creation settings). Click Yes to proceed with the import.

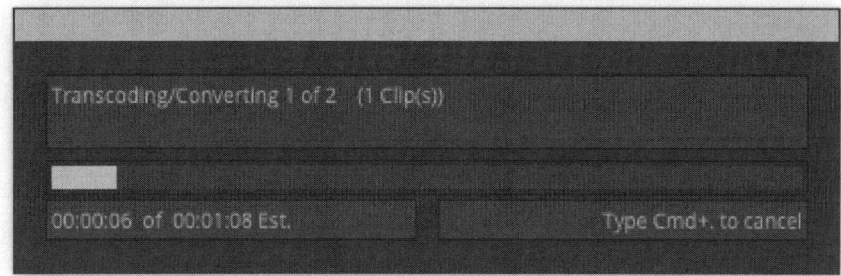

Figure 4.14 The Import progress bar

When the import is complete, the target bin will now contain a Master Clip for the imported media file. Notice in Figure 4.15 that the video clip icon is similar to that of a linked clip, but the icon lacks the 2 links of a chain on the right side. This tells you that the project has imported the media file, not linked to it. And like a linked file, the imported clip has also adopted the name of the source media file.

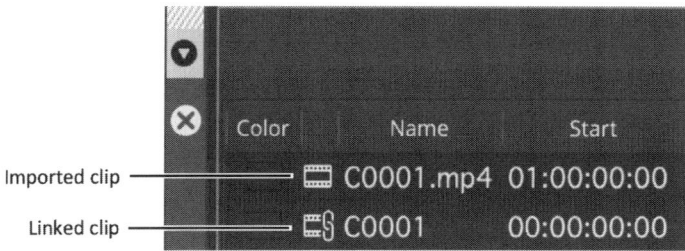

Figure 4.15 The imported Master Clip vs a linked Master Clip.

Changing Clip Names

File names created in a camera are often insufficient descriptions of the media they represent. In the example above, to know what clip C0001 is, you will need to open it in the Source monitor and play it or switch the bin to Frame View. Once you have viewed the clip, you can change its name in the bin. Perhaps **House snowing 01** is an appropriate description. There are more shots of snowing on the house, so each subsequent shot could be renamed and numbered in turn, e.g. **House snowing 02**, etc. After you have ingested the media files, renaming clips is an important part of setting up a project for editing. It makes sorting and locating clips much easier as you work in a project.

To rename an imported or linked clip:

1. Click the clip name to enter text editing mode.

2. Type a new name for the clip.

3. For the name to be accepted, click the clip icon or press the **Enter/Return** key. The curser will jump down to the next clip and remain in text editing mode.

Even though you may have changed the clip name, you have not renamed the file to which it is associated. Media Composer |First remembers the original name of the media file, as it needs that information to help locate the media file when you are working in a project.

 It is important not to change the name of an original media file after you have ingested it into a project and created a clip. If you do, the clip will lose the link to the media file and the clip will go offline. A good rule of thumb is, change the name of the clip, but don't change the name of the media file.

Similarly, you can calso change the name of a sequence by clicking on its name to enter text editing mode. In fact, you can change the name of any object saved in a bin.

> ### Where does Media Composer | First save the Media?
>
> You've learned that linked media clips refer to the original media file wherever it is located, but where has an imported media file been saved? You did nominate a drive in the Media Creation setting, but it is not obvious exactly where on that drive the file has been saved. Media Composer | First provides a tool that will locate the file for you.
>
> To locate the media file:
>
> 1. Select a single clip icon in the bin and from the **Fast Menu** choose **Reveal File**.
>
> 2. An Explorer/Finder window will open and shows the file path and the media file(s) associated with the clip, as shown in Figure 4.16.
>
>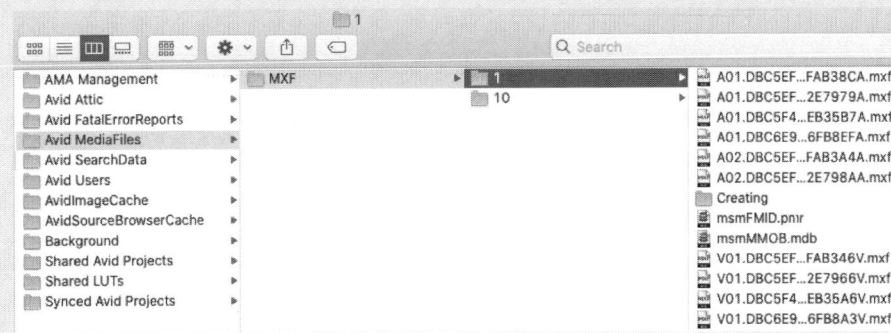
>
> **Figure 4.16** The file path and media files
>
> Media Composer | First creates an Avid MediaFiles folder on the drive you nominated. In that folder is an MXF folder that contains a numbered folder. Within that folder are saved the imported media files. Note that in this example Media Composer | First created an individual media file for each of the video and two audio channels of the original media, resulting in 3 new media files referenced by the one clip in the bin.

Ingesting Audio Media

Like video media, you can link and import audio media. As you have seen, video media often has audio attached while music and sound effects will only consist of audio files.

There is one further consideration when ingesting audio into a project. How many tracks of audio are attached to a media file and how should they be handled?

A single audio channel, like a voice recording, is referred to as **monoaural**, or *mono* for short, while a **stereo** recording, like music or sound effects, is often comprised of two channels – one for the left speaker and one for the right. A video recording is typically accompanied by two channels of audio. Does that make it a stereo recording or two mono recordings? Actually, it could be either. Many video cameras are equipped with a stereo microphone that uses the two channels to record the left and right audio signals. But it is equally possible that those two channels could be used to record entirely separate mono sources. For instance, two separate microphones could be used to pick up the voices of two actors, or an interviewer and interviewee.

When considering how to input audio into Media Composer | First, it is worthwhile deciding whether the two tracks carry paired sound, as in stereo music, or do they carry independent sound, as in two mono recordings of two actors.

Fortunately, Media Composer | First gives you the option of ingesting two channels of audio as either one stereo clip or as two independent mono clip.

Before you link or import an audio file, do the following:

1. Select the **Music** bin in the Bins pane of Media Composer | First.
2. Open the Source Browser and search through the Navigation pane to locate and select the **Music** folder.
3. In the File/Folder Contents pane select the **Input-NEW020101_Techno.mp3** music track.

Importing Audio as a Stereo track Clip

1. In the Source Browser select the **Import** radio button and click the small **gear** icon (as shown in Figure 4.17) to open the Import Settings.

Figure 4.17 The Import Settings button

2. In the **Import Settings** dialog box, select the **Audio** tab.
3. In the Multichannel Audio pane, click the **Edit...** button. The **Set Multichannel Audio** window will open.

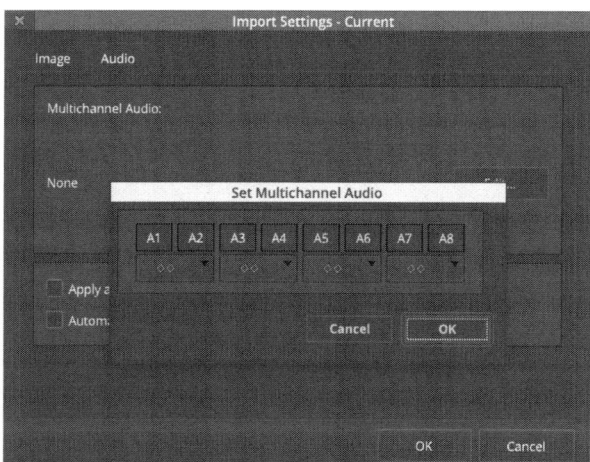

Figure 4.18 Set Multichannel Audio window

4. Click the **Format** button, located under the **A1** and **A2** track indicators. The button will turn green showing that audio channels 1 and 2 from the source media file will be combined into a single stereo track clip in the imported clip, as shown in Figure 4.19.

Figure 4.19 Audio channels A1 & A2 combined as a stereo clip

5. Click **OK** and the Set Multichannel Audio window will close. The Import Settings window will now show **Stereo: A1A2** in the Multichannel Audio pane, as shown in Figure 4.20.

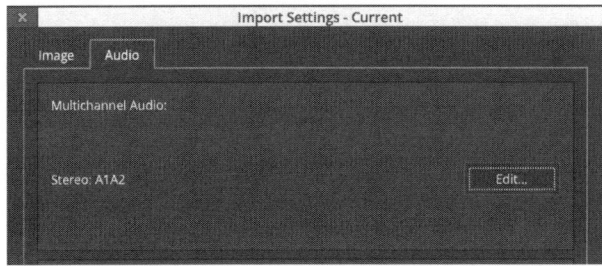

Figure 4.20 Stereo track is set

6. Click **OK** to close the Import Settings window.

7. As with video media, files can either be dragged from the Source Browser to the desired Bin pane, or by clicking the **Import** button at the bottom right of the dialog box (after selecting the appropriate Target Bin, which in this case is **Music**.

8. After the music track has been imported, close the Source Browser.

9. In the Music bin, double click the icon of the newly imported music clip. The clip opens in the Source monitor. (You can also drag the clip icon from the bin into the Source monitor.) In the Timeline window the audio Track Panel displays only one track for the clip, as shown in Figure 4.21. But the track selector shows two overlapping speaker icons in the bottom right corner, indicating this is a stereo track. A1 has both left and right channels combined in a single audio track.

Stereo track icon

Figure 4.21 Stereo Track Selector panel

Importing Audio as a two Mono track Clip

To import the music track again, but this time as a two mono track clip, you will need to reset the Import Settings back to the default.

1. Open the Source Browser and again select the **Import** radio button. Again, click the small **gear** icon next to the Import radio button.

2. When the Import Settings window opens, select the Audio tab. Click the **Edit...** button and turn off the green **Format** button for A1 & A2 by clicking it, or by clicking on the right side of the format button and choosing **Mono**.

3. Click the **OK** button.

   Figure 4.22 shows the Multichannel Audio pane now has the word **None** displayed in it. This means the audio will be imported as a clip representing two independent mono tracks.

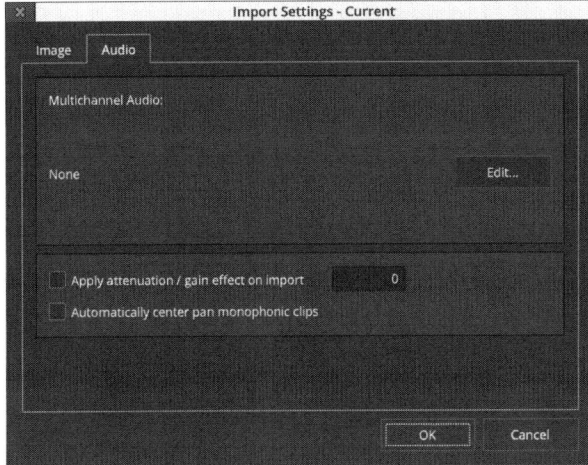

Figure 4.22 The import Settings

4. Click the **OK** button and the Import Settings window closes.

5. In the Source Browser, make sure the **Music** bin is selected as the Target Bin.

6. Click the **Import** button at bottom right in the Source Browser dialog box.

7. After the music clip has been imported, close the Source Browser and double click the icon for the music clip in the bin. The clip opens in the Source window. Look in the Timeline window and see how the audio Track Panel is displayed. In Figure 4.23 the music clip has been split into two separate mono tracks with a single small speaker icon in the bottom right corner of each Track Selector, indicating they are mono tracks.

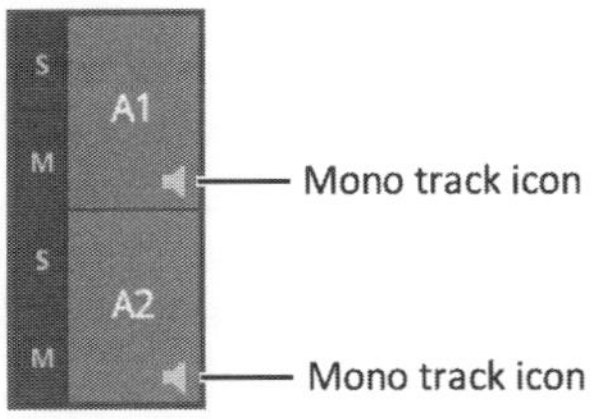

Figure 4.23 Mono Track Selector panel.

Linking Audio as Mono or Stereo Tracks

Audio can also be linked to create clips with either mono or stereo tracks. The process is very similar to the steps you followed when importing audio.

1. Open the Source Browser and select the **Link** radio button.

2. Click the same small **gear** to the right of the Import radio button and this time the Link Settings window will open, as shown in Figure 4.24.

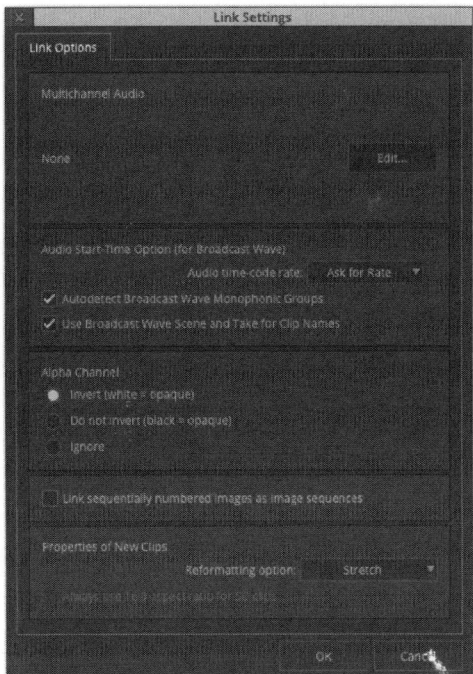

Figure 4.24 Link Settings

1. Use the **Edit...** button in the Multichannel Audio pane to set linked audio as either mono or stereo tracks. Click the **OK** button to close the Link Settings.

2. Click the **Link** button at bottom right of the Source Browser dialog box, and a clip that is linked to the music file will be created in the targeted bin. As with imported media, the Track Selector in the timeline will display either two mono tracks or a single stereo track.

> ### Ingesting Media with Drag-and-Drop
>
> You can ingest media to your project by dragging media files directly from an OS window to a bin. The default behavior is to import them, but you can use a modifier key to link the clips instead.
>
> To import media files:
>
> - Drag the files from the OS window to an open bin.
>
> To link to media files:
>
> - Hold the **Alt** key (Windows) or **Option** key (Mac) and then drag the files from the OS window to an open bin.
>
> If you plan to import media using drag-and-drop, it is best to check your Input settings first, since the files will be imported using the current settings.

Ingesting from Camera Cards

So far, to help you get familiar with using the Source Browser to input media, the media files have been relatively easy to find – a folder with media files inside. But most cameras save media files within a complex folder and file structure that can make locating media files difficult. To complicate matters further, manufacturers tends to create folder and file structures unique to their own cameras.

Figure 4.25 shows the folder structure of the Sony F3 camera, as shown in the Navigation pane. As you can see, the camera has multiple folders inside folders.

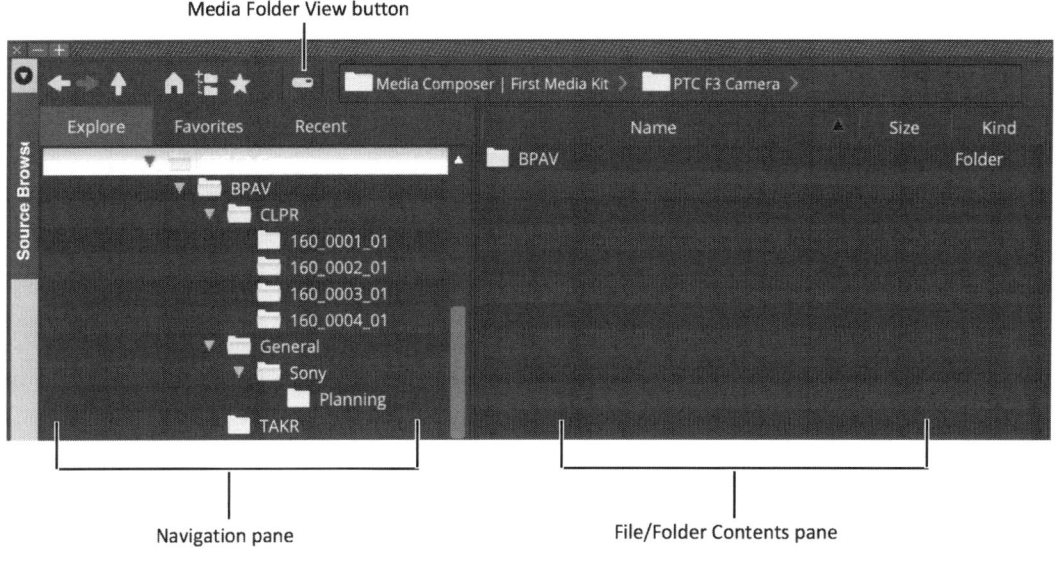

Figure 4.25 Sony F3 camera folder structure

To help you locate media files, the Source Browser has a shortcut method that can search files for you.

- With the top-level folder selected in the Navigation pane, click the **Media Folder View** button.

The Source Browser interrogates all the sub-folders and finds all the media files contained inside them, as shown in Figure 4.26. Notice how all the sub-folders disappear from the Navigation pane and the media files are now displayed in the File/Folder Contents pane.

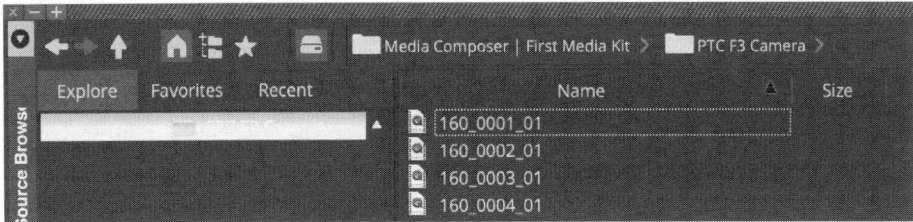

Figure 4.26 Sony F3 camera media files displayed

Deleting Unwanted Clips from a Bin

To delete a clip:

1. Select the unwanted clip(s) in the bin by clicking the clips icon.

2. Press the **Delete** key on the keyboard.

   A window will appear, asking you what you want to delete. As shown in Figure 4.27, linked clips provide no option for deleting the original media files while imported clips will allow you to delete the copies of the original media files that were created during the import process. Both linked and imported media master clips can be deleted from the bin.

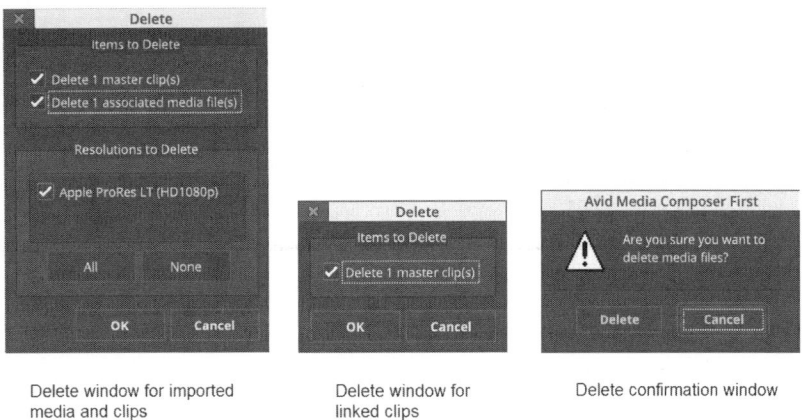

Delete window for imported media and clips

Delete window for linked clips

Delete confirmation window

Figure 4.27 The Delete window differs for imported master clips vs linked master clips.

3. Click the **checkboxes** to select the items to delete, and then click **OK**. If you selected media files to be deleted, a confirmation box will appear.

4. Click **OK** to continue, or **cancel** to close the window without deleting.

Warning: Media deletion is permanent. You cannot undo a media deletion. Anytime you are deleting media, it is best to double-check your selections.

Media Management

In Lesson 3 you learned how to create bins in which to save clips. In this lesson you learned that when you link to or import a media file, you will create a clip that is saved in a bin.

The difference between a clip and a media file is important to understand. A clip is just a small bit of data, or *metadata*, relating to a linked or imported media file and in particular the location of that media file. The media file is the actual pictures and sound you work with when editing a story. When you open and play a clip from a bin, Media Composer | First locates the related media file and shows it to you in the Composer window.

A clip is saved within a Media Composer | First project while a media file is typically saved on a separate storage device, e.g. an external hard drive.

If Media Composer | First cannot locate a video file referred to by a clip, the Source window will display the **Media Offline** message, as shown in figure 4.28. Audio-only clips, such as music, do not display the Media Offline message if their corresponding media files cannot be located.

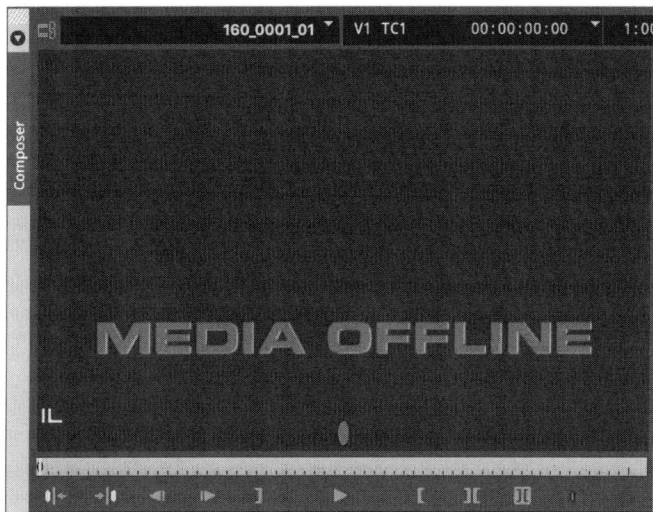

Figure 4.28 Media Offline message is displayed when video media cannot be located.

There are a number of possible reasons why media files might not be found by Media Composer | First:
- The hard drive or memory card is disconnected from the computer or not turned on.
- The media files have been moved from the location that they were in when the clip was created.
- The media files have been deleted.
- The media files have been corrupted.
- The media file name has been changed after the clip has been created.

Managing Clips and Bins in a project

On small projects it may seem unnecessary to save your clips amongst multiple bins, but it is often surprising how quickly projects can grow in size as you work on them. Regardless of a project size, however, it is always good practice to start by having at least a bin for sequences and a bin for clips. Media Composer | First creates these bins for you automatically. The need for additional bins will become apparent as your work on a project progresses. For instance, you might decide that you want to create separate bins for clips related to specific scenes in your film, a bin for music, another for sound effects, and so on. Clips can easily be dragged between bins or copied and duplicated from one bin to another. You can also change the names of clips in bins to better describe the shot.

In studios and broadcast news stations with a team of editors, there are strict conventions with which bins need to be created and named for each story. For an assistant editor, project organization is a big part of the job. Clear organization makes it easier for everyone to work on a project together, and in the professional world, working together is more common than working alone. It is essential to develop good habits early on by clearly naming bins and keeping clips well-organized within them.

Managing Media Files

Media files are your number one asset in any project. Like anything important, you should take the appropriate measures to protect them.

Managing media files begins at their source. It is never wise to work with the original media files that are still saved on the device that recorded them, e.g. a camera or audio recorder. If the device is needed for another job and disconnected from the computer, or the device fails, or the files are corrupted then you have lost your assets and consequently the project is lost. In this unfortunate scenario, media referred to by your clips will go offline.

The steps to safeguard your assets, and therefore your project, are illustrated in Figure 4.29.

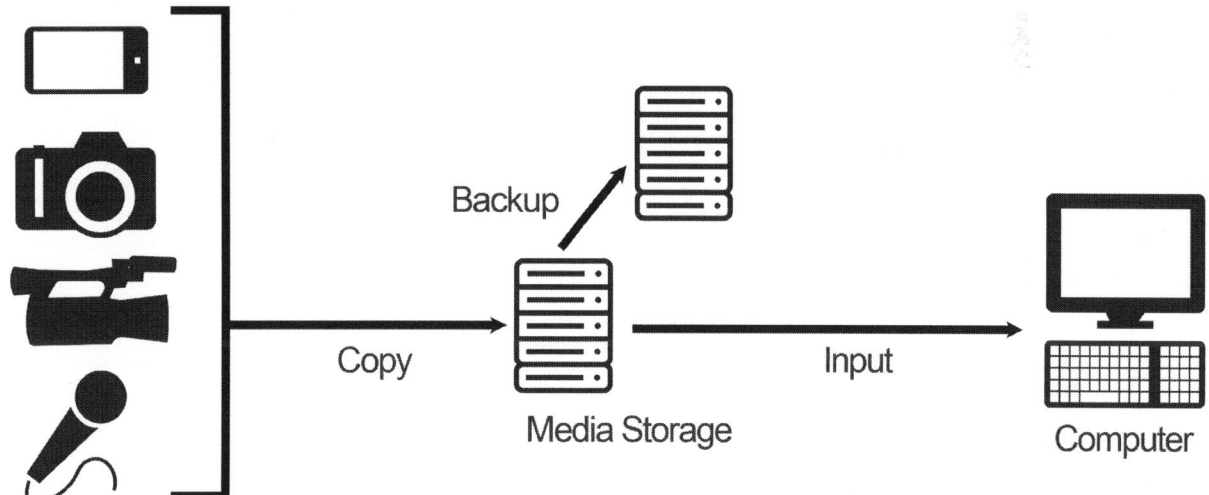

Figure 4.29 Managing media files

1. As soon as possible, copy original media files from the recording device to a fast hard-drive or solid-state drive that has sufficient capacity for the project. These copied files become your master working media files.

2. Make an identical backup copy of your master working media files. If your working media files become corrupted or accidentally deleted from the master copies, you can quickly recover them from the backup copies.

3. Link to or import the media files into your Media Composer | First project. If you import files, you will need additional drive space for the media file copies it creates.

Review/Discussion Questions

1. What is the difference between linking and importing media?

2. When you link to or import a media file, what is saved in a bin?

3. What is the difference between a Clip and a Media File?

4. True or false: When linking media, you can remove the original source drive or camera card containing the media and your media will remain online.

5. When dragging media files from their storage drive to a Media Composer | First bin, in order to link to the files (rather than import them), which modifier key must you press?

6. True or false: When deleting an imported clip, you have the option of deleting both the clip and the media file.

7. True or false: While deleting a linked clip, you only have the option to delete the clip (not the media file).

8. The Link Settings and Import Settings are opened from the Source Browser. What do they allow you to do when linking or importing audio media files?

9. Describe the difference between the icon for a linked clip and an imported clip.

10. Why is it important to backup your master media files?

11. Before importing a media file, you need to open the Media Creation settings. What does the Media Creation settings allow you to configure?

EXERCISE 4

 Exercise Break 4.1
Put what you have learned into practice.

GOALS

- Link to media files
- Import media files
- Save the project

1. Launch Media Composer | First and create a new project named **My Second Project_(student ID)**.

2. Create a new bin (in addition to the two auto-created bins). Name the bins **Sequences**, **Clips**, and **Music**.

3. Open the **Clips** and **Music** bins.

4. Open the Source Browser and click the **Link** radio button at bottom left.

5. In the Navigation pane, locate and select the **Rock Climber QTs** folder.

6. In the File/Folder Contents pane, select all the **.mov** video files. Do not include the 3 music .wav files (named **179_short_we-are-young-we-are-free**) in the selection.

7. Link to all of the .mov video files. Make sure the linked clips are saved in the Clips bin.

8. Before you import one of the .mov video files that you have already linked to, you will need to determine the frame size and frame rate of the footage.

9. Open Explorer (Windows) or Finder (Mac) and locate the **Rock Climber QTs** folder. Select one of the **.mov** video files and open it in a media player like Quicktime player. Locate and note the information that tells you the frame size and frame rate of the file. In Quicktime Player the information is found in the Inspector (Window>Show Movie Inspector).

10. From the menu bar in Media Composer | First, select **Avid Media Composer > Preferences > Project > Media Creation**. Set **Apple ProRes** as the **Video Resolution** and nominate an appropriate **Target Drive** for the imported media file. Take a screen capture before closing the Media Creation window.

11. Open the Source Browser to import one of the .mov video files. Click the **Import** radio button at bottom left and the Project Properties window should open. Set the **Raster** and **Edit Rate** to match the frame size and frame rate of the .mov video files. Take a screen capture of the Project Properties window before clicking **OK**.

12. Select any one of the **.mov** video files from the File/Folder Contents pane.

13. Make sure that **Clips** is your Target Bin and click the **Import** button at bottom right of the Source Browser.

14. If an alert appears noting incompatible media format, click OK and follow the prompt to link and consolidate/transcode the imported media.

15. The selected media file will start to import, and a Progress Bar will pop up indicating how long the process is taking. When the file has finished importing, check to make sure you have a new clip in the **Clips** bin. The clip icon should indicate it is an imported video clip.

16. Now link to the music track **179_short_we-are-young-we-are-free_0037**. Select the **Link** radio button and use the Link Settings (the gear icon) to create a stereo audio clip. Save the audio clip in the **Music** bin. (You will need this track later as you edit your Rock Climber story.)

17. Click the **Import** radio button and this time import a different music .wav file using the Import Settings (the gear icon) to create an audio clip with two mono tracks. Save the audio clip in the **Music** bin.

18. Provide screen captures of the clips in both bins so the clip icons clearly show that there are both imported and linked clips in the bins and the bin names are visible at the top of the screen captures.

19. In turn, open each audio clip in the Source window and take screen captures of the Track Panel in the Timeline window. The screen captures should clearly show that one audio clip consists of a single stereo track and the other of two mono tracks.

20. You have now input media into your project, ready to start editing in the next lesson.

21. From the **File** menu, select **Close Project** then **Quit** Media Composer | First.

LESSON 5

Drag and Drop Editing

In Lesson 3 you learned how to drag and drop a clip into the timeline to start a sequence and how you can add clips to the sequence in the same way. In this lesson you will refine this drag and drop method. You will learn how to use only part of a clip instead of the whole clip and how, in addition to adding new clips to the sequence, you can replace existing clips with new ones.

The exercise at the end of the lesson will be to start editing the sequence in your **My Second Project_(Student ID)** project. It will also give you the opportunity to discover for yourself a couple of additional features in Media Composer | First as you drag and drop clips to the timeline.

Media: Rock Climber

Duration: 40 Minutes

GOALS

- **Adding IN and OUT marks to clips**
- **Understanding how Segment Modes work with drag and drop editing**
- **Understanding Overwrite and Splice In editing**
- **Replacing shots in the timeline**
- **How to use the Track Panel when editing**
- **Adding voice over to the sequence in the timeline**

Deciding Which Part of a Clip to Use

For any given moment in a film, you as the editor decide what the audience needs to see and hear, when they need to see and hear it, and for how long. The camera supplies all of the raw material from which you select the best shot, and then the best part of that shot. You then decide where in the sequence the shot best serves the needs of the story.

But your first choices aren't always going to be the *right* choices. You will often want to try different approaches and see if one arrangement of shots works better than another. Media Composer | First provides many tools that make the editing process simple and straight forward.

Getting Started

In order to follow the steps in this lesson, launch Media Composer | First and open your **My Second Project_ (Student ID)** project. You should already have created bins and input media files ready to start editing.

Selecting Your First Shot

Open the *Clips* bin and the *Sequences* bin. From the *Clips* bin, locate the following clips and preview each in turn by opening them in the Source monitor.

R05_55 Rock-EditStock

R8_114 SLOW Wall Fingers-EditStock

R8_117 SLOW Wall Fingers Reverse-EditStock

R8_105 SLOW Wall Stare-EditStock

Think about how the four shots might be used to create a short sequence. Notice that in each of the two wide shots of the climber walking towards the rock face, he slides his right hand across the boulder. There is also the close-up of his hand moving across the rock. There are a few ways in which you could edit these four shots together – the steps outlined in this lesson are only one approach you might take.

Now that you have previewed all the clips, you don't need to search for them again in the bin. At the top of the Source monitor, click on the **Clip Name** menu displaying the clip name that is highlighted in green, as show in figure 5.1.

Figure 5.1 Clip Name menu

All the clips that you have viewed are listed in the drop-down list. Select the clip **R8_117 SLOW Wall Finger Reverse** and it opens in the Source monitor.

Figure 5.2 Clip opened in Source monitor

1. Play the clip and park the Position indicator on the frame just before the climber begins to put his hand on the rock face.

   To select that frame as the starting point of the clip, either:

   • Click the **Mark In** button under the Source monitor.

   • Press the **I** key on the keyboard. (It is easy to remember 'I' for 'In'.)

2. Play the clip and count approximately 2 ½ of his steps along the wall. It is a slow motion shot so it will run about 6 seconds. Park the Position indicator, and either:

   • Click the **Mark Out** button under the Source monitor.

   • Press the **O** key on the keyboard. (It is easy to remember 'O' for 'Out'.)

Notice that the green Position bar under the Source monitor shows you Mark In and the Mark Out indicators, which appear similar to their corresponding buttons below the position bar, as shown in Figure 5.3

Figure 5.3 In & Out Marks

When the Source monitor is the active window, the Center Duration display at the top of the Composer window is an easy way to see the duration between the In and Out marks.

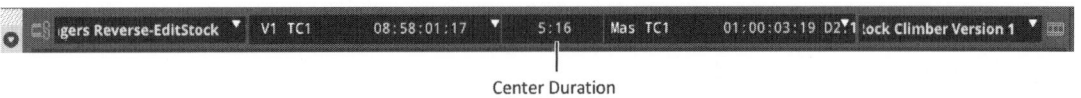

Figure 5.4 Center Duration

3. To play the clip between the Mark In and the Mark Out, press the number **6 key** on the QWERTY section of your keyboard.

4. If you change your mind about the **In** point or the **Out** point, just redo the marks where you want them, and the marks in the green Position bar, as well as the Center Duration value, will be updated.

Setting Up the Timeline for the Edit

Before you drag and drop a clip into the timeline, there are a couple of buttons at the top of the Timeline window that will be useful to you:

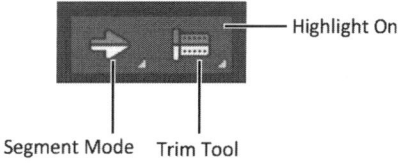 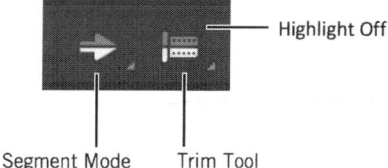

Figure 5.5 Segment Mode & Trim Tool

The **Segment Mode** determines how clips are placed in the timeline when you drag and drop them. It also controls how you can move them around once they are in the timeline. The split red/yellow arrow tells you that the Segment mode consists of two different tools. The active tool is dependent on the position of the mouse pointer in the Timeline window.

The light grey highlight surrounding the arrow icon tells you that the tool is turned on and active. But for the moment, to keep things simple:

- Click on the tool to <u>turn off</u> the highlight so the Segment Mode is disabled.

The **Trim Tool** determines how you can adjust the length of clips once they have been added into the timeline. Like the Segment Mode, the split colors also tell you there are two different trim tools available. The light grey highlight also indicates the tool is active. And again, to start with:

- Click the tool to <u>turn off</u> the highlight so the Trim Tool is disabled.

Performing the First Edit

To add the marked section of the clip to the timeline:

1. Click and drag the marked clip from the Source monitor to the Timeline window.

2. The Select window opens asking you to choose which one of the open bins to save the new sequence in, as shown in figure 5.6. The window will only show you the bins that are open. If the window doesn't show you the bin you want, click the **cancel** button. Open the bin you need and again drag and drop the clip to the timeline. Now select the Sequences bin and click **OK**. Alternatively, you could click on **New Bin** and create a bin from within the select window.

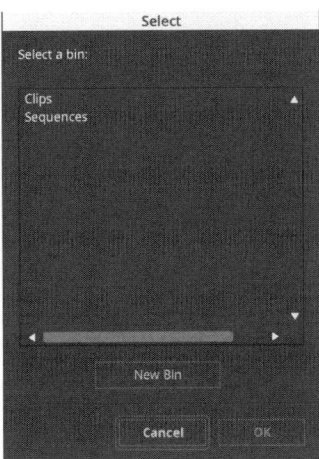

Figure 5.6 Select the bin in which to save the sequence

The timeline will now show you the video and audio track containing only the section of the clip that you marked. Go back to the start by dragging the blue Position indicator (in either the Timeline window or under the Record monitor) to the left. Play the sequence to check the result.

Figure 5.7 Timeline & Record monitor showing the marked section of clip edited into the sequence

3. Before going on to the next edit, locate the sequence in the Sequences bin and rename it **Rock Climber Version 1**.

 Editors employ various naming conventions to keep track of the many versions of a sequence that they create as they work on a project. An early version is often referred to as a Rough Cut while a polished version may be called a Fine Cut. Whatever convention you decide to use, keep it simple and consistent.

Notice what has happened to the Segment Mode button as seen in figure 5.8. It is still inactive because it does not have the light grey highlight around it, but it has now lost its red/yellow split colors and is a solid red arrow instead. This indicates that by default, when you drag and drop a clip to the timeline you have performed what is called an **Overwrite edit**.

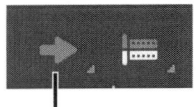

Figure 5.8 The Red Segment mode

An **Overwrite** edit always replaces footage if you drop a clip over the top of an existing segment in the timeline. The only exception is when you drop a clip at the end of the sequence. It that case the clip will just be added to the end of the timeline.

Overwriting a Clip Onto the Timeline

Using the same process, select and mark the second shot:

1. Open the **R8_114 SLOW Wall Fingers** clip in the Source monitor and locate the frame that you will start with.

2. Play the clip, and shortly after he places his hand on the wall, he swings his left leg forward as he walks. Mark the **In** point about half-way through the step when his left leg is parallel to his right leg. His left leg should be in much the same position as it was at the end of the first shot you used.

3. The **Out** point is after he moves his hand off the wall and just before the camera begins to pan away from him. The marked section of the clip should be around 6 ½ seconds long.

4. Drag and drop the clip from the Source monitor to the end of the timeline. Notice that it will snap to the end of the first clip.

   By default, when you add a clip to the timeline, it will either:

   - snap to the end of the timeline
   - snap to the beginning (head) of the timeline
   - snap wherever the Position indicator is parked in the timeline.

5. Just as an experiment (since you can't do any real damage to the edit at this point), undo the edit using **Control/Command + Z** and try snapping the clip to the head of the timeline and see what happens. The Red Segment mode has allowed the second clip to Overwrite the first clip.

6. Undo the edit again, and this time park the blue Position indicator halfway through the first segment in the timeline. Drag and drop the new clip so it snaps to the Position indicator. The new clip will Overwrite the second part of the first clip.

7. Undo the edit again and redo the original edit, snapping to the new clip to the end of the timeline.

Using the keyboard command Control/Command + Z to undo an edit is a very quick way to restore the timeline if you don't like what you have just done. It avoids the frustration of having to do another edit to get back to where you were. Many editors regard the simple Undo function as one of the most useful tools in Media Composer | First. Control/Command + Z provides multiple levels of undo, allowing you to step back through up to 100 previous actions. You can also use the Edit menu to Undo and Redo previous actions.

8. Play the timeline and watch the edit. If the cut between the first and second shots looks smooth, with the action of the left leg being continuous from the end of the first shot to the start of the second then you have performed one of the most common editing tricks editors employ - a continuity edit. As the name suggests, there is a continuity of movement from one shot to the next, making the transition between shots so smooth and seamless that the audience never notices the edit.

A good experiment to try later is to edit those same two shots together, but this time deliberately create a mismatch in the action of the left leg or the hand on the wall. See if the edit is just as smooth and seamless.

Using the same process, select and mark the third shot:

9. Locate the clip R8_105 Slow Wall Stare and **Mark In** just after the climber speaks (in slow motion). **Mark Out** about 5 seconds later. Use the Center Duration display to help work out the duration.

10. Drag and drop the clip so it snaps to the end of the timeline.

Splicing a Shot Onto the Timeline

For this edit, you will use a slightly different technique. Instead of editing the shot to the end of the sequence, you want to insert a shot between the second and third clips.

Dragging and dropping a clip will allow you to snap it to an existing edit point between segments in the timeline, but if you use the current default red Segment mode, you will Overwrite the third shot instead of slotting the new shot in between. To solve this, you will need to change the Segment mode from a red arrow to a yellow arrow.

1. Right-click on the red Segment mode button and a submenu will appear, as you can see in figure 5.9. Notice that by default the red Segment mode has its check box selected and the yellow check box is empty.

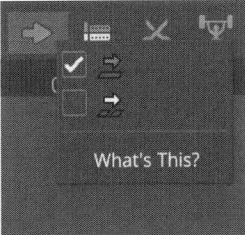

Figure 5.9 The red Segment mode (overwrite) check box is selected.

2. Deselect the red Segment mode and check the box to turn on the yellow Segment mode. Click anywhere in the interface and the submenu closes. Make sure the grey highlight surrounds the yellow Segment mode arrow, indicating that the mode is active.

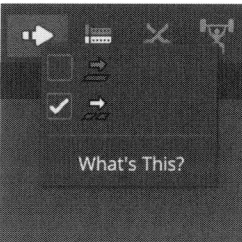

Figure 5.10 The yellow Segment mode (splice) check box is selected

3. The yellow Segment mode allows you to perform **Splice In** edits. A **Splice In** never replaces any footage already in the timeline. It will always insert the new shot in at the edit point. Any segments in the timeline to the right of the edit will move later to make room for the new shot while any segments to the left will remain where they are.

4. Load the **R05_55 Rock** clip into the Source monitor and pick the best 3 seconds of the shot. If you want to make the duration longer or shorter, just change the frame on which the Position indicator is parked and redo the mark In or mark Out points. The old marks will be replaced.

5. Drag and drop the new clip from the source monitor to the timeline so it snaps to the edit point between shots 2 and 3. Shot 3 will move down the timeline to make room for the new clip.

It's worthwhile noting that because the red Segment mode is the default, dragging and dropping will always perform an overwrite edit regardless of whether the red Segment Mode button is turned on or off. If you want to perform a Splice In edit, the yellow Segment mode must be selected and turned on, indicated by the light grey highlight. If you have the yellow Segment mode selected but not turned on, dragging and dropping will result in an Overwrite edit.

If you would prefer the Splice In edit to be the default Segment mode, then you can change it under the edit tab of the Timeline Settings. You find it by going to the menu bar and selecting:

Avid Media Composer>Preferences...>User tab>Timeline>Edit tab>Default Segment Tool.

Replacing a Shot in the Timeline

Let's assume that you decide that you don't like the third shot in the sequence – the low angle shot of the rock. You can easily use the red Segment mode to replace that shot. But instead of using the Source monitor to decide the duration of the shot, you can use the length of the clip in the timeline. You only need to use the Source monitor to mark in where you want the new shot to start.

To replace the third shot:

1. In the Track Panel at the beginning of the timeline, click the track panel to turn off track A2 on the sequence side so only the V1 and A1 tracks are active. They will be highlighted blue while the A2 Track Selector will be grey, as shown in figure 5.11.

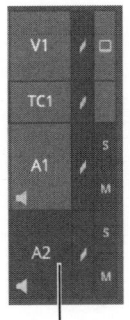

Track A2 turned off

Figure 5.11 The Track Selector panel for the sequence

2. In the timeline, park the blue Position indicator anywhere within the segment you want to replace (in this example, it's the third segment).

3. At the top of the Timeline window, click the **Mark Clip** button. The entire segment in the timeline is marked from in to out. Alternatively, you can press the **T key** on the keyboard.

Notice that only the segments on the **V1** and **A1** tracks are highlighted between the Mark In and Mark Out indicators. If the Track Selector for A2 had been turned on, then it would have forced the entire timeline to be marked. You only need to activate the tracks that you want to work on. You can also ignore the timecode TC1 Track Selector as you cannot add video or audio into the TC1 track.

1. In the **Clips** bin, locate the **R05_54 Trees-EditStock** clip and open it in the Source monitor.

2. If you scrub through the clip by dragging the Position indicator at the bottom of the Source monitor, you see that nothing much changes in the tree shot, so it is safe to set a **Mark In** at the beginning of the clip. You don't need to add a Mark Out.

3. Turn on the red Segment mode and drag and drop the new clip so it snaps to the Mark In point in the timeline. The segment is replaced.

4. To remove the marks from the timeline, click the **Clear Marks** button. This button appears to the right of the Mark Clip button at the top of the Timeline window. Alternately, you can press the **G key** on the keyboard.

You can use marks anywhere in the timeline to Overwrite shots. For instance, you could add a Mark In half way through one shot and add a Mark Out half way through another. Provided the duration of the replacement shot is at least as long as the time between the marks in the timeline, the red Segment mode will Overwrite the marked section of the sequence, only on the tracks that have been made active in the Track Panel.

Adding Voice Over

The red Segment mode can also be used to add audio to the timeline. To avoid overwriting pictures when you only want to add sound, you again need to use the Track Panel to enable and disable tracks.

1. Locate the clip **R02_02(b) Interview** (in the **Clips** bin) and open it in the Source monitor. At around 08:30:00 in the clip, **Mark In** and **Mark Out** around the words, *'The approach to the rock is one of the bigger things that captured me into rock climbing.'*

2. Because you do not want to affect the pictures on V1 or the sound on A1, turn off the Track Selectors on the left side of the Track Panel. But you do want to edit the climber's voice onto track A2 of the timeline, so you now turn the A2 Track Selector on. In figure 5.12, you'll see that V1 and A1 on the sequence side are greyed out while the A2 Track Selector is highlighted blue. You can also turn off the V1 Track Selector on the Source side of the Track Panel so only the A1 track of the source clip is highlighted green. The active A1 track of the source clip will automatically align itself against the active A2 track of the sequence. This is called Auto Patching.

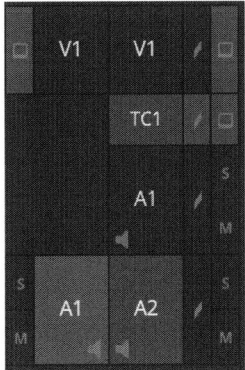

Figure 5.12 The Track Panel set up so the source track A1 will edited onto the sequence track A2.

3. In the timeline, park the blue Position indicator, or add a **Mark In,** where you would like to add the voice over. Just after the cut to the second shot of him walking would be an appropriate place. Drag and drop the clip from the Source monitor to A2 of the timeline so it snaps to the Position indicator or the Mark In. The voice over is now included in your sequence.

 It is also possible to add video only to the sequence in the timeline without modifying the audio tracks. To do this, you would turn off all the audio Track Selectors and leave both the source V1 and record V1 tracks turned on.

Review/Discussion Questions

1. What does adding a Mark In and a Mark Out to a source clip allow you to do?

2. What keyboard shortcuts allow you to add a Mark In and a Mark Out?

3. What tool controls how a clip is edited into the timeline?

4. What is an Overwrite edit?

5. What is a Splice In edit?

6. Which color Segment mode achieves an Overwrite edit?

7. Which color Segment mode achieves a Splice In edit?

8. How do you mark a clip from In to Out in the timeline?

9. True or false – when you have a Mark In and a Mark Out in the timeline you only need to add a Mark In to the Source clip.

10. What do the Track Selectors in the Track Panel allow you to do?

EXERCISE 5

 Exercise Break 5.1
Put what you have learned into practice.

GOALS

- Use segment mode to replace a shot
- Use segment mode to add clips to the sequence
- Consider the suitability of shots that you edit into the sequence
- Use sync locks to preserve sync in the timeline
- Publish to YouTube

1. Launch Media Composer | First and open your **My Second Project_(student ID)** project. Open the **Rock Climber Version 1** sequence.

Replacing a shot

The third shot in your sequence is of trees blowing in the breeze. When you first edited it into the sequence it looked OK. But since you added the voiceover, it obviously doesn't work as well. Can you suggest why?

Alfred Hitchcock is regarded as one of the world's most influential filmmakers and became known as the 'Master of Suspense'. He was an expert at knowing what shot to use and when to use it. He also knew that an audience could infer meaning from shot choices and the order in which they were edited together. It is worthwhile spending a few minutes watching Hitchcock explain the principle of 'montage', the term used to express the essential art of joining shots together to tell a story and create meaning. Below is a link to a YouTube video in which Hitchcock is interviewed on the subject.

https://www.youtube.com/watch?v=TNVf1N34-io&index=3&list=PLE52445E53E71CB18&t=0s

As a variation on Hitchcock's explanation, let's now consider why the tree shot in your sequence doesn't work as well as it might. When there was no voiceover, the sequence shows the rock climber walking, then stopping and looking up. You then cut to the shot of the trees and by inference that is what he is looking at. That was a fair enough assumption. Perhaps he is checking the weather to see how windy it is. But when you added the voiceover, the audience knows something more about what he is doing. He is approaching the rock to climb it. The shot of the trees is now contradicting what he is saying and as a result the meaning is confused.

1. Find the original shot, **R05_55 Rock-EditStock** that you replaced with the trees and overwrite it back into the sequence. Locate the clip and open it in the Source monitor. It may still have the original Mark In and Mark Out visible in the Position bar.

2. In the timeline, use the **Mark Clip** button or the **T** key to mark In to Out of both V1 and A1 of the tree segment.

3. Using the red Segment mode, drag and drop the *R05_55 Rock-EditStock* clip to overwrite the tree segment.

4. Play the sequence to see whether the replacement shot is more appropriate in the context of the story than the tree shot.

Add more voiceover

5. At about 09:03:00 in the clip R02_02(b) Interview, the climber says, *'It gives me a chance to meditate, um, to think about what I'm about to do as I get, ah, to the rock.'* **Mark In** and **Mark Out** around that statement.

6. Park the blue Position indicator or add a **Mark In** just after the cut to the third segment in the timeline - the newly reinstated rock face shot.

7. You don't want to edit the video from the interview clip into the sequence, so in the Track Panel turn off the green V1 Track Selector for the source clip and the blue V1 Track Selector for the sequence.

8. Use the red segment mode to add the audio to track A2 of the timeline by dragging the clip down to A2 before you release the mouse. The audio tracks will Auto Patch as you do this. A1 from the source will now edit onto A2 of the timeline. (As you continue to edit, keep all the voice grabs on A2 of the timeline and keep any other audio on A1 of the timeline.)

Add more interview

Now back at the end of the sequence, overwrite another interview statement to the end of the close up shot of the climber.

9. At about 09:31:00 in the clip R02_02(b) Interview, the climber says, 'I, ah, usually put down all my bags and just look up and really just take in where I am and, ah, I put on my shoes and, ah, start putting all my equipment on and, ah, tie myself to the rock and get going.' **Mark In** and **Mark Out** around that statement.

10. In the timeline, turn on the green V1 and A1 Track Selectors for the source clip because you want to add both video and audio to the sequence.

11. Use the red Segment mode to drag and drop the clip to the end of the sequence, making sure audio is edited onto track A2 and video onto track V1.

Splice in a new shot

12. Locate and open the **R8_112 SLOW Fingers Wall-EditStock** clip in the Source monitor. **Mark In** and **Mark Out** around the part of the shot in which he is running his hand along the wall. It should be about 3 ½ seconds long. You need video and audio, so make sure the V1 and A1 Track Selectors are turned on for both the Source and Record sides of the Track Panel.

13. Use the yellow Segment mode to splice in the clip between the first two shots in the timeline.

14. Play the sequence to satisfy yourself that the new shot works between the two wide shots of the climber walking. Watch the edits carefully to see if continuity has been maintained between the first 3 shots. The position and movement of the hand should flow smoothly from one shot to the next?

But notice what has happened. You have spliced the clip into tracks V1 and A1 of the timeline, so all the segments on V1 and A1 have moved down the timeline to make room for the new clip. However, the segments on A2 of the timeline have not been affected. They have stayed exactly where they were. When you play the sequence, it still seems to work OK until you get to the interview at the end. The sound is now out of sync with the pictures.

To solve the problem, do the following:

1. Undo the edit using **Control/Command + Z**.

2. In the Track Panel, click on the **Sync Lock** button, as shown in figure 5.13. The timeline will now maintain the sync relationships between all tracks even when you only edit new material into some of the tracks. To lock sync on all tracks, click the **Sync Lock** button next to the TC1 Track Selector. To only lock sync between pairs of tracks, you can turn on the individual **Sync Lock** buttons beside the Track Selectors.

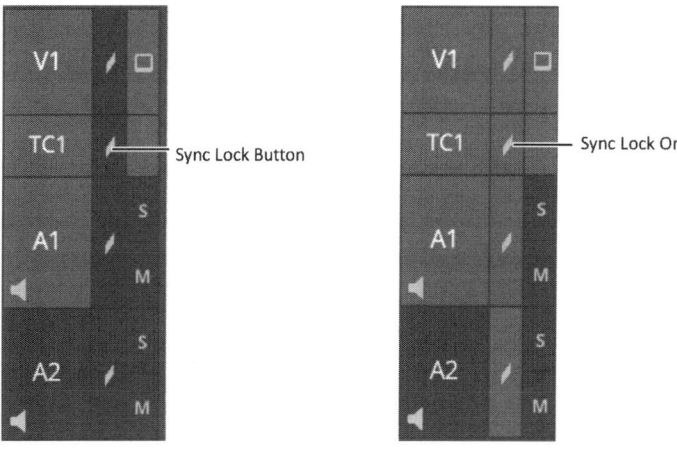

Figure 5.13 The Sync Lock

3. With all sync locks on, redo the Splice In edit and see how the voice on track A2 now maintains its sync relationship with all the other tracks. **The audio segments on A2 move down the timeline to maintain sync with the interview video that has also moved down the timeline when you spliced in the new clip.**

4. Publish the work you have done so far to YouTube.

LESSON 6

Refining the Sequence

In lesson 5 you started editing your Rock Climber sequence by using the red Segment mode to Overwrite clips into the timeline and replace a shot in the timeline. You also used the yellow Segment mode to Splice In a shot between two existing clips in the timeline and you used the Sync Lock to maintain cohesion on the timeline between the video and audio tracks.

In this lesson, you'll improve your sequence by again using the Segment modes, but this time using them to change the order of shots, and also to remove shots.

Media Used: The Rock Climber

Duration: 30 minutes

GOALS

- Reorder segments using Segment Mode (Extract/Splice-In)
- Clean up narration with Segment Mode (Lift/Overwrite)
- Divide segments with Add Edit
- Delete segments from the timeline

Moving Segments in the Timeline

When cutting a montage, it's common to change the order of shots as you explore different creative options. The yellow Segment mode is the tool of choice for doing this kind of work. In lesson 5 you learned how the yellow Segment mode allows you to Splice In a new shot by slotting in a new clip between existing clips on the timeline. But the yellow Segment mode also allows you to move clips once they are in the timeline.

Copying a Sequence

When you are considering making changes to a sequence, it is always a good idea to make a copy of it first and then make changes to that copy. That way, if you don't like the changes you've made, you can always go back to the original version.

Let's start by opening your **My Second Project_(Student ID)** project.

5. Locate your sequence *Rock Climber Version 1* in the Sequences bin but don't open it in the Record monitor.

6. Select the sequence, and from the menu bar at the top of the screen, click **Edit>Duplicate**. The copy will be saved in the Sequences bin with *.Copy.01* added to the end of the sequence name.

7. With the sequence name selected, type a new name, **Rock Climber Version 2**.

8. Now open version 2 by dragging the sequence to the Record monitor/Timeline window. The sequence name displayed in the upper right-hand corner will change to reflect the active sequence's name (in this case, it will read **Rock Climber Version 2**). Any changes you make to this version will not be reflected in version 1.

The Extract/Splice-in Segment Mode

The yellow segment mode (Figure 6.1) is more correctly called the Extract/Splice-In Segment mode.

Figure 6.1 The yellow arrow, Extract/Splice-In segment mode, is the best tool for reordering segments in the sequence.

When you click and drag a clip within the timeline, this tool 'extracts' the clip from its original position and at the same time removing the empty space left behind. When you drop the clip, the tool 'splices' it in at its new position, and all following clips move later in the timeline to make room.

Rearranging Shots

The first change you will make is to use the yellow Segment mode to Extract a segment, move it, and Splice it in at the beginning of the sequence.

1. In the sequence, locate the second shot, the clip **R8_112 SLOW Fingers Wall**. It is the closeup shot of the hand running along the wall and it should be between the two wider shots of the climber walking beside the rock.

2. Make sure the yellow Extract/Splice In Segment mode is selected and active, indicated by the light grey highlight.

3. To avoid the risk of breaking sync between tracks, turn on the **Sync Lock** button next to the TC1 Track Selector in the Track Panel.

4. In the timeline, click the video segment of the clip **R8_112 SLOW Fingers Wall**, as shown in figure 6.2. Both segments on V1 and A1 should become highlighted to show they have both been selected.

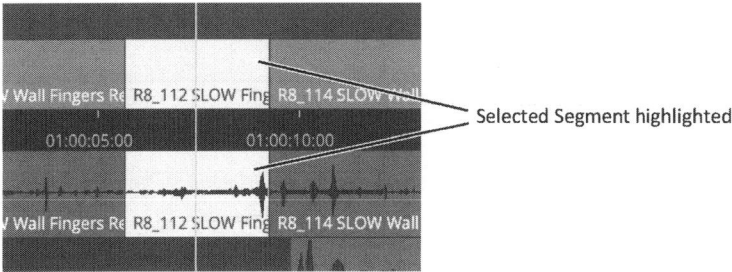

Figure 6.2

If only the segment on V1 is highlighted (Figure 6.3) you can turn on **Link Selection Toggle** (Figure 6.4) to allow both segments to be selected by the Extract/Splice In segment mode. You'll find it amongst the tools at the top of the Timeline window. Alternatively, you can **Shift+Click** each segment to select all the segments that you want to move.

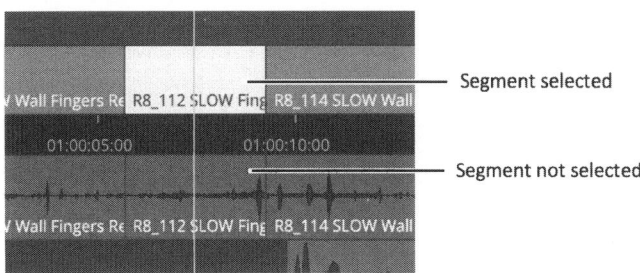

Figure 6.3

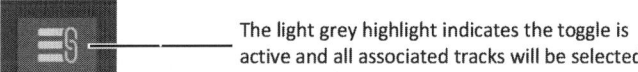

Figure 6.4 The Link Selection Toggle

5. With the segments on V1 and A1 selected, click and drag the shot to the left until it snaps to the beginning of the timeline. The order of the shots will now be rearranged. When you play from the start of the sequence you can decide which version works best.

- Notice that Media Composer | First dynamically updates the sequence as you drag the segments in Extract/Splice-In Segment mode. This makes it easy to see what is going to happen in the sequence even before you release the mouse to execute the edit.

- By turning off the **Link Selection Toggle**, you can move an individual video or audio segment along the timeline without moving other segments that are associated with it. This means you have the ability to move segments independently of each other. But be warned – it can be easy to get your video and audio out of sync. For instance, if you only move a video segment, other video segments will also shift position to accommodate the one you are moving, but audio segments will remain where they are. The result can be a video track out of sync with the audio.

- You don't always have to snap segments to predefined points in the timeline. By holding down the **Control (Windows)/Command (Mac)** key while dragging, you can move a segment anywhere along the timeline. Be careful though. Using the yellow Segment mode to drop a segment within another clip will split the clip as the timeline makes room for the one you are moving.

You may have noticed that the action doesn't quite match on the cut between the hand movement in the closeup shot and the hand movement in the wide shot. At the end of the closeup, the hand is still on the wall but in the wide shot the hand is just moving onto the wall. But don't worry, Media Composer | First has tools that can fix that kind of continuity problem. You will explore them in the next lesson.

The Lift/Overwrite Segment Mode

You learned in Lesson 5 that the red Segment mode (Figure 6.5) allows you to Overwrite segments in the sequence—replacing whatever may already be in the timeline. You saw this when you used the red Segment mode to replace one segment with another.

Figure 6.5 The red arrow, Lift/Overwrite segment mode

However, the red Segment mode is better named the **Lift/Overwrite Segment** mode. When you use this tool to drag and drop segments within the timeline you will be leaving gaps from where you moved the segment – you will have 'lifted' the segment, leaving a blank space behind in the track. When you drop the segment, it 'overwrites' whatever may already be on that track, replacing it with the segment you have moved.

Unlike the Extract/Splice-in Segment mode, the big advantage of the Lift/Overwrite segment mode is it doesn't move other segments in the timeline. Apart from the segment that you are moving, all other segments remain exactly where they are. As a result, it is much easier to preserve sync in the timeline when using the Lift/Overwrite Segment mode.

A good example of using Lift/Overwrite is to clean up the voiceover of the rock climber.

Audio Waveforms

An audio waveform is a graphical representation of the sound edited into a track of the timeline, shown in figure 6.6.

Figure 6.6 The audio waveform displayed in an audio track of the timeline

Knowing how to use the audio waveform can be very helpful when trying to identify sounds that you want to remove from a sequence. For example, editors spend a lot of time and effort removing *'ums'* and *'ahs'* in interviews and reducing unnecessary gaps in speech.

Waveforms are like ripples in a pond when a stone disturbs the surface of still water. The height of the waveform shows how loud a sound is at any one moment in time. The taller the waveform the louder the sound. The shape of the waveform indicates the frequencies of sound being reproduced at that moment. With a little experience, you will be able to identify different sound by the appearance of the waveform. This is particularly useful when trying to locate spoken words. Each word can look like a small bundle of ripples with gaps in between that represent the pauses or breathes between words.

To Display the Waveforms in an Audio Track

You can either turn on or off the waveforms in all audio tracks, or you can view waveforms in specified tracks.

To view the waveforms in all tracks:

1. Click the **Fast Menu** at bottom left of the Timeline window.

2. In the menu that appears, make sure that **Audio Data > Allow Per Track Settings** is not enabled (if it is enabled, a check mark will appear next to the menu item).

3. Enable **Audio Data > Waveform** by clicking the menu item. When enabled a check mark will appear by the menu item. All audio tracks in the timeline will display their audio waveforms.

4. To turn waveforms off, open the **Fast Menu** and select **Audio Data > None**.

To view the waveforms in individual tracks:

1. From the Fast Menu enable **Audio Data > None** then select **Audio Data > Allow Per Track Settings**.

2. At the top left of the Timeline window, click the small disclosure triangle beside the timecode display, shown in figure 6.7. A set of additional tools called the Track Control panel opens beside the timeline Track Panel.

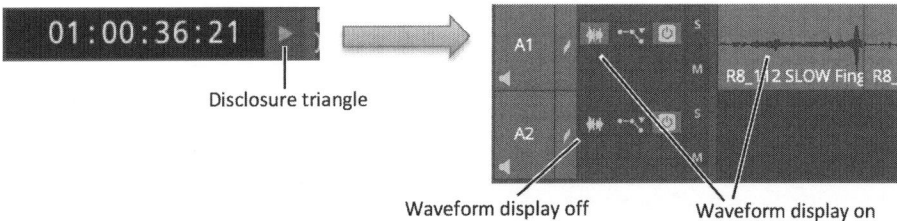

Figure 6.7 The Track Control panel

To help you see the waveform more clearly, you can expand out the horizontal width of the timeline so the gaps between words become easier to see. At the bottom of the Timeline window, click and drag the slider in the Scale Bar, as shown in figure 6.8. Your view of the segment will increase in horizontal width as you drag to the right (zooming in). Drag to the left and it shrinks in width (zooming out).

Figure 6.8

Another useful way to identify sounds in the timeline is to Solo a track so that it is the only track you can hear. In the Track Panel, click the **S button** beside the record track that you want to isolate, and you will hear only that track through your speakers. The other audio tracks will automatically be muted so you cannot hear them.

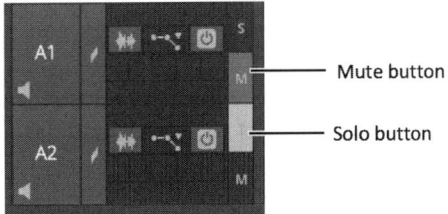

Figure 6.9 The Solo & Mute buttons

Using the Add Edit Button

The Add Edit button can be found in the tool bar at the top of the Timeline window.

Figure 6.10 The Add Edit button

The Add Edit allows you to divide a segment in the timeline, as if you had sliced clip(s) into two pieces at the point where you park the blue Position indicator.

Figure 6.11 shows the timeline with the voiceover, *'The approach to the rock is one of the bigger, ah, things that capture me into rock climbing.'* In this line you want to remove the sound *'ah'*.

Play the segment and simultaneously listen and watch the audio waveform.

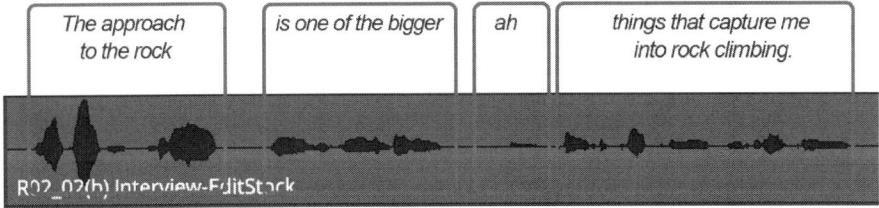

Figure 6.11 A2 in the timeline showing the audio waveform with the accompanying voiceover script.

You only want to clean up the voiceover which is on audio track 2, so in the Track Panel of the Timeline window, turn off all Track Selectors except for A2 on the record side.

To clean up the voice over:

1. In the timeline, park the blue Position indicator just in front of the word, '...*ah*.'

2. Click the **Add Edit** button in the tool bar at the top of the Timeline window (or alternatively press the **H key** in the keyboard). An edit has now been applied to the segment on A2 at that position in the timeline, and the single audio clip has been split in two.

Move the blue Position indicator and look where it was parked on A2. Figure 6.12 shows the Add Edit. This small white '=' sign straddling the edit shows that the frames each side of the edit are contiguous i.e. they are sequential frames in the clip.

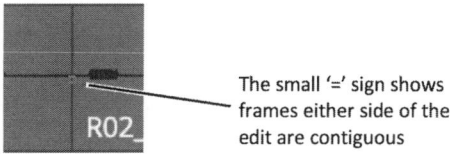

Figure 6.12 The Add Edit in the audio segment

3. Reposition the blue Position bar just in front of the words, '...things that capture me into rock climbing.' It is a very narrow gap in the waveform so be careful where you park the Position indicator. Remember, you can use the Scale Bar to see more horizontal detail in the timeline.

4. Click the **Add Edit** button again and the segment will be divided at the frame on which you are parked.

5. Use the red **Lift/Overwrite Segment** mode to select the segment between the two Add Edits. Figure 6.13 shows the selected segment is highlighted in grey.

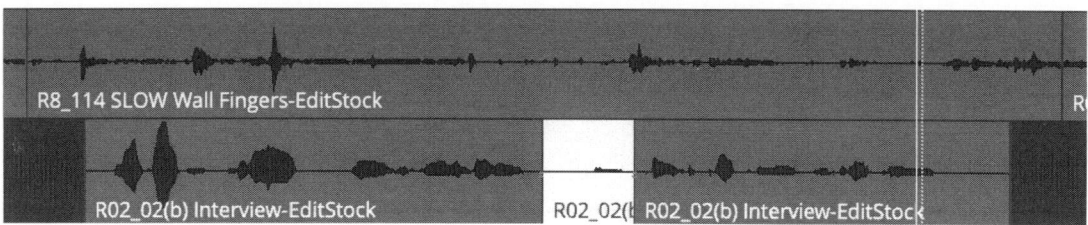

Figure 6.13 Selected segment

6. With the segment in the timeline selected, press the **Delete** or **Backspace** key on the keyboard. Figure 6.14 show the result - the segment is removed from the timeline. Because the red Segment mode Lifts material out of the timeline, it leaves a gap, and the other segments remain where they are.

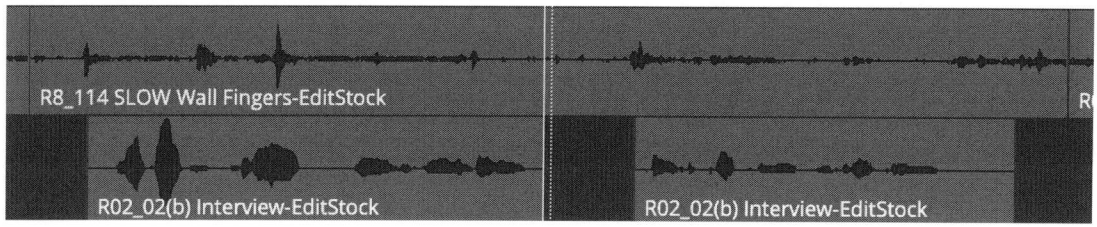

Figure 6.14

7. Now use the red Segment mode to drag the second part of the voiceover clip to the left until it snaps to the first part, as shown in figure 6.15. Because the red Segment mode Overwrites, it replaces the gap and no other segment on the track changes position in the timeline. The risk of breaking sync is therefore avoided.

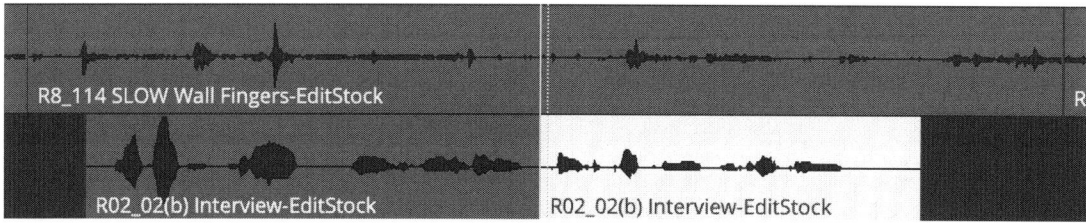

Figure 6.15 The selected segment slides to the left to overwrite the gap.

Play the voice over to hear how much better the sentence sounds. Remember, if you don't like the result, you can always undo the edit and try again.

Deleting Segments From the Timeline Using Extract/Splice-in

You have seen how the red and yellow segment modes allow you to add clips to the timeline and move those clips within the timeline. You have also used the red Segment mode to remove segments from the timeline. The yellow Segment mode can also remove segments, but the risk of breaking sync exists, so use it cautiously.

To delete a segment using Extract/Splice-In:

1. Select the yellow **Extract/Splice-In** segment mode.

2. Click on a **segment** you want to delete. With the Link Selection Toggle button turned on, all associated segments in the timeline will be highlighted.

3. Press the **Delete** or **Backspace** key on the keyboard.

   The segments are deleted from the Timeline and the gaps are closed.

When deleting a segment using this method, Media Composer | First removes the material via the Extract function.

In Figure 6.16, the R8_112 SLOW Fingers Wall segment (the one you moved to the start of the timeline) has been selected using the Extract/Splice-In segment mode. Both the video and the associated audio segment are highlighted.

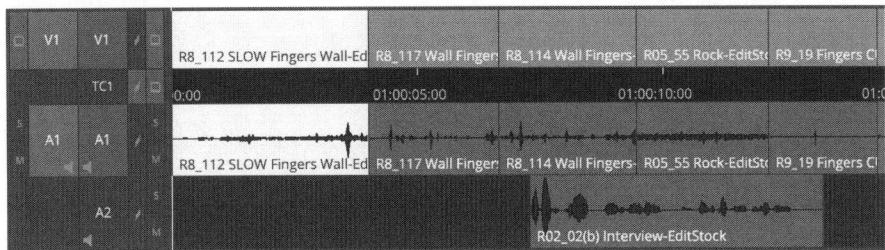

Figure 6.16 Both segments are selected using the yellow segment mode.

Figure 6.17 illustrates that when the segments are deleted, the gaps created on tracks V1 and A1 are closed, but the segments on A2 remain where they are. The result is that the interview later in the timeline is now out of sync - the video on V1 of the climber speaking has been moved towards the beginning of the timeline while the associated audio on A2 remains where it is.

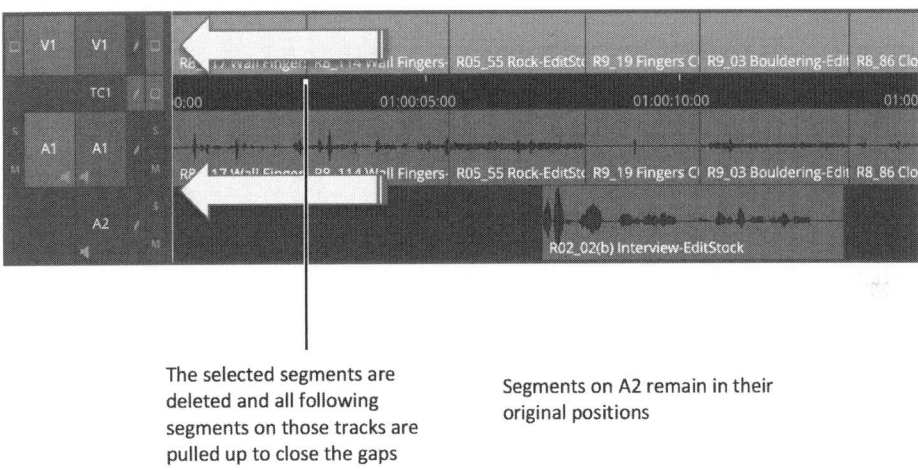

The selected segments are deleted and all following segments on those tracks are pulled up to close the gaps

Segments on A2 remain in their original positions

Figure 6.17 Both segments are extracted and the gaps closed.

Automatic Selection of Segment Modes

You can choose to turn on either or both Segment modes from the Segment mode submenu. If you turn on both Segment modes, the Segment mode button is split half red and half yellow to indicate that you can now choose between the modes as you work within the timeline. They become 'context sensitive', i.e. dependant on where the mouse pointer is positioned over a segment in the timeline.

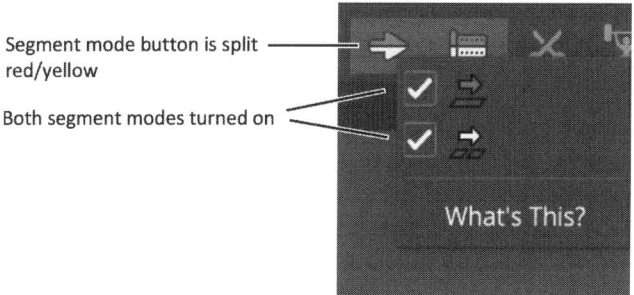

Figure 6.18 Segment mode selection submenu

Figure 6.19 illustrates how the position of the mouse pointer determines which Segment mode will be active in the timeline. Posigin the cursor over the top half of a segment and the red Lift/Overwrite mode will be active when you click. Click in the lower half of a segment and the yellow Extract/Splice-In mode will be active.

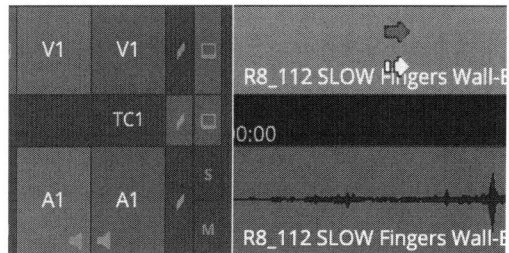

Figure 6.19 Automatic selection of Segment modes

Review/Discussion Questions

1. What three functions does each of the segment modes allows you to do when working with the timeline?

2. What is the correct name for the red Segment mode?

3. What is the correct name for the yellow Segment mode?

4. How can you remove a shot from the sequence and leave a gap (or filler)?

5. What does this button do?

6. What does this button do?

7. Why is the yellow segment mode often well-suited for video and the red for audio?

8. What is the danger in using the Extract/Splice-In segment mode to add, move or delete segments in the timeline?

9. How can you automatically select the Segment mode you want to use in the timeline?

10. What is the keyboard shortcut for Undo?

EXERCISE 6

 Exercise Break 6.1
Put what you have learned into practice.

GOALS

- Use segment mode to remove marked sections of a clip
- Use segment mode to move clips in the sequence
- Use segment mode to add more shots to the sequence

Continue Editing the Rock Climber Sequence

1. Launch Media Composer | First and open your **Rock Climber_(student ID)** project. Open the sequence.

2. In the second voiceover statement the rock climber says, *'It gives me a chance to meditate, um, to think about what I'm about to do as I get, ah, to the rock.'*

3. Use Add Edits and the red Lift/Overwrite Segment mode to delete the *'um'* and the *'ah'* from the statement. Then use the red Segment mode to snap the segments together and close the gap between them.

    Remember, if you want to reposition a single segment without snapping it to a predetermined point in the timeline, you can hold down the **Control (Windows)/Command (Mac)** key while using the Segment mode. To move more than one segment at a time, **Shift+select** each segment with the Segment mode.

    The last clip in the timeline is the interview in which he says, *'I, ah, usually put down all my bags and just look up and really just take in where I am and, ah, I put on my shoes and, ah, start putting all my equipment on and, ah, tie myself to the rock and get going.'* There are four *'ahs'* in this statement that you can remove.

    Because there are no other segments in the timeline after this interview, you can safely use the yellow Extract/Splice-in Segment mode to clean up the interview. There is no risk of pulling any following segments out of sync. But because you do want to maintain sync within the interview, you need to extract both video and audio from the timeline.

4. Turn on the blue Track Selectors for both V1 and A2 of the timeline. Use Add Edits and the yellow Segment mode to extract each *'ah'* from the interview.

   When you play the interview, sync should be maintained between the pictures and sound, but at every edit you will notice a slight 'bump' in the picture caused by a sudden change in the position of the climber. This is a result of the frames you have removed. These bumps are called 'jump-cuts.' Typically, you would disguise these jump-cuts, so the audience isn't distracted by them. One technique is to overwrite them with footage of the climber scaling the rock wall. However, this is the first time the audience has a chance to see who is talking, so you don't want to overwrite the start of the interview. Fortunately, there is another useful tool that will help you easily mask that first jump cut. You will learn that technique in a later lesson. For now, use the red segment mode to overwrite the other three jump-cuts with footage of him climbing.

5. Turn on only V1 and A1 so you edit both video and audio into the timeline without affecting the voiceover on A2.

6. Park the blue Position indicator, or add a Mark In, just after he says, *'…really just take in where I am…'*

7. There are 3 shots that might work well to illustrate him getting started on his climb.

8. **R9_02 Bouldering-EditStock** – use approximately the first 4 seconds.

9. **R8_81 SLOW Chalk Bag-EditStock** – use approximately 5 seconds from when he moves his left hand from off the rock to his chalk bag. This is a slow motion shot that doesn't quite suit the shots either side of it, but you can fix that up later too, using another excellent tool.

10. **R9_19 Fingers CU-EditStock** – use approximately 2 seconds. He moves his hand into shot 4 times. The third take works well. Try to position this shot so the hand slaps on the rock just after his last words, *'…and get going.'*

11. At about 11:02:00 in the clip **R02_02(b) Interview**, the climber says, *'To me rock climbing isn't necessarily how hard you can climb or um, what grade of ah, what grade of rock you can climb. It's really about touching each hold and just, and I guess just challenging yourself to be better than you were last time.'* **Mark In** and **Mark Out** around that statement. Edit it into V1 and A2 of the timeline after the last shot – the close up of the hand slapping the rock.

    Because this is at the end of the sequence, you can use either Segment mode to slide this interview about 7 seconds down the timeline to provide a gap in which you can edit more shots of him climbing. To help you know how far you are sliding the segment, look in the area between the position bars of the Source and Record monitors, as shown in figure 6.20. As you begin to move the segment, a small window opens up and displays how many seconds and frames you have slipped the segment down the timeline.

Figure 6.20 Time display in Segment mode

Up to this point he has talked about preparing for the climb, but now he has started. The closeup shot of his hand slapping the rock is a good visual punctuation mark. In the next lesson you will introduce music that will help you to change the pace of the story and give it more visual energy before he starts talking about the climb itself.

12. After sliding the clip down the timeline, play the interview and locate all the 'ums' and 'ahs'. He also repeats a few words. Use the techniques you have learned so far to clean up the voice track without breaking sync.

13. Don't edit any shots into the 7 second gap or overwrite the jump cuts. You will later use the rhythm of the music track to guide the pacing of the new shots.

14. Publish to YouTube the work you have done so far.

LESSON 7

Music and Audio

As you learned in Lesson 6, sound plays a significant role as you edit a story. Viewing audio waveforms can help you quickly and efficiently find edit points. In this lesson you will explore the range of tools available to take better control of the audio as you edit a sequence.

The exercise will introduce a simple way of dipping music levels under a voice.

Duration: 40 minutes

Media Used: Rock Climber

GOALS

- Display source clip audio waveforms
- Using Digital Audio Scrub
- The Track Control panel
- Using Clip Gain to adjust audio levels
- The Solo and Mute buttons
- Adding audio crossfades
- Deleting crossfades in the timeline

1. Open your **My Second Project_(Student ID)** project.
2. Locate your **Rock Climber Version 2** sequence and duplicate it. Rename the duplicate **Rock Climber Version 3**.
3. Open the **Rock Climber Version 3** sequence in the Record/Timeline windows.

Locating Audio Cues

In Lesson 6 you discovered how to display the waveforms of all audio tracks in a sequence by opening the Timeline window **Fast Menu**, then selecting **Audio Data > Waveform**. Alternatively, you can display the waveform of individual tracks through the **Track Control** panel shown in Figure 7.1. To enable individual track waveforms, first setup the **Audio Data** menu by selecting **None** and **Allow Per Track Settings**.

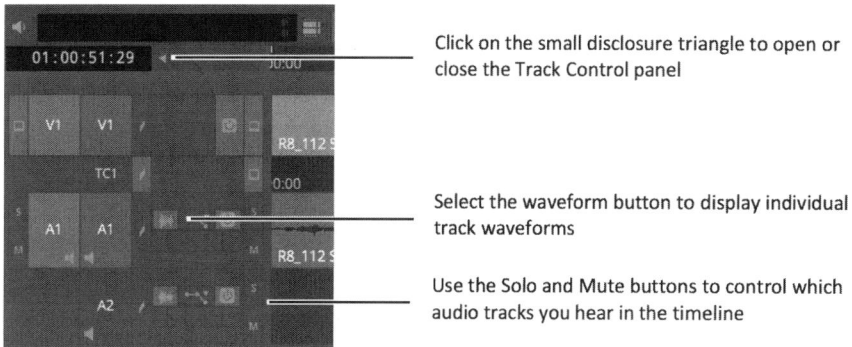

Figure 7.1 The Track Control panel contains useful per-track audio controls.

 Hold the Alt key (Windows) or Option key (Mac) to activate waveforms on all tracks simultaneously when clicking on a single track's waveform button.

Improving the Visibility of the Waveform

In Lesson 6 you learned how to use the Scale Bar at the bottom of the Timeline window to expand the width of the timeline, so that you can see more horizontal detail in the waveforms. Depending on the recorded volume of the audio, the vertical height of the waveform may be quite small or quite large within the track. Music clips, for instance, often appear as solid black waveforms that fill the track from top to bottom. That is because they are generally very loud. To compensate for this, you can adjust the height of the waveforms independently of the height of the audio track.

- To increase the height of the waveform display, select the track(s) to adjust (using the Track Selectors) and then press **Ctrl+Alt+L (Windows)** or **Command+Option+L (Mac)**.
- To reduce the height of the waveform display, select the track(s) to adjust (using the Track Selectors) and then press **Ctrl+Alt+K (Windows)** or **Command+Option+K (Mac)**.

Toggling Source/Record in the Timeline

You can display the waveform for source material in the same way that you display waveforms for segments in the timeline. This can be helpful when deciding in and out points of dialogue in master clips.

To see source waveforms, switch the timeline display from showing the sequence to showing the tracks of the source clip.

To display audio waveforms for the source clip **R02_02(b) Interview**:

1. Load the clip into the Source monitor.
2. In the bottom-left corner of the Timeline, click the **Toggle Source/Record in Timeline** button.

 **Figure 7.2** The Toggle Source/Record in Timeline button

When active, the button glows bright green, and the position indicator in the timeline changes to the same bright green (as shown in figure 7.3), indicating that you are looking at Source material.

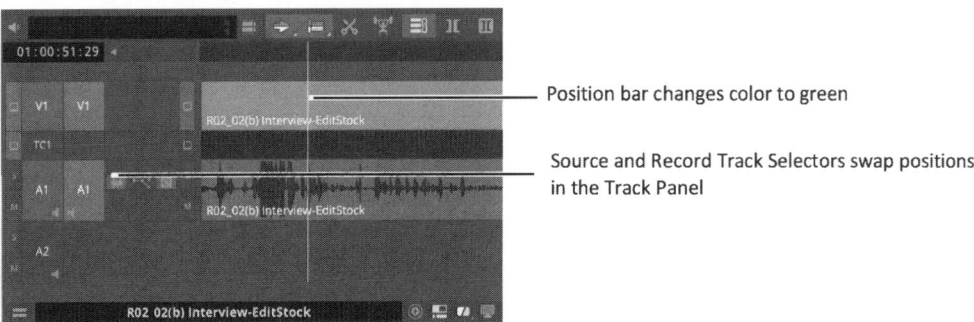

Figure 7.3 The bright green position indicator alerts you to the fact that you are looking at the source material.

The Timeline now displays the Source tracks instead of the sequence. This is especially evident in the Track Panel. The two green Source-side track selectors now appear on the right, and the three Record-side track selectors now appear on the left.

You can enable the view of the source track audio waveform in exactly the same way that you did previously for the timeline by clicking the **waveform** button in the Track Control panel.

As an example, for the source clip **R02_02(b) Interview**:

3. Navigate to approximately 9:03:00. This is one of the voiceover clips you have already used. (You will need to use the timecode display at the top of the Source monitor as the timecode window in the timeline still refers to the sequence.)
4. If need be, use the timeline's Scale Bar to expand out the horizontal detail in the source waveform.
5. Play the Source clip until you find the gap just before he says, '*It gives me a chance...*' and add a **Mark In**.
6. After his words, '*...I get to the rock.*' add a **Mark Out**.

Figure 7.4 shows how the marked area of the clip is highlighted and the marks appear in the TC track of the timeline.

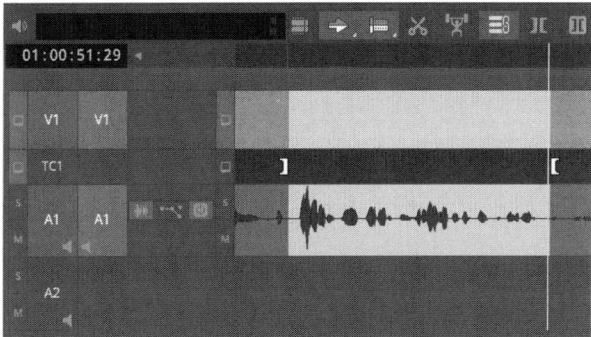

Figure 7.4 The marked area of the source clip is highlighted grey.

7. Toggle out of the source view before you continue editing otherwise you will not see new segments being added to the sequence. Remember, a green Position indicator means you are looking at the source clip in the timeline while a blue Position indicator means you are looking at the sequence.

Using Digital Audio Scrub

As a further aid to locating audio cues, you may find it useful to enable **Digital Audio Scrub**.

Digital Audio Scrub plays the digital audio samples associated with each frame as you move the position indicator through the sequence. This lets you to hear the audio recorded with each individual frame you move over, allowing for very precise audio editing. For example, you may have difficulty identifying in the waveform the exact point between spoken words - Digital Audio Scrub can help you pick the exact frame on which to cut. Digital Audio Scrub works by either dragging the Position indicator, or by using the Step Forward/Step Back buttons on the keyboard or interface.

To access the **Toggle Digital Audio Scrub** button, you may need to map it to the tool bar at the top of the Timeline window. To do this:

8. From the **Tools** menu, open the **Command Palette**.

9. At bottom-left of the Command Palette window, make sure the **'Button to Button' Reassignment** radio button is turned on.

10. Under the **Play** tab, locate the **Toggle Digital Audio Scrub** button.

11. Click and drag the button icon to a blank button in the tool bar at the top of the Timeline window.

12. Close the Command Palette.

To enable digital audio scrub:

- Hold the **Shift** key while dragging through the Timeline to temporarily activate Digital Audio Scrub.

- Use the **Toggle Digital Audio Scrub** button to switch Digital Audio Scrub on and off.

Adjusting Audio in the Sequence

So far, in editing your Rock Climber sequence, you have basically ignored whether the sound accompanying the illustrative footage has been distracting or too loud or too soft. You have of course been able to use the Solo and Mute buttons to help you hear what you need to hear while editing.

However, in the final program, a sudden change in sound volume or quality between audio segments can be jarringly noticeable to the audience. In the same way that editors carefully decide what are the best shots to use at any given moment, they also pay close attention to the sound – what does the audience need to hear?

Prioritization being key to audio elements, being able to hear voices clearly and at the correct level is the first consideration. Then the natural sound, or effects audio, is balanced against the voices. Finally, music volume is adjusted so it doesn't compete for your attention with voices or effects.

Setting Up for Audio Work

There are a couple of settings that make adjusting audio levels and balance quick and easy.

In the Track Control panel for each audio track:

1. Click the **Audio Data** button, as shown in figure 7.5. It opens the Audio Data drop menu, shown in figure 7.6.

Figure 7.5 The Audio Data button

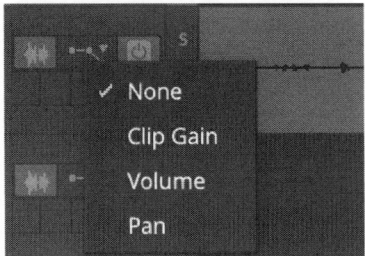

Figure 7.6 The Audio Data menu

2. Select **Clip Gain** in the **Audio Data** menu. Clip Gain is enabled on the track.

 Holding Alt/Option in the Track Control Panel activates the item for all tracks. Otherwise, all selections are on a per-track basis.

Each audio segment in the Timeline will now show a series of horizontal lines superimposed over a less prominent audio waveform – this is a Decibel Graph. Also, appearing in the bottom-left corner of each clip, is a very small white icon, representing an audio fader. Click on the icon and a fader will appear, allowing you to control the audio level of that segment, as you can see in figure 7.7.

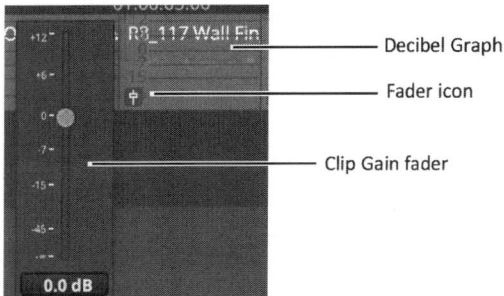

Figure 7.7 With Clip Gain enabled, the audio segment reveals a mini fader

The Audio Tool

When working with audio, you may wish to look at more precise meters than those at the top of the Timeline window. Media Composer | First also includes large audio meters that are easier to read. The large audio meters are called the Audio Tool. (The Audio Tool does do other things, hence the name "Tool," but it is primarily a big pair of meters.) Use these meters when you need to accurately measure audio levels.

To open the Audio Tool:

- Press **Ctrl+1 (Windows)** or **Command+1 (Mac)**.
- Select **Tools > Audio Tool**.

You can increase the size of the Audio Tool by dragging the bottom right corner of its window down until the meters reach their maximum size. You can also move the tool to a convenient position on your computer screen, or dock it in the paneled user interface.

So, what is the "right" audio level? As a rule of thumb, the audio in your sequences should generally be between –26dB and –8dB, as measured by the digital values on the left side of the meter. Voice level is typically around –12dB within that range.

Using Solo and Mute

The Solo and Mute buttons, shown in Figure 7.8, are also helpful in isolating the audio that you need to adjust without being distracted by competing sound on other tracks.

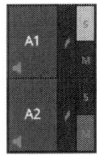

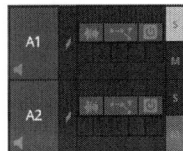

Figure 7.8 The Solo and Mute buttons are always visible and accessible in the Timeline tracks, whether the Track Control panel is open or not.

It is possible to solo more than one track. This is ideal for isolating just a couple tracks out of the full mix, such as the music and sound effects without the dialogue or vice-versa.

Adjusting the Volume of a Segment

To adjust clip gain (in this case, of the voice track (A2) of your **Rock Climber Version 3** sequence):

1. Turn on the **Solo** button for A2 of the timeline. This means you will only hear the rock climber speaking and not be distracted by any of the natural sound accompanying the climbing footage.

2. With **Clip Gain** turned on for A2, Click the **Fader** icon in the corner of the first segment on A2 of the timeline. A pop-up fader window appears.

3. Click and drag the **Fader** to adjust the level. Adjust the fader to read a value of +6.0dB. Play the segment and look at the **Audio Tool** to see the voice levels. The levels should look about right.

4. You can tell by how 'fat' the waveform is that the voice is fairly loud in the first segment but in the second the voice level tails off to become much quieter. So, in the second segment, adjust the fader to +9.0dB.

5. Continue down the timeline and adjust each segment on A2 so the voice level is averaging at around -12 dB on the left-hand scale as you play each segment.

6. When you have finished adjusting the level of each segment, play the entire sequence to make sure the voice level is of a consistent volume throughout.

7. The fader pop-up window will close automatically when you click elsewhere in Timeline.

To adjust the Clip Gain of the A1 natural sound/effects audio track:

1. Turn off the **Solo** on A2 so you can hear both the voice and effects audio tracks. The advantage now is that because you know the voice levels are correct, you can judge the loudness of the effects track by ear. If the volume of the effects is dominating or competing for your attention compared to the voice, then it is too loud.

2. Work down the timeline and adjust each segment on A1 so you can hear the sound without it drowning out or distracting you from listening to the voice. Often with background audio, less is more.

Replacing Effects audio

If you decide that any audio segment on A1 is just not working well enough, then consider finding a replacement. You can do this during the exercise to follow. Using what you learned in an earlier lesson, mark an audio segment from **In** to **Out** in the timeline and overwrite it with audio that you think works better. Often you find it in other clips in the bin. Remember to turn off the V1 and A2 Track Selectors because you are only replacing the sound on A1 and not the video or voice.

Adding audio crossfades

Another useful way of improving an audio track is to smooth out hard cuts with crossfades. Sometimes a sudden change in the quality of the sound can be just as distracting as a change in volume. For instance, it is very noticeable in the sequence when the background sound cuts to that of running water as the shot changes from the climber looking up to the shot of the rock face. An audio crossfade can smoothly blend the sound of the water into the preceding and following audio segments.

Try this in your Rock Climber sequence:

1. **Solo** A1 of the sequence in the timeline and have only the A1 Track Selector turned on.

2. Park the blue Position indicator close to an edit between two segments on A1. You don't need to be right on the edit point, just closer to it than to any other edit.

3. Click the **Quick Transition** button in the tool bar at the top of the Timeline window, shown in figure 7.9.

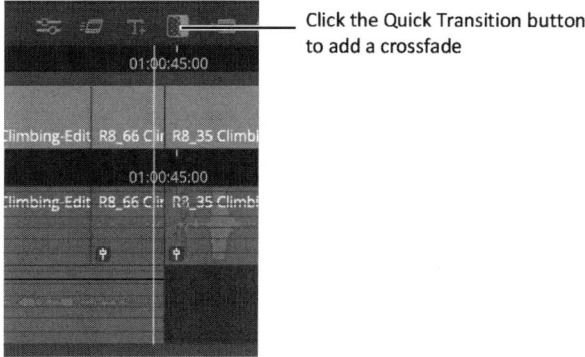

Figure 7.9 Park near the edit point in the timeline and click the Quick Transition button

4. When the Quick Transition dialogue box opens, as shown in figure 7.10, select from the following drop menus or enter numeric values, then click **Add**.

   - **Add**: Dissolve
   - **Position**: Centered on Cut
   - **Duration**: 24 frames
   - **Start**: 12 frames before cut

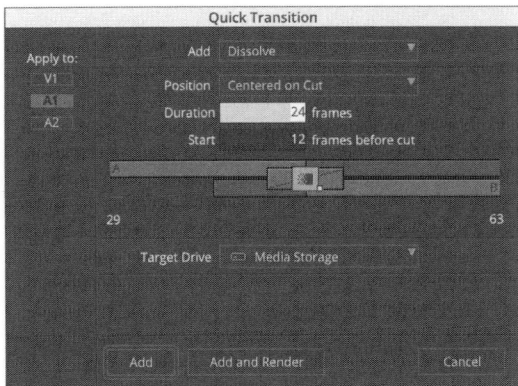

Figure 7.10 The Quick Transition dialogue box

When the dialogue box closes, a dissolve icon appears across the audio edit in the timeline, as seen in figure 7.11.

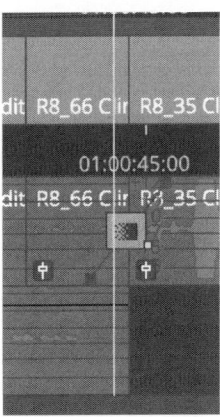

Figure 7.11 A dissolve effect icon appears across the edit in the timeline.

- A crossfade between the two segments relies on there being sufficient overlap of audio on both sides of the edit. Insufficient media on either side will require you to adjust the transition parameters until a successful crossfade can be achieved.

- Play the crossfade and if you don't like the result, park on the effect icon in the timeline and click the **Quick Transition** button again to modify the parameters.

- If you want to remove the crossfade, park on the effect icon in the timeline and click the **Remove Effect** button in the tool bar at the top of the Timeline window.

Figure 7.12 The Remove Effect button

Review/Discussion Questions

1. How do you open and close the Track Control panel?

2. How can you change the vertical detail of an audio waveform in the timeline?

3. What does Digital Audio Scrub allow you to do?

4. Where do you turn on Clip Gain?

5. What does Clip Gain allow you to do?

6. Which audio track should you adjust first to achieve correct levels?

7. How can you listen to a single audio track?

8. How can you turn off an audio track so you cannot hear it?

9. What does the Audio Tool provide?

10. How do you add a crossfade to an audio edit?

EXERCISE 7

 Exercise Break 7.1
Pause here to practice what you've learned.

GOALS

- Create a new audio track and edit in music
- Use add-edits, Clip gain and crossfades to improve the audio mix
- Add more rock climbing footage to the sequence

Continue editing the Rock Climber sequence

In this exercise you will add a music track to the timeline and adjust its audio levels.

1. Launch Media Composer | First and open your **My Second Project_(student ID)** project. Load the **Rock Climber Version 3** sequence in the Record monitor.

   In the Lesson 4 exercise, you linked to one music track and imported another. In your project's *Music* bin, you should find those two music tracks. There was also a third music track that you probably didn't input into the project.

   View the Music bin in Text view. The track you need for your sequence is **179_short_we-are-young-we-are-free_0037**. It should be a stereo clip that runs for 37 seconds. You linked to it in Exercise 4.

2. Open the clip in the Source monitor and check the Track Selector in the Timeline window to make sure it is a stereo track.

   Notice that the green Track Selector for the stereo track is positioned at the bottom of the Track Panel, with no blue Record Track Selector beside it. You need to create a stereo Record track in the timeline.

 Media Composer | First will only allow you to edit a stereo Source track into a stereo Record track. Similarly, you can only edit a mono Source track into a mono Record track.

3. Create a new stereo audio track in the timeline by going to the menus at the top of the Media Composer | First interface and selecting **Timeline>New>Audio Track>Stereo**. You can also do a right-mouse click in a blank area of the Timeline window and select **New>Audio Track>Stereo** in the pop-up menu.

4. Play the music track in the Source monitor. It is a fast paced, high energy track that is unsuited to the first 'meditative' part of the story. However, it will work well as the climber gets started. In the Timeline, park the blue Position indicator just after the hand slaps the rock in closeup. Add the entire music track onto A3 of the timeline.

5. Notice when you view the audio waveform of the clip in A3 that the waveform is a solid block of grey or black. Reduce the height of the waveform in A3 by first turning on the A3 Track Selector and turning off any other audio Track Selector. Then press **Ctrl+Alt+K** (Windows) or **Command+Option+K** (Mac) until you can clearly see the shape of the audio waveform, as shown in figure 7.13.

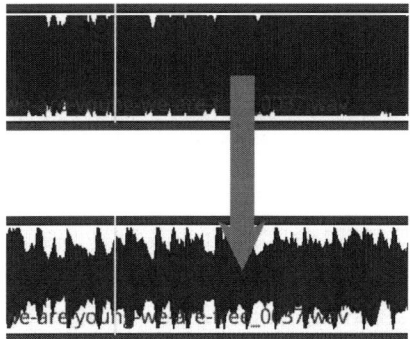

Figure 7.13 Reducing the height of the waveform display

6. When you play the timeline, you will not be able to hear the voice or the effects audio because the music overpowers both tracks.

7. For record track A3, from the Track Control panel turn on **Clip Gain** and pull down the fader until the music peaks at about -14 dB on the meters in the **Audio Tool**.

8. Play the sequence and notice that when the voice starts, the music is still too loud by comparison. Using what you have already learned, here is a quick and easy way of lowering the music level so it dips under the voice.

9. Make sure only the Track Selector for A3 is turned on. Just before the narration begins, place an

10. **Add Edit** on A3.

11. Place another **Add Edit** in the A3 track just after the narration ends.

12. Notice that the section of the segment between the Add Edits now has its own fader. Pull down the fader so the music level is well below the voice level. The red '=' signs straddling the Add Edits is telling you that something is different between the contiguous segments. In this case, the audio levels are different.

13. To smooth out the sudden change in audio levels, apply crossfades to both of the Add Edits by using the **Quick Transition** button. Adjust the duration of the crossfades so they produce pleasing changes in levels – not too quick and not too slow.

14. Now overwrite more climbing shots in the gap after the closeup of the hand. If you cut to the rhythm and beat of the music, there is probably room for 5 or 6 shots. Try to find a series of shots that depict a progression of climbing up the rock wall. If you like, you can overwrite the interview grab up to just before he says, '…*how hard you can climb*…'.

15. Publish to YouTube.

LESSON 8

Introduction to Transition Effects

In Lesson 7 you learned how to use the Quick Transition feature to add crossfades to an audio track. Quick Transition can also be used to add dissolves and other transition types between video segments in the timeline.

This lesson's exercise will be to continue editing your Rock Climber sequence and apply some transition effects.

Media Used: Rock Climber

Duration: 40 minutes

GOALS

- Apply video Quick Transitions
- Modify Quick Transitions
- Modify transitions in the Timeline
- Understand 'handles'
- Remove effects
- Add transitions from the Effect Palette
- Modify effects from the Effect Editor
- Save an Effect Template

Creating Visual Transition Effects

Of all visual effects used in film and television the most common are dissolves and fades. They can add drama, resolve a difficult cut point, convey the passage of time or location, or even indicate an altered state of consciousness. Media Composer | First uses the same basic method to create dissolves between pictures as it does for crossfades in audio. Because these are the most commonly used effects, the Quick Transition feature provides an easy way of applying them to a sequence.

Perhaps more important than *how* to apply transition effects is *why* you might want to use them. This will also be explored in this lesson.

 A dissolve blends together the images between adjacent shots in the sequence. A fade blends the image to, or from, black. Fades are commonly used only at the beginning or end of a scene.

1. Open your **My Second Project_(Student ID)** project.
2. From the **Sequences** bin, locate your **Rock Climber Version 3** sequence and duplicate it. (**Edit > Duplicate**)
3. Rename the duplicate **Rock Climber Version 4**.

You can use this version to add video transitions. If you don't like the end result you can return to Version 3, make another duplicate and try again.

Adding Quick Transitions

The Quick Transition button, shown in figure 8.1, is the fastest way to add a video dissolve or an audio crossfade to a cut point.

To add a video dissolve or fade, turn on the Track Selector for the desired video track in the timeline. To add an audio crossfade you turn on the appropriate audio Track Selector. You can simultaneously add a dissolve and crossfade by having both video and audio Track Selectors turned on.

Figure 8.1 The Quick Transition button

To quickly add a 1-second dissolve to the sequence you have created so far:

1. Only have the V1 Track Selector turned on and park the Position Indicator close to the edit between the first two shots in the *Rock Climber Version 4* sequence.
2. Click the **Quick Transition** button or press the **Backslash** key [\] on the keyboard.

    The Quick Transition window opens, as shown in Figure 8.2.

3. Click the **Add** button or press the **Enter** key.

The dialog box will close and the default transition—a one-second dissolve centered on the cut —will be applied to the edit point on the active track. A dissolve icon will also appear across the edit point in the timeline.

Of course, you won't always want a 1-second dissolve for a transition, so let's explore the other controls.

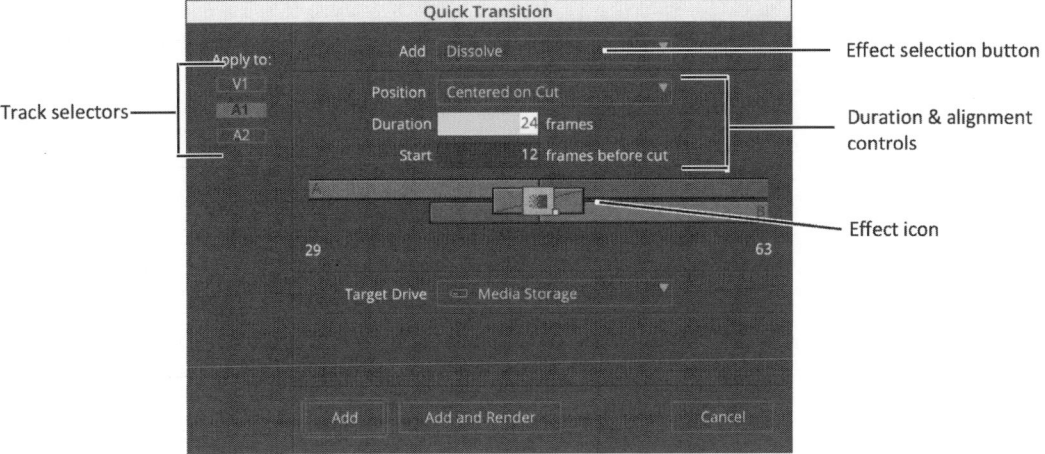

Figure 8.2 Using the Quick Transition dialog box is the easiest way to create a transition effect.

Customizing Quick Transitions

The Quick Transition window is divided into a number of sections.

Using the **Add** menu at the top of the dialogue box, you can select from a few dissolve-related transition effects. Click the drop menu to see what options are available but choose **Dissolve** to start with.

Below the Add menu are a few choices for modifying the duration and alignment of the transition. Included in this section is a scaled graphical representation of the transition, showing the alignment and 'handles'. This can help you to understand any duration or alignment problems that may occur.

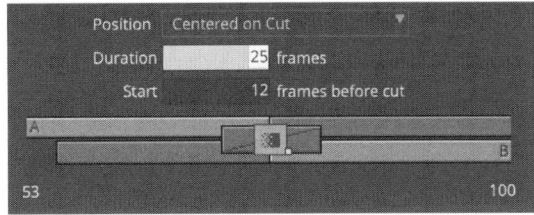

Figure 8.3 Alignment section of the Quick Transition dialog box

At this point, it's important to understand the concept of "handles"; To create a transition, you must have more source media in the media file than was edited into the timeline. The 'outgoing' segment (the A-side shot) and the 'incoming' segment (the B-side shot) need to overlap for the duration of the transition, as shown in figure 8.4. This extra media required on either side of the edit is referred to as the *handle*.

Or, in other words, the *handle* is the unused portion of the master clip.

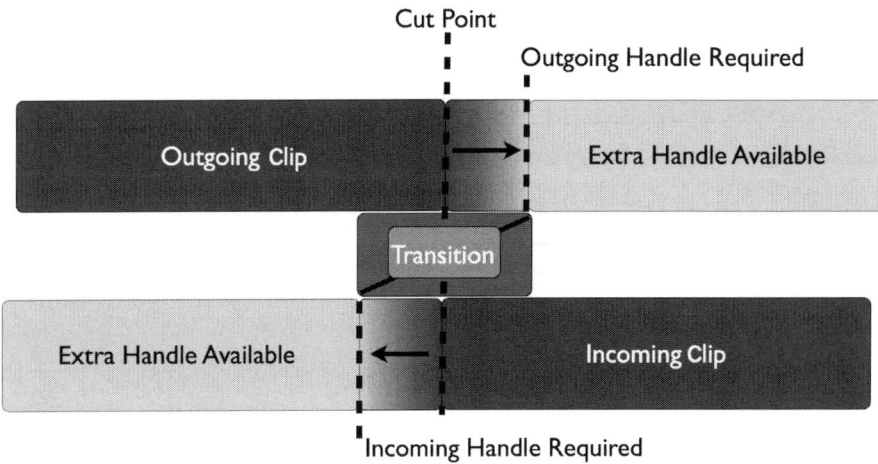

Figure 8.4 Handle diagram

If you type a duration in the dialog box that requires more handle than is available in the media file, Media Composer | First will automatically adjusts the duration of the handle to give you the longest possible transition.

By default, the Quick Transition dialog box will apply a dissolve transition that is centered on the cut point, meaning an equal number of frames for the dissolve happens before and after the cut points. This requires the outgoing and incoming segments to have at least enough handle for half the duration of the transition, as you can see in figure 8.5.

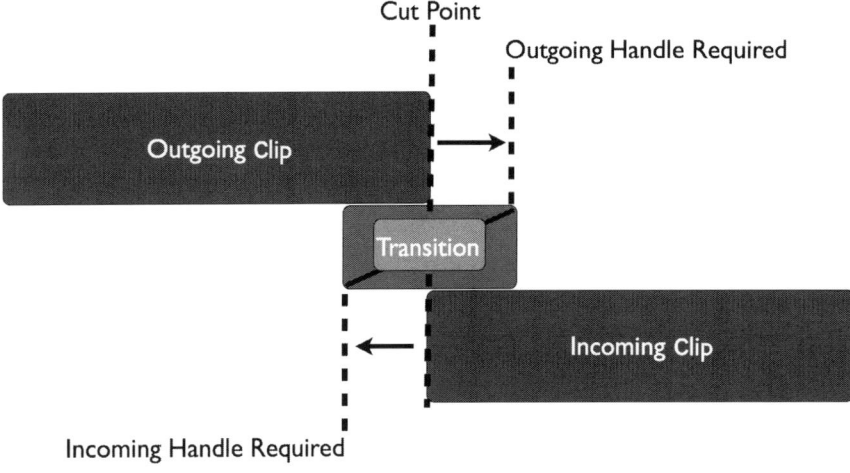

Figure 8.5 Transition alignment diagram

You can change the alignment so the transition starts on the cut, instead of being centered on the cut. This means the outgoing segment will need to have a handle length equal to the entire transition but the incoming shot doesn't need any extra handle as it already "starts at the cut."

If Media Composer | First determines that you don't have any handle on the incoming shot, it will reconfigure the dissolve alignment to achieve the best outcome.

4. To see how this works, park the blue Position indicator near the cut just after the climber says, '... really just take in where I am...'.

5. Click the **Quick Transition** button or press the **Backslash** key [\] on the keyboard and see how the Quick Transition reconfigures to achieve the best possible dissolve, as shown in figure 8.6.

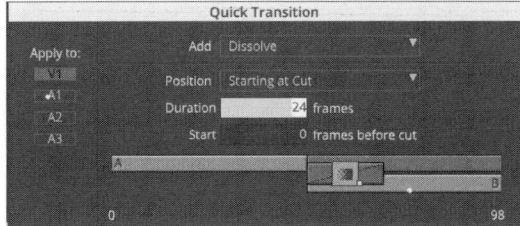

Figure 8.6 Transition alignment and duration changes to suit the handle lengths

In this case, the outgoing A side has enough handle for a dissolve while the incoming B side has no handle available at all. To achieve a dissolve, Quick Transition changes the Position to 'Starting at Cut'. It also calculates that the default Duration of 24 frames can be achieved. Given the handle length available, you could make the duration greater or less than 24 frames, but the transition will still only be able to start at the cut.

 Another way to adjust a transition within the Quick Transition window is to drag the left or right edge of the purple graphical effect icon to change its duration. You can also drag within the purple effect icon to change its alignment.

Clicking the **Add** button will result in the creation of a real-time effect. If you were to click the **Add and Render** button, Media Composer | First would render the transition, creating a new media file that is as long as the effect, and combines the outgoing and incoming handles. This can be helpful to ensure real-time playback if you find your computer pauses or stutters when it tries to play a transition.

In the Quick Transition dialog box, the left section of the dialog box is used for **track selection**. The tracks selected before you click the Quick Transition button determine the track(s) that will have the effect applied, but if you forget to select the correct Track Selectors in the Timeline window before clicking the Quick Transition button, or you change your mind, you can change the selected tracks here.

Modifying Transition Effects in the timeline

Once you have added a transition, the Timeline displays a transition icon over the cut point. A diagonal line indicates the duration and position of the transition, while the graphic design of the icon tells you the transition is a dissolve, as you can see in figure 8.7. When you look at the effect icon in the timeline, notice that there are also handle controls at each end of the diagonal line. You can click and drag those controls to change the duration of the transition. If you click and drag the icon you can change the start position. The mouse pointer changes into a small left-right pointing arrow when you click on the control handles to alter the duration and the mouse turns into a hand for changing the position.

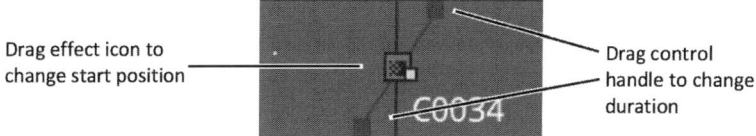

Figure 8.7 Modifying a transition from within the timeline

If you start modifying the transition from within the timeline, the Composer window reconfigures to show you 6 small screens – the Transition Corner Display.

Figure 8.8 The Composer window reconfigures to show the outgoing and incoming frames of the transition.

The top 3 images show you the start, middle and end frames of the outgoing shot over the duration of the transition. The bottom 3 images show you the start, middle and end frames of the incoming shot. The images update dynamically as you adjust the duration and position of the transition in the timeline.

 You cannot drag an effect beyond the cut point, nor can you drag an effect beyond the ends of the handles.

 You can press the Alt key (Windows) or the Option key (Mac) before you drag a transition handle to lengthen or shorten the transition equally in both directions.

If you are not seeing these handle controls, or if you do not want to modify the transition from within the timeline, you can show or hide the controls by clicking the <**Transition Manipulation** button, as shown in figure 8.9. The button is located at the top of the timeline window.

Figure 8.9 The Transition Manipulation button

When to Use a Transition Effect

Watch your favorite films and TV shows, and you will see that most edits are straight cuts. But, when you start looking at music videos, movie and game trailers, and other short, highly stylized pieces, you can find plenty of examples where transition effects are used instead of cuts.

Let's consider whether a dissolve is appropriate at the cut between the first two shots in the Rock Climber sequence. When you started editing, the intention was to try to achieve continuity style cuts between the opening clips, in which the action flowed seamlessly from one shot to the next. This worked quite well until you rearranged the shots, and now the position of the hand is different between the action at the end of the first shot and the start of the second shot.

In some cases, using a dissolve is a good way to disguise a discontinuity of action like this. However, a dissolve can also suggest that a period of time has elapsed between shots or there has been a change of location between shots. In your opening series of shots neither of these is true. So, while a dissolve may mask a discontinuity of action it may also infer something else that contradicts what you are trying to achieve (there is a much better solution that we will look at in a later lesson). Given this contradiction, let's remove the transition from this edit.

Removing Transition Effects

As you learned in Lesson 7, the Remove Effect button is in the Tool bar at the top of the Timeline window.

Figure 8.10 The Remove Effect button

To remove a transition effect using Remove Effect:

1. Park the Position indicator near the transition effect.

2. Select the **track(s)** that contains the transition effect(s) to be removed. (Deselect any tracks you want to leave unaffected.)

3. Click the **Remove Effect** button. The effect will be removed.

You can also remove a transition effect using the Transition Manipulation button:

1. With the **Transition Manipulation** tool active, click on the transition **effect icon**. The effect will be highlighted.

2. Press the **Delete** key. The effect will be removed.

Adding Multiple Transition Effects

Media Composer | First allows you to easily add Quick Transition effects to a series of edits. This is a great little time-saver in situations, like in a montage, where you may want to add dissolves to several edits in a row. There is a section of your sequence that might lend itself to this approach.

When the music starts, you have edited a series of quick shots together that depict the rock climber energetically scaling the wall. While straight cuts work well, employing dissolves or dips to black might enhance the impression that, more than just requiring effort, it is taking time to achieve.

To add a dissolve to multiple cuts:

1. Select the **track** in the Timeline window Track Panel on which you want to apply the effects.
2. Mark the cuts with a **Mark In** point before the first cut and a **Mark Out** point after the last cut. The marked series of edited will be highlighted, as shown in figure 8.11.

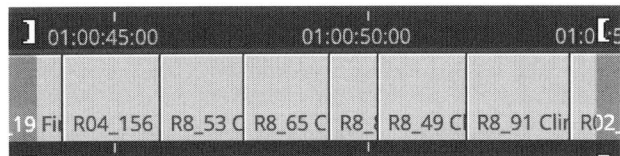

Figure 8.11 Edits between marks

3. Click the **Quick Transition** button or press the **\ (backslash)** key to open the Quick Transition dialog box.
4. Select the **Apply to All Transitions (IN->OUT)** checkbox that now appears in the dialog box.

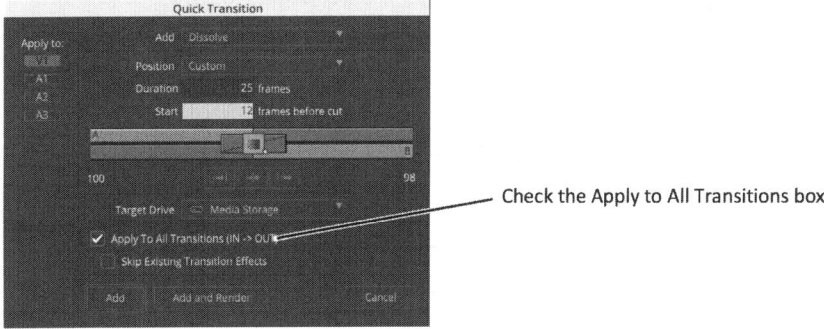

Figure 8.12 The Apply to All Transitions (IN -> OUT) option

5. Click the **Add** button.

All the edits between the In and Out marks now have a transition applied to them. Figure 8.13.

Figure 8.13 All edits with transitions

Accessing effects from the Effects Palette

While the Quick Transition dialog box provides quick access to the most commonly used effects, all effects, including dissolves and fades, can be accessed through the Effects Palette. There are a few ways to access the Effect Palette, the most straightforward of which being to choose **Effect Pallet** from the **Tools** drop-down menu. The window will initially appear as a floating window but can be docked to the paneled user interface – figure 8.4 shows the Effect Palled as a tab shared with the bins window.

The Effect Palette displays a list of all available effects. Across the top of the palette are buttons to show "Filters" (also known as Segment Effects), Transition Effects, Audio Track effects, and Audio Clip effects. These four categories help to keep things organized and easier to find.

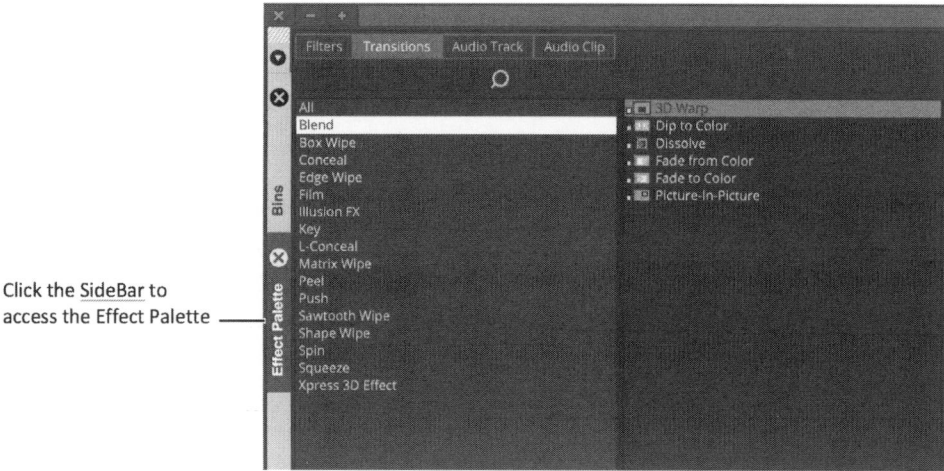

Click the SideBar to access the Effect Palette

Figure 8.14 The Effect Palette

The left side of the Effect Palette lists effect categories, and the right side lists specific effects within the selected category. When you select a category on the left side, all the effects in that category are displayed on the right.

 A green dot next to an effect icon indicates that the effect is a real-time effect. It does not require rendering.

To add a dissolve from the Effect Palette:

1. Open the **Effect Palette**

2. Select the **Transitions** button at the top of the palette.

3. Select the **Blend** category in the left-hand column.

4. From the list of effects in the right-hand column, drag the **Dissolve** effect icon onto a cut in the Timeline.

5. When the cut highlights, release the mouse to apply the effect.

To replace an existing transition effect with a different transition effect from the Effect Palette:

1. Drag a **transition effect** from the right side of the Effect Palette over an existing transition in the Timeline.

2. When the Timeline effect highlights, release the mouse to replace the effect.

 Note that the range of transition effects available in the Blend category of the Effect Palette is similar but not exactly the same as those available in the Quick Transition.

Modifying Effects in the Effect Editor

To change any of the parameters for an effect, open the Effect Editor.

To open the Effect Editor, in the timeline park the blue Position indicator on the effect that you want to modify. Make sure the Track Selector is turned on for that track. Do one of the following:

- Choose **Tools > Effect Editor.**

- Choose **Windows>Workspaces>Effects**.

- Click on the **Effects** workspace button on the right-hand side of the Media Composer | First interface.

- Click the **Effect Mode** button in the tool bar at the top of the Timeline window, as shown in figure 8.15.

Figure 8.15 The Effect Mode button

The Effect Editor organizes parameters in collapsible groups. The types of parameters available vary according to the effect you are modifying. In the case of a dissolve, **Foreground** is the only parameter you can change. Clicking a disclosure triangle next to the parameter opens the group and displays available adjustments, as shown in Figure 8.16. Any changes you make are instantly previewed in the Composer window.

Figure 8.16 The Effect Editor

What happens along with this is more subtle, but very critical. In the Composer window, the Record monitor has now become the Effect Preview monitor. The monitor no longer shows you the entire sequence but only displays the selected effect, which is highlighted in the Timeline. The position bar under the monitor, which normally encompasses the entire sequence, now navigates only through the selected effect.

When working in Effect mode, it's best to get in the habit of using the position bar in the Effect Preview monitor to scrub through the effect. Don't scrub using the Timecode track in the Timeline. If you click the Timecode track, the Effect Editor will close. This is normal behavior.

Depending upon how you opened the Effect Editor, the Composer window may be configured as a single Effect Preview monitor or as a two-monitor display.

- Opening by clicking the **Effect Mode**> button or via the menu **Tools > Effect Editor** results in a two-monitor configuration where the left-hand screen functions as the normal Source monitor, as shown in figure 8.17.

Figure 8.17 The Effect Editor and the Effect Preview monitor in a two-screen configuration

- Opening the Effect Editor through the **Effects** workspace menu or workspace sidebar results in a single larger Effect Preview monitor, as seen in figure 8.18.

Figure 8.18 The Effect Editor and the Effect Preview monitor in a single-screen configuration

In whichever viewing mode you prefer to work, the Effect Editor allows you to change the **start position (or alignment)** of the dissolve and its **duration**. Click the Transition Alignment button to reveal a list of options, or type a duration for the effect in the Transition Duration field.

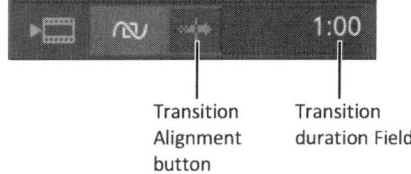

Figure 8.19 The Transition Effect Alignment & Duration buttons

You can click the **Play Loop** button in either the Effect Editor or the Effect Preview monitor to loop playback through the effect, shown in figure 8.20. To stop the looping playback, just click anywhere other than the button (for example in the Effect Preview monitor).

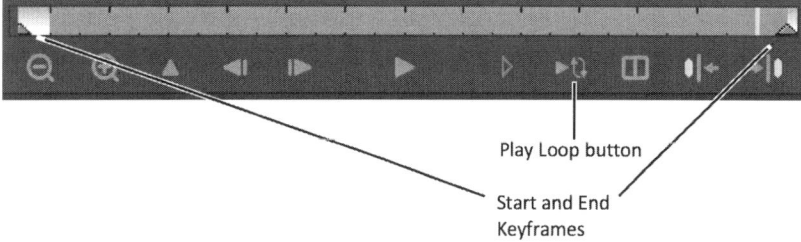

Figure 8.20 The Play Loop button and Keyframes under the Effect Preview monitor

Keyframes allow you to modify a dissolve in a way that's not possible through the Quick Transition dialog box. Typically, you expect a dissolve to start on the outgoing image (the "A" side) and transition through to the incoming image (the "B" side). The keyframes each have a value assigned to them that controls that transition from one image to the next. Those values are determined by the **Foreground** slider in the Effect Editor.

Try this experiment:

Click on the **Start** keyframe under the Effect Preview monitor or the equivalent **Start** keyframe in the Effect Editor. They mirror each other and when selected will be highlighted purple, as shown in figure 8.21.

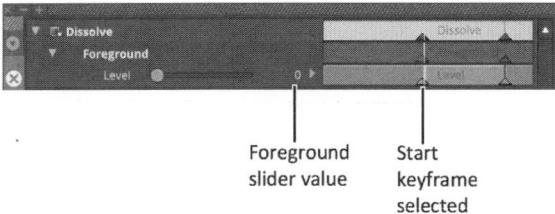

Figure 8.21 The Start Keyframe and Foreground slider value in the Effect Editor

Notice that the **Foreground** slider has a value of 0 when the start keyframe is selected. This means the outgoing image (A side) is fully visible.

Click on the **End** keyframe so it turns purple (see figure 8.22). The **Foreground** slider has now changed position and has a value of 100, meaning the incoming image (B side) is now fully visible.

Figure 8.22 The End Keyframe and Foreground slider value

The time between the Start and End keyframes is the duration of the dissolve.

If you now select the **Start** keyframe and change the **Foreground** slider value to 100 and then select the **End** keyframe and change its **Foreground** slider value to 0, you will have produced a very unusual result. Close the Effect Editor or alternatively click in the timeline's timecode track. Play the new dissolve to discover the potential and power of keyframes to modify effects. Your dissolve now works in reverse, starting with the B side and ending with the A side.

Creating an Effect Template

After creating a great effect, you may want to reuse it in other parts of your sequence. For this, you can save effects as templates and use them repeatedly without having to re-create them. The icon in the upper-left corner of the Effect Editor (see Figure 8.23) is used to save effect templates into a bin. Click and drag the icon to any bin, thereby saving it as a template for later use.

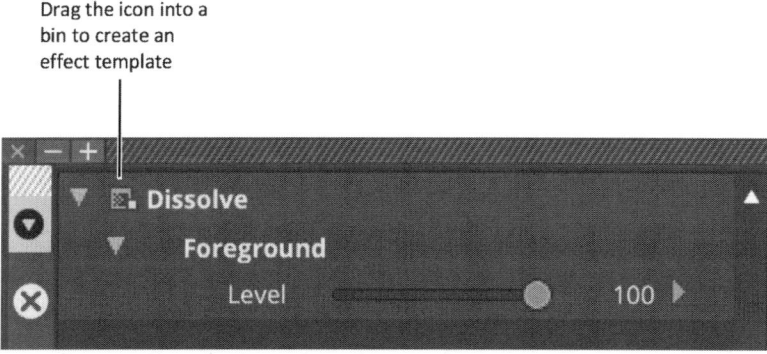

Figure 8.23 The effect icon allows you to save the effect as a template.

To save an effect template from the Effect Editor:

- From the upper-left corner of the Effect Editor, drag the **effect icon** into a bin.

To apply effects templates from a Bin:

- From the bin, drag an **effect template** for a transition effect onto an edit in the timeline or onto a previously applied transition effect in the Timeline (if you want to replace an effect).

 **Any open bin that contains an effect template will be displayed as a category at the bottom of the Effect Palette (named for the bin in which the effect resides). Selecting the Bin category will display all the effect templates from that bin on the right side of the Effect Palette.**

Review/Discussion Questions

1. If you want to add multiple dissolves to a series of cut points using the Quick Transition dialog box, how do you identify the cuts that will get the dissolves?

2. What is a handle, and why is it important in the context of transition effects?

3. What must you do to ensure a Quick Transition is added only to a video cut point, and not an audio cut point?

4. True or False: The Transition Corner display shows the first, middle, and last frames of the A-side and B-side of the transition.

5. True or False: Dragging a transition from the Effect Palette onto an existing transition in the Timeline replaces the existing transition.

6. True or False: To save an effect template, you drag the effect icon from the upper-left corner of the Effect Editor into the Effect Palette.

7. What function must be enabled before you can modify a transition effect from within the Timeline to change its duration or position?

8. What does the Foreground parameter in the Effect Editor allow you to adjust?

9. When you open the Effect Editor what happens to the Record monitor in the Composer window?

10. When the Effect Editor is open, do you scrub through an effect from the timeline or the Effect Preview monitor?

EXERCISE 8

Exercise Break 8.1
Pause here to practice what you've learned.

GOALS

- Add transition effects to the sequence
- Modify the effects
- Create an Effect Template
- Publish to YouTube

Add Transitions To the Rock Climber Sequence

1. From your **My Second Project_(Student ID)** project, open your **Rock Climber Version 4** sequence.

2. Use the **Remove Effect** button to delete any dissolves that may be on edits in the V1 track.

3. Use either the Quick Transition or the Effect Palette to add a **Dip to Color** to each of the edits during the start of the music and before the following interview. Don't be afraid to experiment with the duration of the transitions to see how they affect the feel of that series of shots. You can add a transition to each edit in turn or apply them to all transitions at once.

4. When you are happy with the transition duration, open the Effect Editor for one of the transitions and see that the Dip to Color effect has a Background Color parameter that you can change. Click on the disclosure triangle to reveal the **Hue, Saturation** and **Luminance** sliders. Experiment to see if a color other than black works for these transitions in the sequence. White might be an interesting alternative.

5. If you decide on a custom color, create an Effect Template by dragging the effect icon from the Effect Editor to a bin.

6. Now replace all the original transitions with the template from the bin.

7. Publish your work so far to YouTube.

LESSON 9

Using 3-Point Editing

So far you have learned how to build and modify a sequence by dragging and dropping segments into the timeline. This is a very tactile way of working and suits many editors. Beyond the drag and drop approach is the concept of 3-point editing - rather than relying on using the mouse and the user interface, 3-point editing offers keyboard shortcuts that can help you edit faster and more accurately.

Your exercise will be to continue editing your Rock Climber sequence by using 3-point editing instead of the drag-and-drop method.

Duration: 40 minutes

Media Used: Rock Climber

GOALS

- Build your sequence using splice and overwrite using three-point editing techniques
- Remove material from the sequence using Lift and Overwrite
- Manage tracks to maintain sync

1. Launch Media Composer | First and open your **My Second Project_(Student ID)** project.
2. To protect your work done to date, it is a good idea to duplicate the sequence **Rock Climber Version 4** and rename the duplicate **Rock Climber Version 5**.
3. Open the **Rock Climber Version 5** sequence in the Record/Timeline windows.

Building Your Sequence with Splice-In

As you have already learned by using the drag-and-drop method, the two most common ways to add shots to a sequence are *Splice-In* and *Overwrite*. Splice-In adds more material to the sequence. Overwrite replaces material that is already there. If you are adding a new shot to the end of a sequence, then it generally doesn't matter which tool you use, as there are no pre-existing segments to either move with a Splice-In or replace with an Overwrite. In that case, either tool will simply add the new segment to the end of the sequence.

Splicing Video Clips

"Splice" is a term that Avid borrowed from traditional film editing. To add a new shot to a reel of film, the editor would insert it by cutting the existing film at the point where the new shot was supposed to start. Adhesive tape was then used to join the new shot, or segment, at each end, inserting it between the cut ends of the film. With the new piece added, the film was longer. In Media Composer | First, the Splice-In function works in much the same way. It adds the new shot into the sequence by creating a cut point and inserting the segment between the existing frames. The new shot makes the track longer—which also, frequently, makes the sequence longer.

 Other NLEs often call this type of edit an insert edit or a ripple edit. If you are familiar with insert editing in Final Cut Pro or Premiere Pro, you already understand how the Splice-In function works.

Splice-In is often used to build a scene. If you're adding segments in sequential order to the end of the timeline, then it behaves in a similar way to Overwrite. But splicing a shot between existing segments shows its real value. Splice-In pushes all subsequent, or downstream, material further down the Timeline (to the right). As shown in Figure 9.1, when adding a new shot between others, shot Y (and every other shot after it, like shot "Z") is pushed along and the track becomes longer.

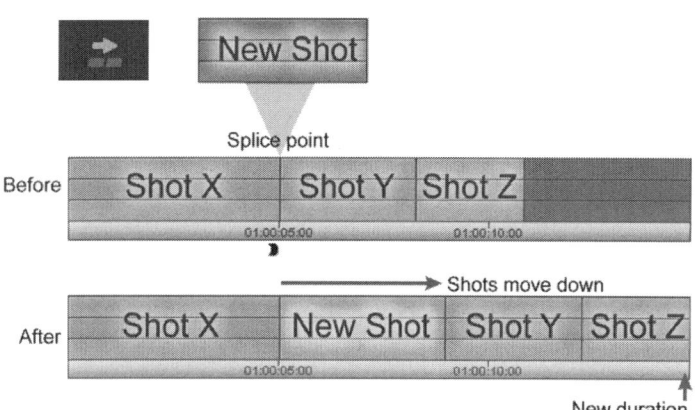

Figure 9.1 Splicing a segment between others moves all subsequent segments down the Timeline to the right.

The yellow Splice-In button is found in the tool bar under the Source monitor. Its keyboard equivalent is the **V** key. To the right of the Splice-In button is the red Overwrite button.

Figure 9.2 The Splice-In and Overwrite buttons under the Source monitor

Setting up to perform a Splice-In edit is very similar to setting up to drag-and-drop a clip into the timeline except that rather than using the mouse, it is easier to execute the edit using the keyboard.

1. At about 14:18:00 in the clip R02_02(b) Interview, the climber says, '*There's a point in routes when you get to a really difficult part but if you don't commit to it and know you're going to get it you're not going to get it.*' **Mark In** and **Mark Out** around that statement.

   To splice the shot into the sequence using Splice-In:

2. In the Timeline, place the **position indicator,** or mark an **In** point, about 4 or 5 seconds after the last interview words, '*…to be better than you were last time.*' This is where you want to splice the shot into the sequence. Mark an In point at this location (If you don't, the system will splice at the location of the position indicator)

3. In the Timeline window's Track Panel, turn on the Source **V1** and **A1 Track Selectors** and the Record **V1** and **A2 Track Selectors**. Ensure other tracks are deselected. The audio tracks should auto-patch so A1 from the source aligns next to A2 of the record. The two video track selectors should be next to each other.

4. To develop your keyboard skills, press the **V** key on the keyboard (or alternatively click the yellow **Splice-In** button). The clip is spliced into the sequence.

5. At about 14:45:00 in clip R02_02(b) Interview, the climber says, '*When you mess up on a route and fall, you just have to get right back on it.*' **Mark In** and **Mark Out** around that statement.

You want to edit this new clip to the end of the previous clip (the clip before the 4-5 second gap you just created), so you need to move the blue Position indicator to the first frame of black after that previous segment.

To snap the Position indicator to the first frame of black:

1. In the timecode track of the timeline, **Ctrl-click (Windows)** or **Command-click (Macintosh)** near the edit point.

2. Depending on where the Position indicator is parked, click either the **Go to Previous Event** or **Go to Next Event** button under the Record monitor. Figure 9.3. The Position indicator will snap to the nearest edit point on any track. Keep clicking the button until the Position indicator snaps to the edit point you want.

Figure 9.3

3. Use the **V** key to splice the new interview clip to the end of the previous interview segment.

4. In the Clips bin, locate clip R8_35 Climbing Fall-EditStock. **Mark In** just before he loses his grip and falls and **Mark Out** just before he starts talking. But keep his yell. It provides a great punctuation mark in the story. The duration between marks should be about 3 seconds.

5. Snap to the edit point between the two interview segments.

6. Ensure the audio Track Selectors are aligned so source A1 is next to record A1 and the two V1 track selectors are next to each other.

7. Because you need to maintain sync between the video of the interview on V1 and its corresponding audio on A2, you need the segment on A2 to move down the timeline at the same time the segment on V1 moves. To achieve this, also turn on the A2 Track Selector on the record side of the Track Panel. Figure 9.4. Even though you will not be editing anything into A2, the track is active, so the segment in A2 will move down by the same amount as the segment in V1 when you perform the Splice-In.

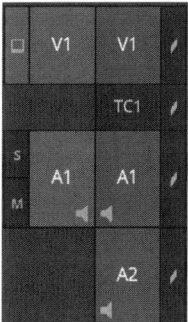

Figure 9.4

8. Use Splice-In (V) to edit the clip into the timeline between the two interview segments. Figure 9.5 illustrates how sync is maintained by having all track selectors turned on for the tracks that need to maintain sync.

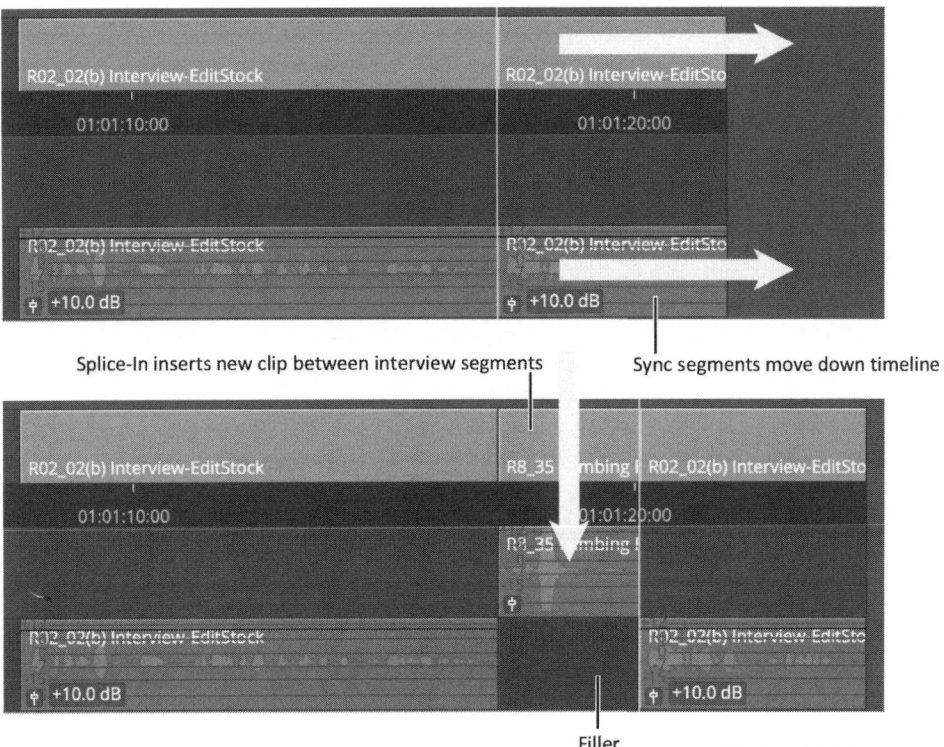

Figure 9.5 Maintaining sync between segments

 Tracks always matter! Check your track selection in the Track Panel before you perform an edit.

Concept: Understanding Filler

Filler refers to the empty space in the Timeline. The term is derived from the blank celluloid film used to keep picture and sound tracks in sync whenever there was a temporary gap in one or the other during the editing process. If you've used other editing applications, you may be familiar with the term "slug." Filler and slug serve the same purpose. Thinking of it as filler rather than empty space is more accurate. In Media Composer, you can manipulate filler in the same ways you edit video or audio segments. You can add edits to it, trim it, apply effects to it, and more. This is different from any other NLE (Non-Linear Editor) on the market, and provides some real advantages, specifically with regard to trimming and in working with effects.

Editing with Overwrite

While Splice-In adds new material to the sequence; Overwrite replaces material already there.

Overwrite is the perfect tool for quickly adding the action shots which visually support the interview.

To edit a clip using Overwrite:

1. Load either the clip **R9_08 Hanging High-EditStock** or **R9_07 Bouldering Wall Continuation-EditStock** into the Source monitor. Decide which one you prefer as a second shot after the one of him falling.

2. You only need to identify or mark a combination of any three points between the source clip and the sequence. Media Composer | First uses two of the marks to calculate the duration of the edit and uses that information to determine where the fourth mark would be. The calculated fourth mark could be an IN or an OUT point. It doesn't matter. The possible options are:

3. Mark an **In** point and an **Out** point in the Timeline and mark an **In** point or **Out** point in the source clip.

   - Alternatively, in the Source monitor, simply place the Position indicator where you want to start using the clip. The system calculates how many frames to overwrite into the sequence to replace the exact number of frames marked in the Timeline. If the clip does not contain sufficient footage, the screen displays the message, "Insufficient source material to make this edit."

4. Mark an **In** point and an **Out** point in your clip and mark an **In** point or an **Out** point in the sequence.

   - Alternatively, in the sequence, simply place the Position indicator where you want the overwrite to begin. The marked clip will be added into the sequence at the IN or OUT point you marked.

5. In this case, marking the IN and OUT in the timeline and the IN on the source shot will probably work best in determining where you want to place the shot. Just after he falls and yells, add a **Mark In** to the timeline. **Mark Out** just after he says, *'When you mess up on a route and fall….'*. In the source clip **Mark In** at the point where you think the cut on action from the closer shot will look the best.

6. Click the **Source Track Selectors** and **Record Track Selectors** for the tracks you want to use for the edit.

7. Press the **B** key on the keyboard (or click the **Overwrite** button).

The marked section in the sequence is overwritten by the material you selected in the clip. The total length of the sequence does not change unless the new shot extends beyond the end of the sequence.

Removing Material From a Sequence

Creating a rough cut is not just a constant process of adding material and making the sequence longer and longer. There are plenty of times when you will want to remove material from the sequence—because you want to change the shot, because you want to remove a portion of it for better timing, or for other creative purposes.

You can remove footage from your sequence and either close or retain the gap that results. You'll be marking the portion you want to remove by placing IN and OUT marks in the sequence.

Lift

Lift removes material from the Timeline, leaving filler in its place. Appropriately, the icon for the Lift button is a strongman lifting a set of weights. The button is located in the tool bar at the top of the Timeline window.

Figure 9.6 The Lift button

Lift is used when you want to remove segments or parts of segments but still maintain the rhythm of a sequence or the synchronization of the picture and audio tracks. This action is the inverse of overwriting; both lifting and overwriting maintain the integrity and duration of the sequence.

To lift material from the Timeline:

1. Mark an **In** point and an **Out** point at the start and end of the material to be removed. It doesn't need to be an entire segment. You can mark just a part of a segment or include several segments between the marks.

2. Select the desired record **tracks** by enabling just the desired **Track Selector** panels.

3. Press **Z** on the keyboard (or click the **Lift** button in the Timeline).

You can use the Mark Clip button (or press the T key) to quickly select a whole clip for removal. Based on the record tracks you have selected and the location of the blue position indicator, the Mark Clip function automatically finds the IN and OUT points of a clip in the sequence.

You were offered a choice of two shots of the climber hanging from the rock face after he falls. To get a feel for the Lift function:

4. Use the **T** key to mark the segment that you used in the timeline.

5. With the V1 and A1 Track Selectors turned on, **Lift** the segment from the timeline.

6. Notice how the **Mark In** and **Mark Out** remain in the timeline after the segment has been removed.

7. Now mark an **In** point on the alternative shot and Overwrite the filler left after you lifted the segment out. The marks in the timeline disappear after you replace the segment.

Of course, to replace the segment you didn't need to lift it out at first. You could have simply overwritten it with the alternative shot.

Extract

Extracting removes material from the Timeline and closes the gap left by its removal. This action is the inverse of splicing. Both extracting and splicing affect the length of a track and/or the sequence. It is represented by a pair of scissors (Figure 9.7) and the button is located next to the Lift button at the top of the Timeline window. In some other applications, 'Extract' is called a "Ripple Delete."

Figure 9.7 The Extract button

Here is a perfect opportunity to use the Extract tool. At the beginning of the sequence, there is a discontinuity of action between the end of the first shot and the start of the second. In the first shot the hand is on the wall while in the second shot the climber is just starting to put his hand on the wall.

To fix the continuity at the cut:

1. In the sequence, mark an **In** point at the start of the second shot. **Ctrl-click (Windows)** or **Command-click (Macintosh)** will allow you to snap to the edit point.

2. Mark an **Out** point just after the climber has placed his hand on the wall and begins sliding it across the rock.

3. Select all the record **tracks** by enabling their **Track Selectors**. This is so you can maintain sync across all tracks throughout the entire sequence.

4. Press **X** on the keyboard (or click the **Extract** button in the Timeline).

How do you know the Position indicator is parked on the Head frame or Tail frame of a Segment? Look in the bottom left or bottom right corner of the Record monitor. When your Position indicator is on the Head frame, you'll see this symbol (Figure 9.8) in the lower-left corner. When your position indicator is on the Tail frame, you'll see this symbol (Figure 9.9) in the lower-right corner.

Figure 9.8 Head frame symbol

Figure 9.9 Tail frame symbol

Review/Discussion Questions

1. What happens to existing segments in the timeline when you Splice-In a segment at a point earlier in the timeline?

2. What happens to existing segments in the timeline when you Splice-In a segment at the end of the timeline?

3. What happens to existing segments in the timeline when you perform an Overwrite edit earlier in the timeline?

4. What happens to existing segments in the timeline when you perform an Overwrite edit at the end of the timeline?

5. With which editing function(s) are you more likely to break sync—Splice-In, Overwrite, Lift, or Extract? Why?

6. How can you ensure that you maintain sync when editing segments into the sequence?

7. What do the functions Go to Previous Event and Go to Next Event do?

8. Why do you only need to define 3 marks to achieve a successful Splice-In or Overwrite edit?

9. What is the difference between Lift and Extract?

10. What keys on the keyboard allow you to Splice-In, Overwrite, Extract and Lift?

EXERCISE 9

Exercise Break 9.1
Pause here to practice what you've learned.

GOALS

- Use 3-point editing to edit clips into your sequence
- Use Splice-In and Overwrite edits
- Use Lift and Extract
- Manage tracks to maintain sync
- Use keyboard shortcuts instead of the mouse

Continue Editing Your Rock Climber Version 5 Sequence

1. There is about 11 seconds in which you can edit more rock-climbing shots into the sequence. The IN point is just after the words, *'to be better than you were last time'*, and the OUT point is just after the words, *'…but if you don't commit to it…'*.

2. Use 3-point editing and the Overwrite tool to edit a series of climbing shots into the 11 seconds. Because the music is still driving the pace of the video, mark the IN and OUT cutting points in the timeline based on the music's rhythm and beat. Mark the IN point in the clip you want to use. Because he is about to talk about difficult parts of the climb, see if you can find shots in which he looks uncertain or having difficulty. Clip **R04_150 Matt Climbing-EditStock** is a good example of indecisiveness in choosing where to grab the rocks.

3. Try using the keyboard shortcuts instead of the mouse to navigate through clips and the sequence. The **J-K-L** keys are particularly useful as they are close to the **I** and **O** keys for marking IN and OUT points. With practice, you can use one hand on the keyboard to find and mark IN and OUT points in both clips and the sequence. Use the **B** key to Overwrite shots into the timeline.

4. If you want to try a different shot, mark a segment in the timeline from IN to OUT (**T** key) and use the Lift tool (**Z** key) to remove it, or simply use Overwrite (**B** key) to replace it.

5. Now use the Splice-In tool (**V** key) to add some more interview to the end of the sequence. At around 15:48:00 in clip **R02_02(b) Interview-EditStock**, he says, *'The end of a perfect day is to top out of a route and to, ah, come down and enjoy the sunset.'*

6. Use the Extract tool (**X** key) to remove the *'ah'* from his words and close up the gap, remembering to maintain sync between tracks V1 and A2.

7. To end, adjust all the audio levels for the clips you have edited into the timeline during this lesson.

8. Publish your sequence to YouTube.

LESSON 10

Using Multiple Tracks

Because sound plays such an important role in filmmaking, Lesson 7 introduced you to the tools available to view audio waveforms, mix audio and create audio tracks. Most of the work you do with audio occurs in the timeline and the ability to simultaneously hear voice, sound effects and music is dependent on you using multiple audio tracks.

Using multiple video tracks can be helpful as you edit a sequence and try different arrangements of clips to see what works best in telling your story. It is also possible to create multiple video tracks in Media Composer | First and in a similar way to audio, you can use video tracks to combine images in the timeline. Lesson 16 will cover that subject.

Media: Rock Climber

Duration: 40 minutes

GOALS

- Creating new video and audio tracks
- Patching tracks
- Using Sync Locks
- Identifying broken sync
- Moving segments between tracks
- Selecting multiple segments

1. Launch Media Composer | First and open your **My Second Project_(Student ID)** project.

2. As in previous lessons, to protect your work to date, duplicate your **Rock Climber Version 5** sequence and rename it **Rock Climber Version 6**. Load the new sequence into the Record monitor/Timeline window.

Overview

Not only do timeline tracks allow you to arrange and combine video and audio segments, but they play an important role in keeping your work organized. In editing your *Rock Climber* sequence, you have used the following track layout:

- **V1**: Picture
- **A1**: Natural Sound (FX audio)
- **A2**: VO (Voice Over and Interview)
- **A3**: Music (stereo)

Figure 10.1 illustrates what your track layout and arrangement of segments might look like so far.

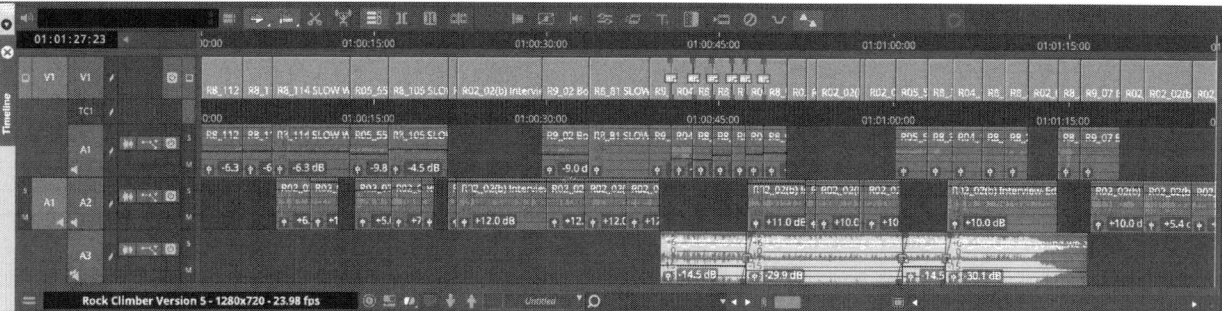

Figure 10.1 The Rock Climber sequence

By keeping the audio on separate tracks, you can immediately see the relationships between each type of sound. It also makes monitoring, editing, adjusting levels and mixing much easier.

In a similar way, it is often helpful to place different types of video clips on separate tracks. For instance, in *Rock Climber*, you might like to edit all the interview clips onto V1 and all the climbing clips onto V2.

 If you want to make it easier to remember how you're using the tracks, you can rename tracks in the Timeline. To do so, in the Track Panel, right-click on a Track Selector number, select Rename Track, and type a new name for the track.

Working with Tracks

Media Composer | First supports up to 4 video tracks and 8 audio tracks.

Adding Video Tracks

In Lesson 7 you added a stereo audio track to the timeline. Now you'll add a video track to your **Rock Climber Version 6** sequence.

To add a video track, do one of the following:

- With the sequence open in the Timeline, choose **Timeline > New > Video Track**.
- Right-click in the Timeline, then choose **New > Video Track**.
- Press **Ctrl+Y** (Windows) or **Command+Y** (Mac) .

By way of revision,

To add a mono audio track:

- With a sequence in the Timeline, choose **Timeline > New > Audio Track > Mono**.
- Right-click in the Timeline, then choose **New > Audio Track > Mono**.
- Press **Ctrl+U** (Windows) or **Command+U** (Mac) .

To add a stereo audio track:

- With a sequence in the Timeline, choose **Timeline > New > Audio Track > Stereo**.
- Right-click in the Timeline, then choose **New > Audio Track > Stereo**.
- Press Shift+**Ctrl+U** (Windows) or **Shift+Command+U** (Mac).

Patching Tracks

When you use the drag-and-drop method of editing, you can directly drag a video or audio clip onto the track where you want it to go.

When you use 3-point editing, you need to connect—that is, *patch*—source video or audio clips to the specific record tracks where you want to edit the clips. Patching tracks enables you to edit a source video track onto any available record video track in the timeline.

Source audio media (audio that is in the source monitor) can only be patched to Record audio tracks of the same type, i.e. a mono source track can only be patched to a mono record track and a stereo source track can only be patched to a stereo record track.

Auto-Patching

By default, Media Composer | First allows tracks to 'Auto-Patch'. Auto-Patching is a setting that allows you to automatically patch tracks based on track activation.

To patch tracks using Auto-Patching:

1. Disable the green Record Track Selectors to which source tracks are currently patched.
2. Now, enable the desired **tracks**, by clicking on the blue Record Track Selectors.

    The enabled Source tracks will jump next to the new enabled Record tracks, indicating the patch has occurred.

You can also use keyboard shortcuts to change the activation of your tracks. This enables you to patch tracks without reaching for the mouse.

To activate/deactivate Track Selectors using the keyboard:

1. Select either the Record monitor or Source monitor in the Composer window.
2. Press the keys shown in figure 10.2 to activate or deactivate a Track Selector.

Figure 10.2 Track Selection activation using the keyboard

If you prefer, you can turn off Auto-Patching and then rely on manually patching tracks.

To turn off Auto-Patching, go to the menu bar at the top of the screen and select:

1. **Avid Media Composer > Preferences...**
2. In the **Settings** window, select the **User** tab.
3. Double click the **Timeline** setting.
4. From the **Timeline Settings** window, select the **Edit** tab.
5. Un-check the **Auto-Patching** check box. Click **OK**.

Manually Patching Tracks

To manually patch a track from a Source clip to a different track in the sequence, do either:

- Click and hold the Source Track Selector button (V1 in Figure 10.3) and drag the arrow to the target Record track on which you want to make the edit. The Source track you selected realigns next to the Record track and becomes highlighted.

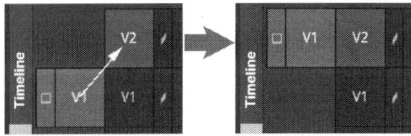

Figure 10.3 Drag from the source track to the target record track to patch the track

- Click and hold the left mouse button with the pointer on the Source track and the system will offer you the available Record tracks you can patch to, as shown in figure 10.4. Roll the mouse over the track choice you want, and the button will become highlighted. Click the button and the tracks patch.

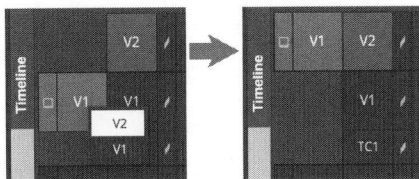

Figure 10.4 You can also patch tracks through the pop-up menu. To access it, click and hold on the source track.

Using Sync Locks

In the exercise for Lesson 5 you discovered how to maintain sync between tracks by turning on the sync locks. This is particularly helpful when you are using Splice-In to add clips between segments that are already in the timeline.

To review – in the Track Panel, turn on the **Sync Lock** button next to the TC1 Track Selector, as you can see in figure 10.5. All tracks in the timeline are now locked so they will maintain sync during 3-point editing.

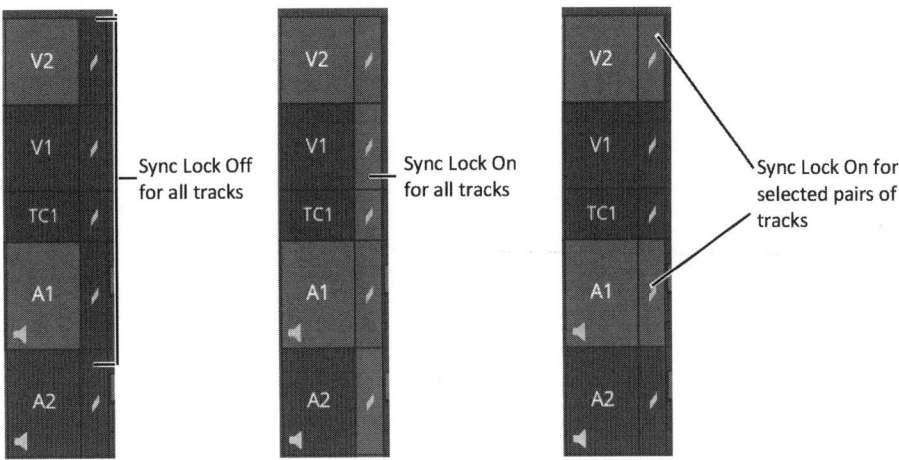

Figure 10.5 Turning Sync Lock on

However, when you are using multiple video tracks, you may not want all tracks to be locked together in sync. For instance, you may have all the interview segments exactly where you want them on tracks V1 and A2 and you don't want them to move as you edit in climbing shots on V2 and A1. As you try editing in new climbing shots and rearranging existing segments, you may only need to maintain sync between the segments on V2 and their corresponding natural sound on track A1.

To maintain sync between specific tracks:

- Turn on the Sync Lock buttons beside the individual Track Selectors of the tracks you want to keep in sync, e.g. V2 and A1.

> **Concept: Recognizing Broken Sync**
>
> It is important to know how to recognize if you have broken sync. Media Composer will indicate if audio and video segments that come from the same source are out of sync by overlaying little numbers and thin lines along the bottom edges of the segments, as shown in Figure 10.6. The value indicates the number of frames they are out of sync.
>
>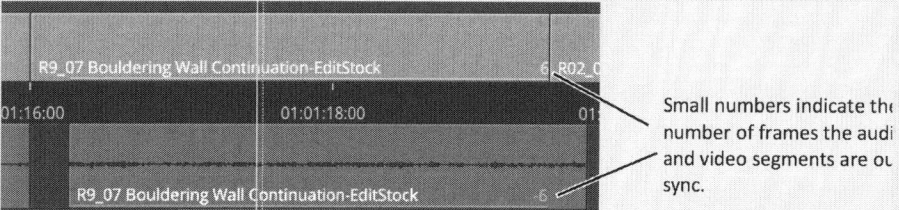
>
> Figure 10.6 The small numbers indicate the amount these segments are out of sync.
>
> For now, if you accidentally break sync, simply use the Undo function, repeatedly pressing **Ctrl+Z (Windows)** or **Command+Z (Mac)** until sync is restored.

Moving Segments Between Tracks

In Lessons 5 and 6 you learned how to use the red and yellow Segment modes to add clips to a sequence and move them horizontally along the timeline. By default, segments will snap to pre-existing edits, a Mark In or the blue Position indicator.

You can also use the Segment Modes to move segments vertically from one track to another.

Table 10.1 shows a couple of additional keyboard shortcuts that will help ensure that you move the segments exactly as you wish.

Table 10.1 Useful Keyboard Shortcuts When Moving Segments

Keyboard Shortcut	Result
Ctrl-drag (Windows)/Command-drag (Mac)	Allows the segment to move freely
Ctrl+Shift-drag (Windows)/Command+Shift-drag (Mac)	Locks the segment to vertical movement only

The table shows that you can move a segment vertically between tracks without letting it slip horizontally along the timeline as you move it.

However, you need to be aware of which segment mode you are using as you move the segment.

In your timeline, locate the two segments just after the climber says, *'but if you don't commit to it, and know you're going to get it, you're not going to get.'* They should show him losing his grip and falling then just hanging from the rock face.

Remember that when the Segment Mode button is turned on it has a light grey highlight around it. If both red and yellow segment modes are active, then the tool's icon appears as a split red/yellow arrow, as shown in figure 10.7.

Figure 10.7 Segment Mode button when both tools are active

In this dual mode, the position of the mouse pointer in the timeline automatically determines which segment tool will be used, as shown in figure 10.8.

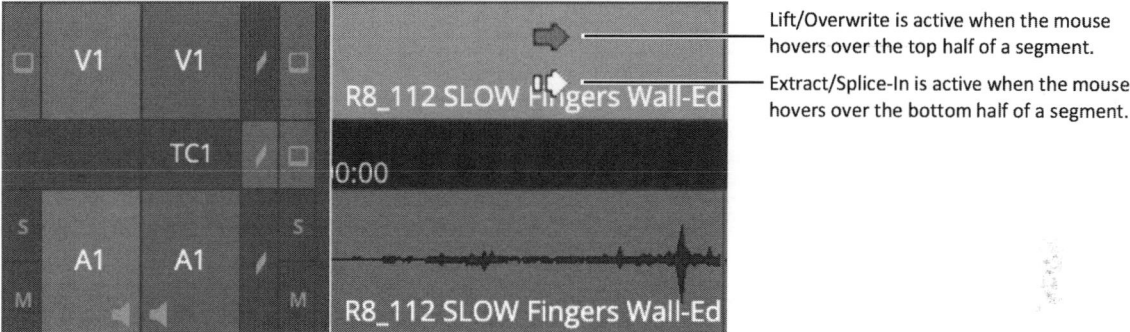

Lift/Overwrite is active when the mouse hovers over the top half of a segment.

Extract/Splice-In is active when the mouse hovers over the bottom half of a segment.

Figure 10.8 Automatic selection of Segment Mode

With the Segment Mode button configured as above, see what happens when you move a segment between tracks.

1. Turn off the **Link Selection Toggle** button so only the video segment will be selected in the timeline.

2. Roll the mouse over the top half of the segment on V1 in which the climber loses his grip. The mouse pointer should change into the red segment mode icon.

3. **Ctrl+Shift-drag (Windows)/Command+Shift-drag (Mac)** the segment from V1 to V2. It should only move vertically between tracks without moving horizontally along the timeline.

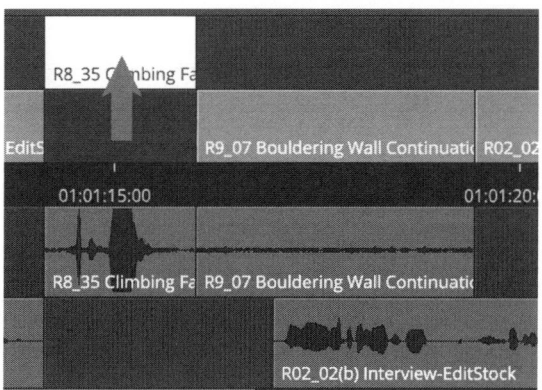

Figure 10.9 Red segment mode lifts the segment from one track and overwrites it on the other.

Undo the move and try it again, but this time use the yellow Segment mode.

4. Roll the mouse over the bottom half of the same segment on V1. The mouse pointer should change into the yellow segment mode icon.

5. **Ctrl+Shift-drag (Windows)/Command+Shift-drag (Mac)** the segment from V1 to V2. Again, it will move vertically, but not horizontally, as shown in figure 10.10. But now the video segments to the right move to close up the gap, with the result that the following video segments on V1 are now out of sync with their respective audio segments on A1 and A2.

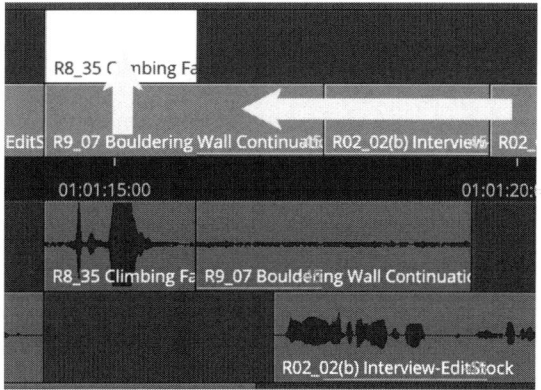

Figure 10.10 Yellow segment mode extracts the segment from one track and splices it in on the other. Following segments close up the gap and sync is broken.

Undo the move again, and this time turn on the **Sync Lock** for all tracks before using the yellow Segment mode.

6. Turn on the **Sync Lock** button beside the TC1 Track Selector.

7. Roll the mouse over the bottom half of the segment on V1. The mouse pointer changes into the yellow segment mode icon.

8. **Ctrl+Shift-drag (Windows)/Command+Shift-drag (Mac)** the segment from V1 to V2. As before, the segment only moves vertically between tracks. Unfortunately, exactly the same problem occurs. Even when Sync Lock is on, the following segments on V1 move to close up the gap.

9. Undo the move once more.

Breaking sync despite Sync Locks being on is not a software error but is an indication that, by default, Sync Locks are set to work only when you are using the 3-point editing tools. However, you can change a setting that allows Sync Locks to function when you drag-and-drop segments between tracks using the yellow segment mode.

Similar to the steps you performed earlier, from the menus at the top of the screen:

10. **Select Avid Media Composer > Preferences... > User tab > Timeline > Edit tab.**

11. Check the box for **Segment Drag Sync Locks**.

12. Click **OK** to close the **Timeline Settings** window.

Now turning on Sync Locks in the timeline will prevent the breaking of sync when you use the yellow segment mode to move segments between tracks.

Try moving the segment again.

13. Turn on **the Sync Lock** button beside the TC1 Track Selector.

14. Roll the mouse over the bottom half of the segment on V1. The mouse pointer changes into the yellow segment mode icon.

15. **Ctrl+Shift-drag (Windows)/Command+Shift-drag (Mac)** the segment from V1 to V2. As before, the segment only moves vertically between tracks. When you release the mouse, Media Composer | First fills the gap on V1 with Filler, thereby preventing the following video segments from moving.

Undo the move once more to see how you can become more efficient by selecting and moving more than one segment at a time.

Selecting Multiple Segments

There will be times when you want to move multiple segments in the Timeline. Using segment mode, you can select multiple segments at once. As with many things in Media Composer | First, there are several ways to do this. Try using each of the methods at different times and decide which method suits you best.

Let's go through each method.

To select multiple segments:

- Enable one or both of the Segment mode arrows. Now, while holding down the **Shift** key, click on each **segment**. In this case, select both the video segments of the climber falling.

    Each segment is highlighted to indicate it is selected. This is useful for selecting a few segments, whether they are contiguous or not. Use this "Shift-click" method to deselect segments as well.

To lasso segments:

1. Starting in the gray space below the time bar but just above the top video track, click-and-drag the **Mouse pointer** down and to the right. This creates a lasso. Figure 10.11.

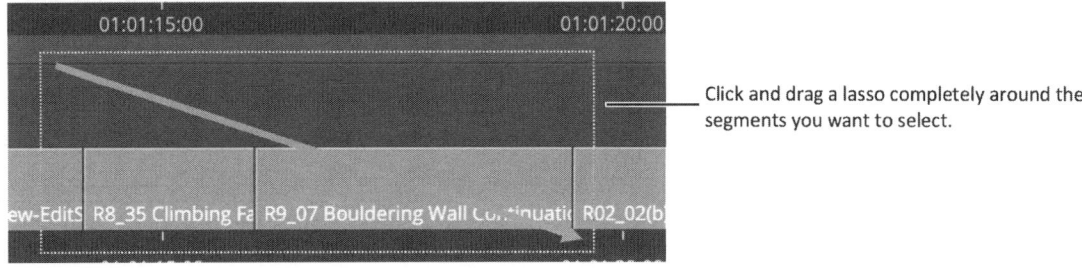

Click and drag a lasso completely around the segments you want to select.

Figure 10.11

Lassoing from left to right is important in this case because lassoing right to left puts you into an entirely different type of editing mode called trimming (specifically a trim type called "Slipping").

2. Continue dragging to draw the **lasso** around the **segments** you want to select. The lasso must completely encompass a segment to select it.

3. Release the **mouse** button to select the segments.

   All segments completely inside the lasso when you release will be highlighted. This is useful for selecting a contiguous group on adjacent tracks.

Finally, you can select a group of segments by track by using dedicated buttons in the Timeline. These are shown in Table 10.2.

Table 10.2 Buttons for Selecting Segments

Button	Name	Description
	To the Left	Selects the segments under the position indicator and all segments to the left on active tracks
	To the Right	Selects the segments under the position indicator and all segments to the right on active tracks
	Select In/Out	Selects all segments between the IN and OUT marks on active tracks

To map the buttons to the top of the Timeline window:

1. From the menu at the top of the screen, select **Tools > Command Palette**.
2. At bottom-left of the Command Palette, make sure the **'Button to Button Reassignment'** radio button is selected.
3. From the **Edit** tab of the Command Palette, drag-and-drop each button in turn to a blank button in the Timeline window tool bar.
4. Close the Command Palette.

To select segments by track:

1. Select the **tracks** containing segments you want to move by enabling their Track Selectors.
2. Optionally, add **In** and **Out** marks to define a region of the sequence.
3. Click the **To the Left**, **To the Right**, or **Select In/Out** button to make your selection.

The segments are selected in the same way as if you had selected them with the segment tool. You can now move these segments together.

Monitoring Tracks

In Lesson 7 you learned how to monitor individual audio tracks through the Solo and Mute buttons in the Track Panel of the Timecode window. You can also control monitoring of the video tracks through the Track Panel, but it works in a slightly different way.

Like audio monitoring, each video track has a Video Monitoring button, but unlike the audio tracks, you can only have one video monitoring button active at any one time. However, you can turn them all off. This is true of both Record video tracks and Source video tracks in the timeline. Figure 10.12 shows how it works with Record tracks.

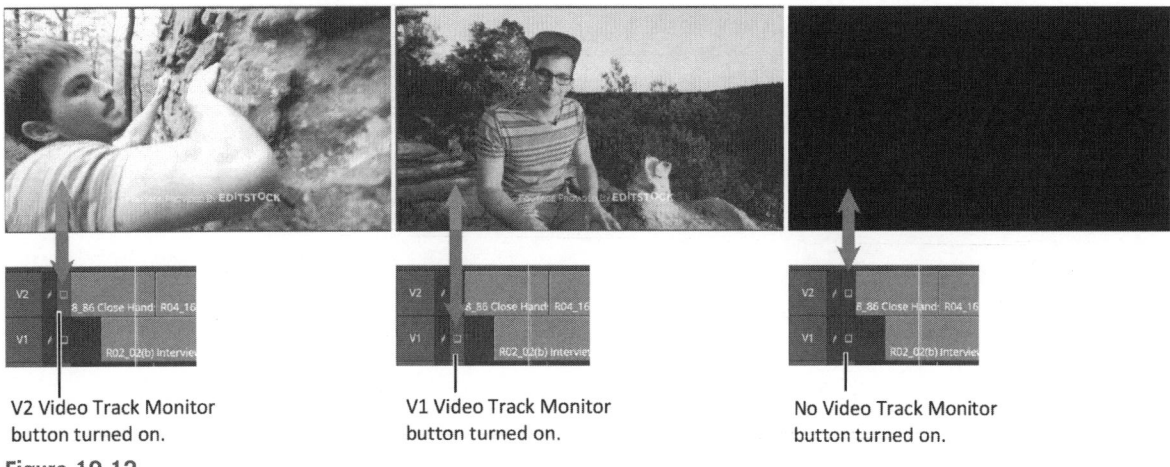

V2 Video Track Monitor button turned on.   V1 Video Track Monitor button turned on.   No Video Track Monitor button turned on.

Figure 10.12

In each screen capture above, the Position bar remains at the same spot in the timeline. When the Video Track Monitoring button for V2 is active, you will see from the V2 track down to all tracks below. In the example above, the blue Position indicator is parked where a climbing shot of Matt on V2 obscures the shot of him in interview on V1 underneath.

When the Video Track Monitoring button for V1 is active, you will see from track V1 down. You can now see Matt in interview because you have effectively stepped under the segment on V2 to see what is on the track below.

If you turn all Video Track Monitoring buttons off, you have turned all the monitoring off and as a result you see nothing but a black screen on the Record monitor.

A Word of Warning

Editors new to Media Composer | First can get caught out by this Video Track Monitoring function. It is easy to inadvertently switch to an underlying track when using multiple tracks and wonder why the footage on the upper tracks has disappeared. More alarming still is inadvertently turning off all Video Track Monitoring. Suddenly the Record monitor goes black and you fear you have lost your work. Turning off the monitoring on the Source side of the Track Panel can be equally distressing. You suspect your media has gone offline but you become confused because there is no Media Offline message displayed in the Source monitor

Review/Discussion Questions

1. How many video tracks and audio tracks can you create in Media Composer | First?

2. When you use the drag and drop method to edit segments into the timeline, how can you move a segment onto a specific track?

3. When you use 3-point editing, how do you decide which track a segment will be edited into?

4. What are the two ways source tracks can be patched to record tracks?

5. What are the shortcut keys that allow you to turn Track Selectors on and off?

6. What restrictions are there when patching audio tracks?

7. How can you recognize when tracks are out of sync?

8. How can you prevent breaking sync when using 3-point editing?

9. What setting can you change to prevent the yellow segment mode from breaking sync when you move segments between tracks?

10. How can you use segment mode to select multiple segments in the timeline? Suggest at least two ways.

11. How do you control monitoring of video in the timeline?

EXERCISE 10

 Exercise Break: Exercise 10.1
Pause here to practice what you've learned.

GOALS

- Use segment mode to move multiple segments
- Use a separate video track to edit more climbing footage into the sequence
- Refine the edit

Finish Editing the Rock Climber Sequence

You have nearly completed putting together the structure of the story. In later exercises you will use some video effects to fix a couple of problems and add some polish, then add titles.

1. Open your **Rock Climber Version 6** sequence.

You need to create some extra room at the end of the timeline.

2. Hold down the **Shift** key and use a **Segment Mode** to select the final two interview video segments on V1 and the corresponding audio segments on A2 i.e. a total of 4 segments. The climber says, *'The end of a perfect day is to top out of a route and to come down and enjoy the sunset.'*

3. Move the segments horizontally down the timeline by about 6 seconds.

4. Turn on the Record Track Selectors for V2 and A1.

5. Look through the *Clips* bin and find a few shots that you can use to depict the climber reaching the top of the rock face and finishing the climb. Edit those clips onto V2 and A1.

Because the video is going onto V2 and the audio is going into A1, you can use the Segment Modes to move and rearrange the segments without fear of breaking sync between V1 and A2.

6. Just to be safe though, turn on the Sync Locks for V1 and A2.

Review the sequence from the beginning and note any areas that will need some attention later. For example, there are several occasions where there are 'jump' cuts in the video segments of the interview – the places where you removed *'ums'* and *'ahs'*.

There may also be some shots where the camera is a little shaky. Later, you can add some image stabilization to improve them. Some shots may also benefit from applying motion effects to either speed them up or slow them down to better suit where they are in the story.

7. Publish the sequence to YouTube.

LESSON 11

Assembling a Dialogue Scene

In the next two lessons, you will take a break from Rock Climber, after briefly reflecting on Rock Climber itself and consider what you were achieving as you edited that short story

In this lesson and the next, you will have the opportunity to explore a different kind of filmmaking - scripted drama - and how Media Composer | First has a set of tools well suited to editing a range of different program styles, from documentary to drama.

Your exercise will be to edit a short scene from a drama called *'Jacuzzi'*.

Media Used: Jacuzzi

Duration: 40 Minutes

GOALS

- Understand the importance of narrative and emotion in telling a story on film.
- Understand 'Circle Takes'.
- Using Color Patches and Markers to identify takes and frames.
- Assembling a Rough Cut
- Trying different takes.

The Unscripted Documentary

Your short **Rock Climber** sequence was from a longer film about an enthusiastic climber, Matt Rodgers. The film is a style of program called an 'unscripted documentary'. Prior to filming, the Producer/Director researched the subject and spent time talking with Matt to understand the 'ins' and 'outs' of the sport. When it came to filming, it was more or less a case of following Matt as he scaled the rock face, and as you have seen, the camera crew did a good job of capturing a range of interesting shots. The Producer/Director then sat down with Matt and filmed an interview so he could explain his passion for climbing.

Before handing the film over to the Editor, the Producer/Director will typically produce a 'paper edit' – a road map outlining the story and the order in which the filmed elements should be told. Depending on the Producer/Director, the paper edit can be anything from a very detailed document to a basic sketch. The amount of detail in the paper edit can be influenced by the degree of confidence the Producer/Director has in the Editor.

Of all crew members, the Editor will probably spend more one-on-one time with the filmmaker than anyone else. Once a good working relationship has been established, it is likely that they will work together on many projects throughout their careers. Armed with the paper edit, the Editor will start looking through all the footage to identify the various story elements. Just as you did, the editor would listen to the interview and find the images that best illustrate what the story is about.

But editing a film is much more subtle than just an exercise in 'show and tell'. What makes a film engaging is tapping into the emotion, the risk, the energy, the sense of achievement or failure so the audience can empathise with the subject, not just understand it. So, in addition to making obvious shot choices that support the story, the editor is building an emotional connection with the audience. And just as you did, cutting according to rhythm and pace is one of the ways editors can convey a sense of quiet meditation or hectic energy.

The Scripted Drama

At its core, the scripted drama has the same goals as the unscripted documentary. It endeavors to engage the audience in both the narrative and the human emotion provoked by life and circumstance. The big difference is that in scripted drama the intention is clear from the start, with a well written screenplay guiding the way. The entire effort of the cast and production crew is to capture that story. The editor's job is to put together a jigsaw puzzle of shots, so the audience experiences the story as a whole and not just the individual pieces.

Telling a dramatic story is much more than conveying what people said or did. Sometimes emotion is better expressed in what wasn't said or done. For instance, the look on a character's face might speak louder than a torrent of words. And, like cutting together the shots of the rock climber, a dramatic sequence often works best when action flows smoothly from one shot to the next. It helps convey a sense that this is a naturally continuous performance rather than a series of separate shots joined together. The goal is to immerse the viewer in the story and not to distract them with your editing style. For this reason, editing is often referred to as the 'anonymous craft'. The more unnoticed the editing is, the more engaged the audience can be in the story.

Getting Started with a Scene from Jacuzzi

Below is an excerpt from the screenplay for the film *Jacuzzi*. It is the script for one short scene. It is a 'dialogue' scene in which much of the story is conveyed through what the characters are saying, yet underlying that is emotional context – how they are feeling. It has been marked up to give you an idea of which takes the Director thought were the best. These are often referred to as "circle takes."

> ### What is a Circle Take?
>
> When Editors begin previewing 'dailies' or 'rushes', i.e. the original camera footage, there is always one thing they would like to know – which of the many takes is the one preferred by the Director? Knowing the answer to that is a good place to kick start the editing process. On set, the Director may tell the Script Supervisor to 'circle that take'. The Script Supervisor will draw a circle around the take number on the script as a clear message to the Editor that the director thinks that take is a good one.
>
> Editors also like to make their own notes as they view the footage. Perhaps one particular take is the best overall but there may be a moment in a different take when a character delivers a line or provides a facial expression, a gesture or reaction that is better than all the rest.
>
> When it comes to the final assembly, the actor may deliver the performance, but the editor delivers the scene.

```
                    INT/EXT. FRONT DOOR - DAY

              A delivery truck is parked in the driveway.

         IVAN's burly assistants, LEEROY (27) and MOOSE (26), have the tailgate
            down and are mid-way through getting a new SPA, still in its plastic
                            wrap, lowered to the ground.


                              IVAN (O.S.)
                       So, you want a refund then?


         DON holds the front door half closed as he talks to Ivan. He shakes
                                 his head: no.


                              IVAN (CONT'D)                        7_36_5
                        You just don't want it?


                              Don nods: yes.
            Ivan stares incredulously for a LONG BEAT, then shrugs.
```

                        IVAN (CONT'D)
                    You're the boss...
                (turns, calls out) Pack it up boys!

    Moose and Leeroy's confused faces peer around the spa.   7_31_1

                        Moose & Leeroy
                            Huh?

                            IVAN
                      He doesn't want it.

                           LEEROY
                    He doesn't want it!?

                            IVAN
                     That's what he says.   7_33_2

    Moose and Leeroy swap a perplexed glance.

                           LEEROY
                But it's already off the truck.   7_33_2
                                                                  continued

                            IVAN
                      Then put it back on.   7_32_2

                            MOOSE
                     Ivan, it's Friday arv'.

                            IVAN
                           I know.   7_33_2

                           LEEROY
           We'll have to go all the way back to the warehouse.

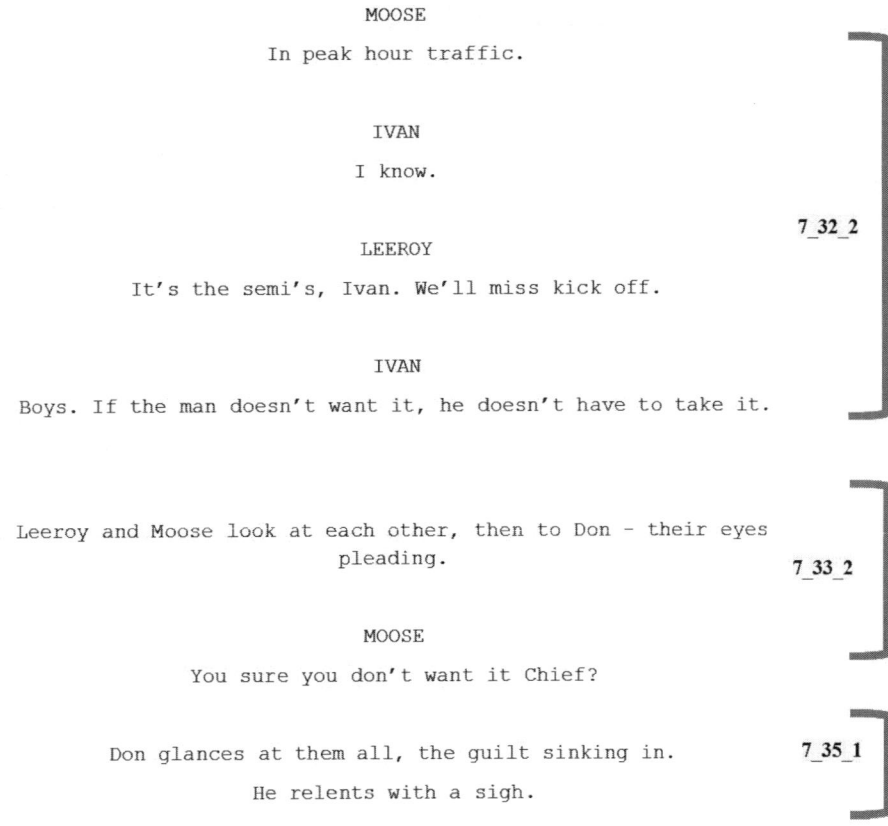

```
                        MOOSE
                In peak hour traffic.

                         IVAN
                        I know.
                                                    7_32_2
                        LEEROY
       It's the semi's, Ivan. We'll miss kick off.

                         IVAN
     Boys. If the man doesn't want it, he doesn't have to take it.


     Leeroy and Moose look at each other, then to Don - their eyes
                              pleading.
                                                    7_33_2

                        MOOSE
              You sure you don't want it Chief?


     Don glances at them all, the guilt sinking in.    7_35_1
                    He relents with a sigh.
```

Open an Existing Project

1. Launch Media Composer | First and open the project, Jacuzzi.

2. The project has 3 bins – one for the **Sequences** and two for the camera footage. Bin **Scene 7** and bin Scene 9 contain the clips from the rushes of two short scenes.

3. Open the **Scene 7** bin. Notice that all the clip icons show the clips have been created by importing the media files. Also notice that the clip names are based on the camera slates at the head of each media file, i.e. Scene **Number_Slate Number_Take Number**. When you look at the Slate Numbers, you see that the scene is comprised of 6 different slates or shots, and apart from Slate 35, all slate numbers have more than one take.

Marking Clips

Media Composer | First has a couple of handy ways for you to identify good takes or worthwhile moments in a clip.

- You can color code clips to help you identify good or 'circle' takes. On the left side of an open bin, is a column labeled color. **Right-mouse click** in a blank color patch next to a clip icon and a color palette opens, as you can see in figure 11.1. Select a color and it is assigned to the patch.

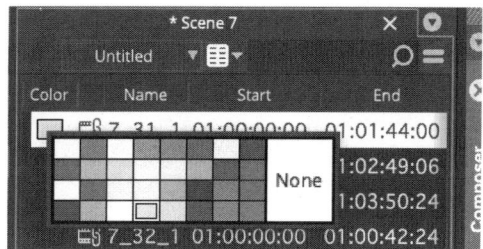

Figure 11.1 Color coding of clips in a bin

In Table 11.1, are listed all the circle takes decided by the director.

- Use the color column in your bin to assign a color patch to each one of these takes. It will make selecting the good shots much quicker when you start putting the scene together.

Table 11.1 Circle Takes

Circle Takes
7_31_1
7_32_2
7_33_2
7_34_2
7_35_1
7_36_5

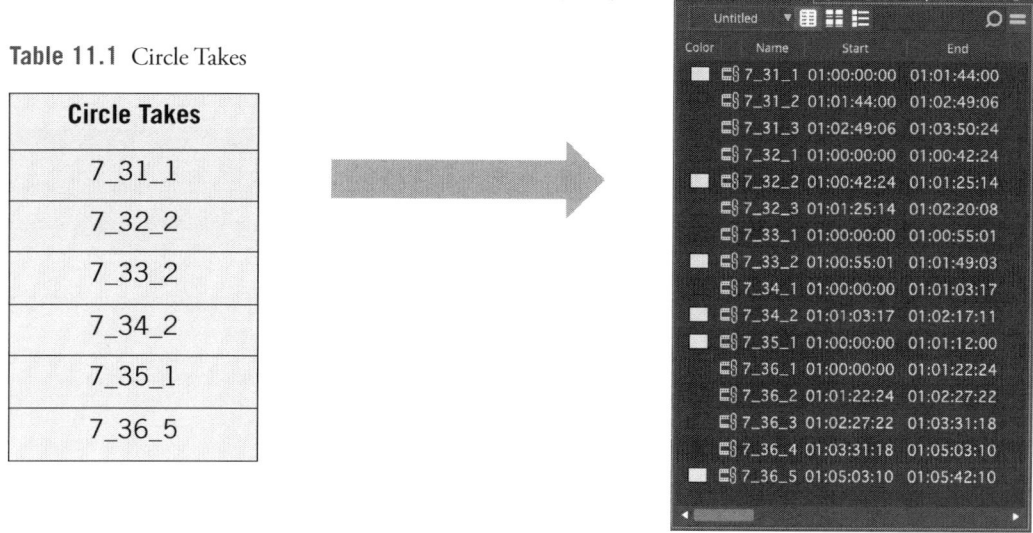

Figure 11.2 Circle Takes color coded in bin.

- You can also add a marker to a single frame in a clip and attach a note to it.

  1. Open the clip 7_31_1 in the Source monitor. The actors stop during their performance and start again later in the take. Park the Position indicator at timecode 01:00:56:00. It is where the actors recommenced the action after their false start. Click on the **Add Marker** button in the tool bar under the Source monitor. Figure 11.3.

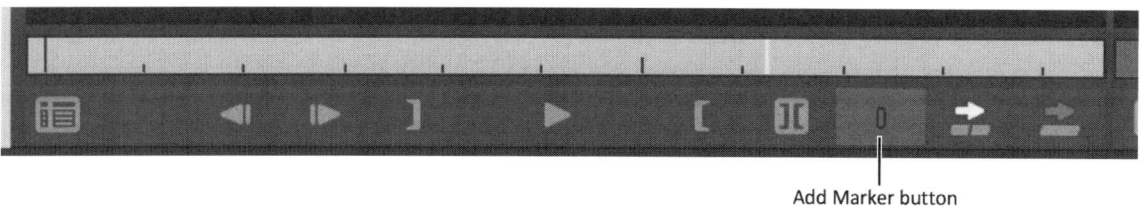

Figure 11.3 The Add Marker button

The Edit Marker dialogue will open. You can type in a name for the marker, assign a color to the marker and add a comment. Click **OK** when you're finished.

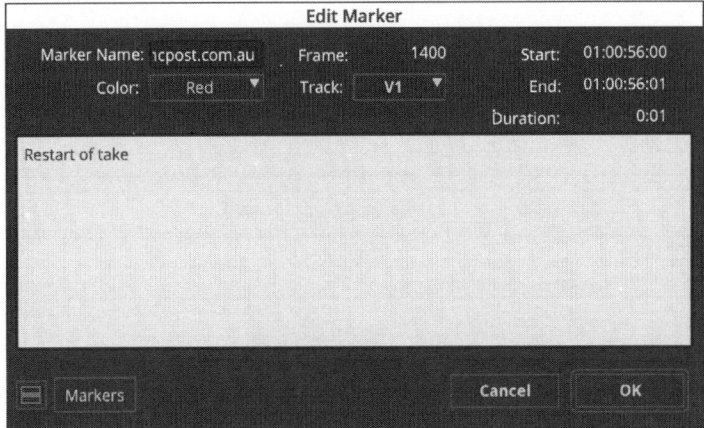

Figure 11.4 The Edit Marker dialogue

The Edit Marker dialogue will close, and a marker will appear behind the Position indicator in the Source monitor's position bar, as shown in figure 11.5. When you park on the marker, a larger marker with the comment attached appears at the bottom of the frame in the Source monitor.

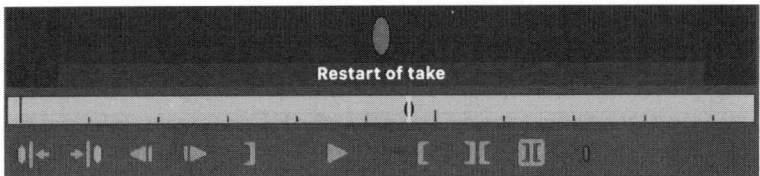

Figure 11.5 The Marker with text visible in the Source monitor.

There are other takes that can benefit from adding multiple markers. For instance, clip 7_35_1 has three versions of Don reluctantly agreeing to take delivery of the jacuzzi, as you can see in figure 11.6.

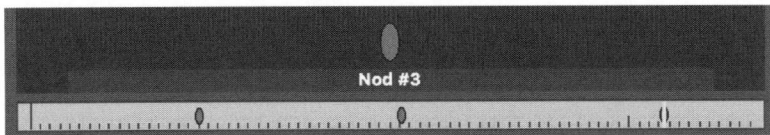

Figure 11.6 Multiple Markers added to a clip

Markers make it very quick and easy to locate each version.

To snap to a Marker:

- Click on the **Marker** in the Position bar and the Position indicator jumps to that time in the clip.

- Map the **Go to Marker** buttons to buttons under the Source monitor. To find the buttons go to **Tools** menu > **Command Palette** > **Move** tab.

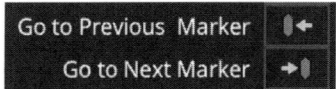

Figure 11.7 Go to Marker buttons in the Command Palette

- From the **Tools** menu select **Markers**. The Marker window opens. Click on a **Marker** in the list, shown in figure 11.8.

#	Marker Name	TC	End	Track	Part	Comment
0003	Don CU	01:01:03:09		V1		Nod #3
0002	Don CU	01:00:37:05		V1		Nod #2
0001	Don CU	01:00:16:23		V1		Nod #1

Figure 11.8 Marker window

It is also possible to add markers to the sequence in the timeline. These can be helpful to identify segments or frames that you need to do further work on, such as applying effects or color correction or where audio needs to be replaced because of poor quality sound.

The Rough Cut

The first assembly is for you to set out the basic structure of the scene and discover if there are any obvious problems with the camera coverage or performances. As the name suggests, a *Rough Cut* is just that, a rough cut. Once you have put together the building blocks of the scene, you can start fine tuning the sequence and fix anything that needs attention (for instance, the microphone boom might be seen in bottom of frame during a good take). Adding markers might help remind you to fix problems later.

With the marked-up script as a guide, start assembling the sequence using 3-point editing. At this stage, base the **In** and **Out** points on the dialogue in the script. But also pay attention to any action occurring at the edit points. Don't be too concerned about matching action at this stage. In the next lesson you will learn how to use the trim tools to improve the pacing and action across edits. Below is a suggested approach to editing the first two shots into the sequence.

1. Open the Sequences bin. (You will see there is a sequence already in there for Scene 9. You will use that sequence in the next lesson.) From the menu bar at the top of the screen select **Timeline > New > Sequence**. An Untitled Sequence.01 will appear in the Sequences bin. Rename the sequence Scene 7 Rough Cut.

2. From the Scene 7 bin, open the clip 7_36_5 in the Source monitor. Just after the director calls 'action', use the **I** key (I for IN) to mark the **In/** point. After Ivan says, *'OK, you're the boss'*, use the **O** key to mark the **Out** (O for OUT).

3. Review the marked section of the clip by pressing the number **6 key** on the keyboard to play the clip from IN to OUT.

4. In the Timeline window, make sure the Track Panel is set up with the Source **V1** and **A1** Track Selectors turned on and aligned next to the Record Track Selectors **V1** and **A1** that are also turned on.

5. Press the **V** key to **Splice-In** the clip into the timeline. After performing the edit, the blue Position indicator will be sitting at the end of the segment, ready for the next shot.

Before proceeding, it is worthwhile to consider why this clip may be an appropriate way to start the scene. There are other possible choices that in the end might work better but you need to start somewhere and there are a few good reasons why this shot might be suitable.

- **The scene commences with Ivan delivering the first line.**
- **The shot shows that Ivan is talking to Don, although Don has his back to the camera.**
- **The shot locates where the action is occurring – at the front door of the home with Ivan outside and Don inside.**

As the editor, you are acting on behalf of the audience. You need to ask what do they need to know and when? Sometimes, for dramatic purposes you want to withhold information from them, but at other times, like this, you may want to keep them informed to avoid any confusion.

6. Load clip *7_31_1* into the Source monitor. **Mark In** just before Ivan says, *'Pack it up boys.'* **Mark Out** after Ivan says, *'He doesn't want it.'* Press the number **6 key** if you want to check the marked section of the clip.

7. Splice-In (**V**) the clip at the end of the first segment in the timeline.

Review the edit in the timeline and see if you have included all the lines of dialogue up to that point in the script. It doesn't have to be a perfect cut. You just need to know you have included everything. You can improve on it later if needs be. Also consider why this may be an appropriate choice for the second shot.

In this part of the scene, Ivan is still speaking, but he is now addressing his workers, Leeroy and Moose. The shot shows where Ivan is standing in relationship to the boys and reveals that the jacuzzi is already unloaded from the truck.

Adding Reaction Shots

The opening shot is one continuous interaction between Ivan and Don. Although Ivan is doing all the talking, he is obviously reacting to non-verbal signals from Don. It is important to show the audience how Don is responding to what Ivan is saying, and in turn that explains why Ivan is saying what he says to Don.

You could choose to Overwrite parts of the first segment on V1 with reaction shots of Don, but if you don't like the results you would need to undo the edits and reinstate the original. A better approach may be to leave the segment on V1 untouched and Overwrite the shots of Don onto V2 of the timeline instead. That way you can try different options and move segments around on V2 without affecting the basic shot on the video track underneath.

1. Create a new video track in the timeline by going to the menus at the top of the screen and selecting **Timeline > New > Video Track**. A new V2 track will appear for the sequence.

2. On the Record side of the Track Panel, turn off the Track Selectors for V1 and A1. You don't want to affect what you have already edited into those tracks. Turn on the Track Selector for V2.

3. In the timeline, **Mark In** just after Ivan says, *'Do you want a refund?'* and **Mark Out** just before Ivan looks surprised and says, *'Oh, you don't want it?'*

4. Open clip 7_34_2 in the Source monitor and **Mark In** after Ivan delivers the line, *'So you want a refund.'* You don't need to add a Mark Out as Media Composer | First will automatically calculate the out point based on the duration between the marks in the timeline.

5. Perform an Overwrite edit by pressing the **B key** on the keyboard. The shot of Don shaking his head will be edited onto V2. Review the edit to see how well it works. Don't be concerned about hearing the crackle of the microphone under the shot of Don. You can fix that up later.

6. Now mark suitable **In** and **Out** points in the timeline for Don's response to Ivan's line, *'Oh, you don't want it?'*. The points should be *after* Ivan delivers the line.

7. Mark the **In** point in clip *7_34_2* for Don's response and Overwrite it (**B**) onto V2.

In reviewing the sequence, ensure the **Video Track Monitor** button in the Track Panel is switched to the V2 track (as shown in figure 11.9) so you can view both video tracks.

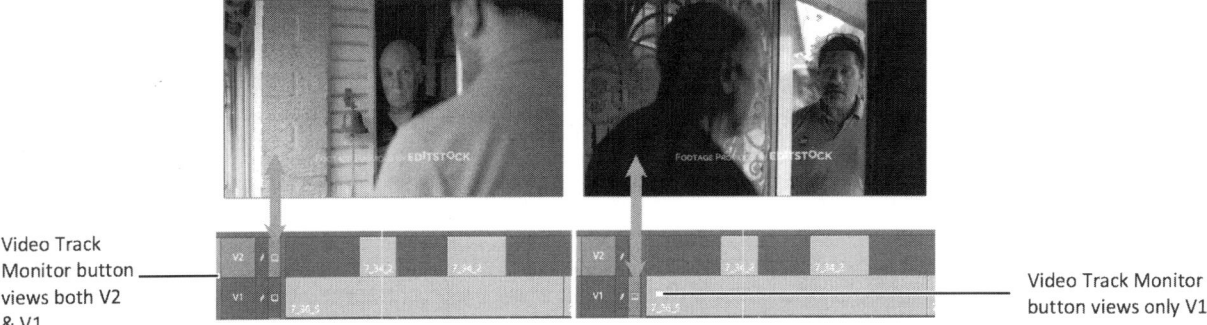

Figure 11.9 Video Track monitoring

Trying Alternative Takes

You can also use additional video and audio tracks to test alternative takes. If you are not sure the take you have used is works the best, Overwrite the video of an alternative version onto a higher-level video track and edit the audio onto another audio track. By default, the timeline already has an A2 audio track that you can use. To monitor the alternative take, switch the **Video Track Monitor** up to the video track you have used and solo the associated audio track.

Replacing Takes

If you want to replace one take with another:

1. Turn on the Track Selectors for the segment you want to replace.

2. Park the blue Position indicator on the segment.

3. Press the **T key** or click the **Mark Clip** button under the Record monitor or in the Timeline window's Tool Bar.

4. Open the replacement clip in the Source monitor and Mark the **In** point.

5. Make sure the Source Track Selectors are patched to the correct Record tracks.

6. Perform an Overwrite edit (B).

In the next lesson you will learn how the Rough Cut can be refined by using Trim Tools to adjust the length of shots and the timing of edits in the timeline.

Review/Discussion Questions

1. What are 'dailies' or 'rushes'?

2. What might a director do to identify good takes for the editor?

3. How can you mark a good take in a bin?

4. How can you mark a specific frame in a clip or sequence?

5. What is a "Rough Cut"?

6. Apart from deciding if a performance is good or not, what else helps guide shot choices when assembling a sequence?

7. How can you add reaction shots without affecting the segments you have already edited into the timeline?

8. When using multiple video tracks, how can you control which video track you are monitoring?

9. When using multiple audio tracks, how can you monitor a single track?

EXERCISE 11

 Exercise Break 11.1
Pause here to practice what you've learned.

GOALS

- Use 3-point editing to continue Scene 7 of Jacuzzi.
- Add more reaction shots of Don.
- Replace segments.

Finish the Rough Cut of Scene 7 of 'Jacuzzi'

To finish the rough cut, use the script as the guide and use each of the suggested circle takes to assemble the sequence. They may not end up being the best shots for the final version, but they will let you know how well the scene works and if there are any problems that need fixing. Always keep in mind that you want the audience to know more than just what is said and by whom. You also want the audience to know how they are feeling about the situation. After you have put together the rough cut you can start fine-tuning the scene.

1. Open the **Jacuzzi** project and open your sequence.

2. Using 3-point editing, follow the marked-up script to finish assembling the sequence.

3. Now decide where it may be appropriate to include another shot or two of Don. Although the interaction is between Ivan and the boys, Don is looking on and feeling increasingly guilty about sending the jacuzzi back. Use the V2 track to include at least one more 'cutaway' of Don as he listens to the conversation.

4. To find where the clip works the best, you can use the red Segment mode to move the segment up and down the timeline. Hold down the **Control (Windows)/Command (Mac)** key on the keyboard to freely move a segment without it snapping to an edit point or the blue Position indicator.

There are three options for the final shot in which Don relents.

5. Add a V3 track to the timeline and edit the two versions you haven't used to V2 and V3. Switch the Video Track Monitor button to review each option in turn. When you have decided which one

works best, use the red Segment mode to move the one you prefer onto V1. (Unless of course the best one is already on V1.) To ensure a segment only moves vertically when swapping tracks, use the red Segment mode and hold **Ctrl+Shift (Windows)/Command+Shift(Mac)** as you drag the segment between tracks. The segment will Overwrite the one on V1.

6. You can delete the unwanted segment/s by selecting them with the red Segment mode and pressing the **Delete** key.

7. There is the poor audio in the first segment when the microphone breaks up, so look for an alternative take of Ivan saying, *'Oh, you don't want it?'* Because on V2 there are reaction shots of Don either side of that statement you should be able to replace just that statement on V1 and A1 without the viewer knowing you have used a different take. But you also need to fix the audio break up just before Ivan speaks those lines.

8. Because 3-point editing works with any three marks, you can fix both microphone break-ups plus replace the video on V1, all in one edit. In the timeline, mark **In** and **Out** around the audio that needs to be replaced on A1, i.e. **Mark In** just before the first microphone break-up and **Mark Out** after Ivan says, *'Oh, you don't want it?'* Now locate the replacement shot and **Mark Out** after Ivan says his equivalent line. You do not need a Mark IN. (If the Source clip does have a Mark IN, you can delete it by pressing the **D** key on the keyboard.) Make sure tracks are patched correctly and perform an Overwrite edit onto V1 and A1 of the timeline.

9. When satisfied with the Rough Cut, publish it to YouTube.

LESSON 12

Trimming Dialogue Scenes

Up till now, making changes to a sequence has basically consisted of clips to be added, removed or moved in the timeline. The Trim tools add another level of adjustment in which segments already in the timeline can be lengthened or shortened and the timing of edits altered. This lesson covers techniques for refining a rough-cut dialogue scene using trim.

Media Used: Jacuzzi

Duration: 40 minutes

GOALS

- Understand the Trim mode
- Entering Trim Mode
- The Trim Mode Interface
- Control the pacing of the edit using Ripple trims
- Create L- and J-cuts for a seamless edit
- Perform dynamic trimming on the fly
- Identify and correct audio problems at the edit point
- Maintain sync and repair broken sync

To prepare for this lesson:

1. Launch Media Composer | First and open the **Jacuzzi** project.

2. From the Sequences bin, create a duplicate of the **Scene 9 Rough Cut** sequence. Play the sequence to get an idea of what the scene is about and the areas that need to be fixed.

Understanding Trim

Trimming is one of the most powerful tools in editing. Simply put, it is the process of adding and removing frames within the timeline to refine the edit. In Media Composer | First, Trim is also an edit mode with special functions.

Trimming is where the real work of editing is done. For example, by adding or removing frames in just the right places, you can energize a dull conversation, increase (or decrease) the apparent tension between characters or extend a poignant moment for maximum impact. Trimming undoubtedly enables you to move from a good rough cut to a great sequence.

Regardless of film genre, there are a few things in common when cutting dialogue. Whether it is a scene of actors performing scripted dialogue, or the "dialogue" of a documentary interview, the editor is concerned with the following:

- Pacing a scene for the right emotional impact
- Keeping everything in sync
- Matching action on a cut if necessary
- Keeping audio edits clean

When trimming sync sound, you obviously need to keep pictures and sound locked together. And, you need to keep the audio edits clean. There shouldn't be any clicks, pops, or partial words at an edit point. (In **Scene 7** of **Jacuzzi** you used 3-point editing to replace part of a take that had poor audio.) Maintaining a continuity of action between shots can also keep the scene running smoothly without visual jumps distracting the viewer. Of these four concerns, the pacing of the scene is the most demanding.

The Trim Tools

Media Composer | First has a number of tools for trimming segments in the timeline. The most frequently used group can be found in the tool bar at the top of the Timeline window, as you can see in Figure 12.1.

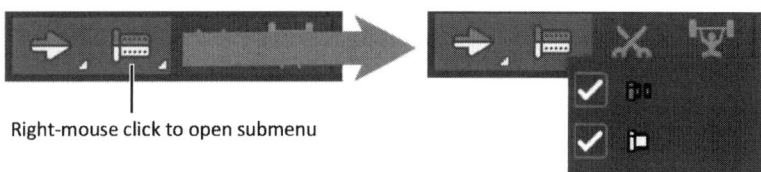

Figure 12.1 The Trim mode button

- Configured in a similar way to the Segment mode tool, a right-mouse click will open a submenu from which you can select either or both of the Trim Tools. When both are turned on, the Trim mode button is split half red and half yellow which allows the automatic selection of either tool based on the position of the mouse pointer in the timeline.

- To activate automatic selection, the Trim mode button must be turned on with a single mouse click. The button will adopt a light grey highlight to indicate it is active.
- You can trim segments on any video and audio track provided the Record Track Selectors for those tracks are turned on.

Figure 12.2 illustrates how the mouse pointer icon changes depending on its position close to an edit in the timeline.

- When the mouse pointer hovers over the top half of a segment it changes to the red Overwrite Trim mode.
- When it hovers over the lower half, it changes into the yellow Ripple trim mode.
- The tool also changes depending on whether the pointer is on the outgoing (A) side or incoming (B) side of an edit.
- Hovering the mouse directly over an edit will change the tool to the white Dual-roller trim mode.

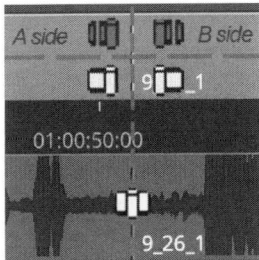

Figure 12.2 Automatic selection of the Trim tools is based on the position of the mouse pointer in the timeline.

The color coding of the Trim tools indicates they behave in similar ways to the segment and editing tools.

- The red Overwrite Trim will **Lift** frames and leave filler behind or **Overwrite** and replace filler. It can also Overwrite frames at the head or tail of a segment in the timeline. Overwrite trim does not change the position of any segment in the timeline.
- The yellow Ripple Trim will **Splice-In** frames or **Extract** frames from the head or tail of a segment. Ripple Trim moves following segments up or down the timeline to adjust for the added or removed frames.
- White Dual-roller Trim removes frames from the segment on one side of an edit and adds an equal number of frames to the segment on the other side. Effectively, it moves an edit point up or down the timeline depending on the direction in which you perform the trim. Segments do not change position in the timeline when using Dual-roller Trim.

Entering Trim Mode

- To enter Overwrite Trim or Ripple Trim, position the mouse on either side of an edit and on the upper or lower half of the track. For Dual-roller Trim, roll the mouse on top of the edit. The mouse pointer changes to the respective trim tool icon. Click the mouse and a set of rollers will appear on the selected side of the edit. Figure 12.3 illustrates the relationships between tool icons and the rollers that appear on edits.
- If the Link Selection Toggle is turned on, rollers will appear on the edit points of all associated video and audio tracks.
- If Link Selection Toggle is turned off, rollers will only appear on the edit you click.
- You can select additional edits by holding down the Shift key and clicking on the edit points.

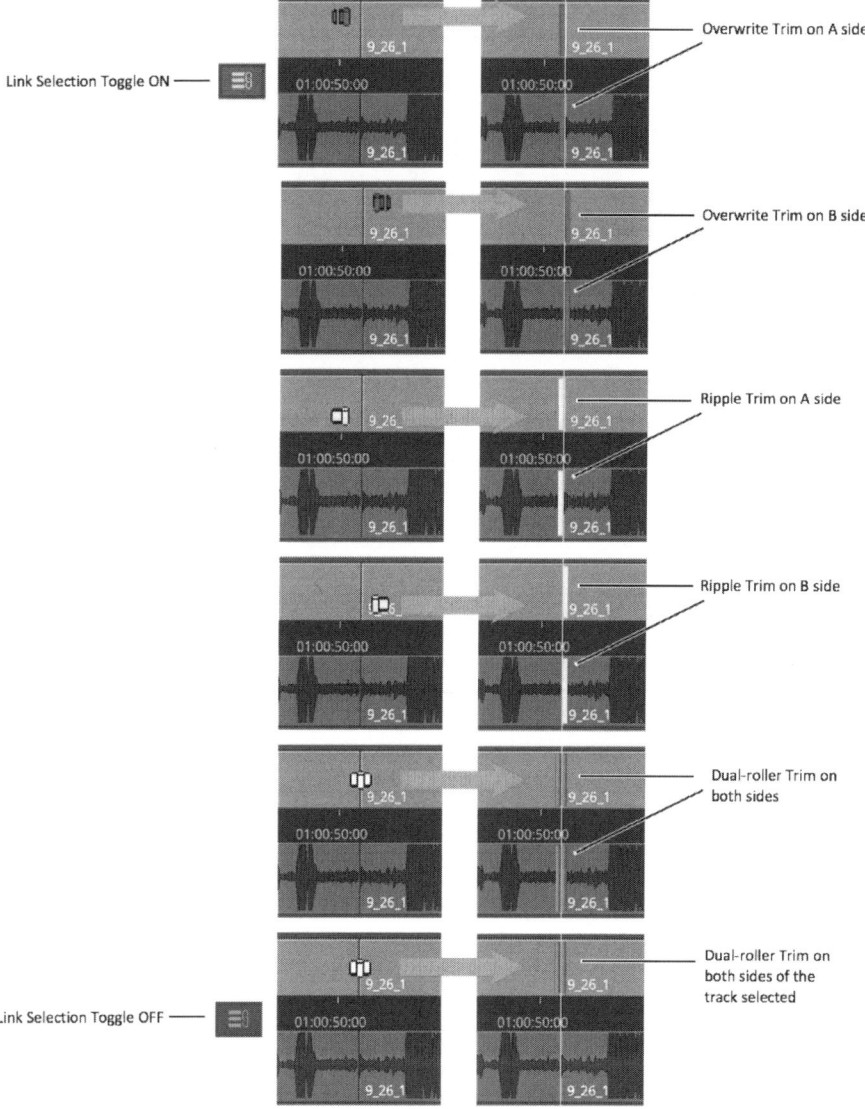

Figure 12.3 Trim Tool rollers applied to edits in the timeline

The Trim Mode Interface

As soon as you enter Trim Mode, the Composer window reconfigures to display the Trim Mode Interface, as shown in figure 12.4.

Figure 12.4 The Trim mode interface

- The **A-side monitor** shows the last frame of the outgoing shot.
- The **B-side monitor** shows the first frame of the incoming shot.
- The **Trim Counter** displays the number of frames either side of the edit that have been added or removed. The purple highlight indicates which side of the edit has trim rollers applied. A positive value in the Trim Counter indicates a trim to the right while a negative value indicates a trim to the left.
- You can also swap between trimming the A side or the B side of the edit by clicking in either the left or right monitor window. The purple highlight in the Trim Counter changes sides accordingly. Clicking on the frame edge between the A and B side monitors selects Dual-roller trim. Both Trim Counters will be highlighted purple as a result.
- The **Trim buttons** allow you to trim frames in either direction. The single arrows allow a single frame trim to the left or right while the double arrows allow a 10-frame trim to either the left or right.
- The equivalent keyboard shortcuts for the Trim buttons are shown in Figure 12.5.

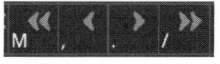 **Figure 12.5** The Trim button keyboard shortcuts

- You can also trim frames by clicking and dragging the roller in the direction you want to trim.
- The **Play Loop** button allows the timeline to continuously play around the edit that you are trimming. The advantage of play loop is that you can use the keyboard shortcuts to trim the edit and the timeline dynamically updates to show you the trim as it plays.
- To exit Trim Mode, click in the **Timecode Track** or **Time Bar** of the Timeline window.

Overwrite Trim

When you are in Overwrite Trim mode, there will be a red roller on either the A side or the B side of the edit in the timeline. Overwrite Trim combines Lift and Overwrite functions.

- When the roller is on the A side:
  - A trim to the left will **Lift** frames from the A side and leave Filler, as shown in figure 12.6.

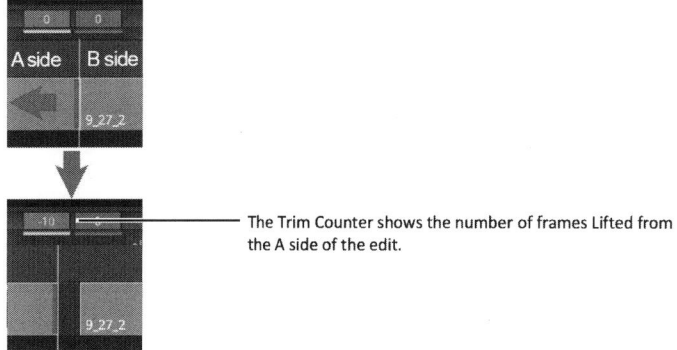

Figure 12.6 A 10-frame trim to the left Lifts 10 frames and leaves filler on the A side.

  - A trim to the right will add frames to the tail of the segment on the A side and **Overwrite** them at the head of the segment on the B side. Figure 12.7. This trim is equivalent to performing a Dual-roller trim at the edit.

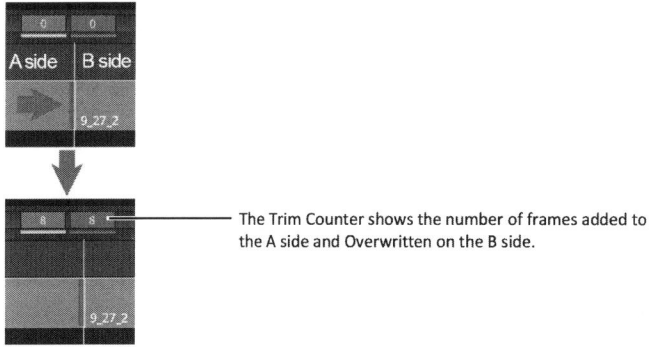

Figure 12.7 An 8-frame trim to the right adds 8 frames to the A side and Overwrites 8 frames on the B side.

- When the roller is on the B side:
  - A trim to the right **Lifts** frames from the B side and leaves filler, as shown in figure 12.8.

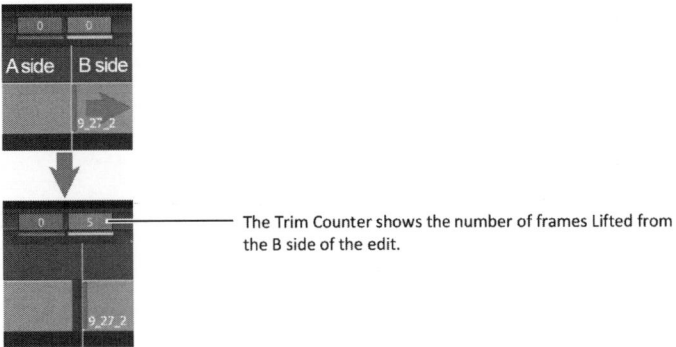

Figure 12.8 A 5-frame trim to the right Lifts 5 frames and leaves filler on the B side.

- A trim to the left adds frames to the head of the B side and **Overwrites** frames on the tail of the A side. This trim is equivalent to performing a Dual-roller trim at the edit.

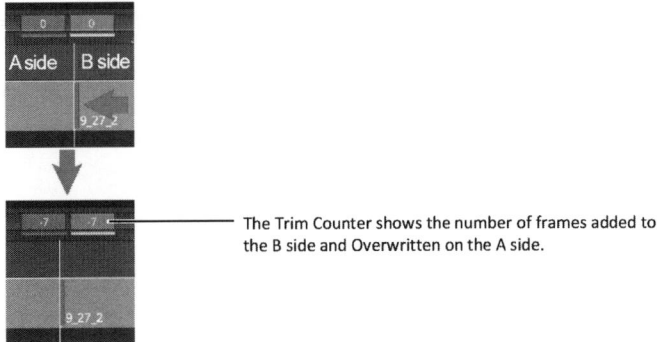

Figure 12.9 A 7-frame trim to the left adds 7 frames to the B side and Overwrites 7 frames on the A side.

Dual-Roller Trim

Dual-roller Trim can produce a very similar outcome to Overwrite Trim but with a distinct advantage. Unlike Overwrite Trim, you don't need to decide which side of the edit to place the roller when you want to add frames to one side and overwrite frames on the other. Dual-roller Trim adds rollers to both sides of the edit, so it doesn't matter in which direction you trim. One roller will remove frames from one side while the other roller simultaneously adds an equal number to the other side.

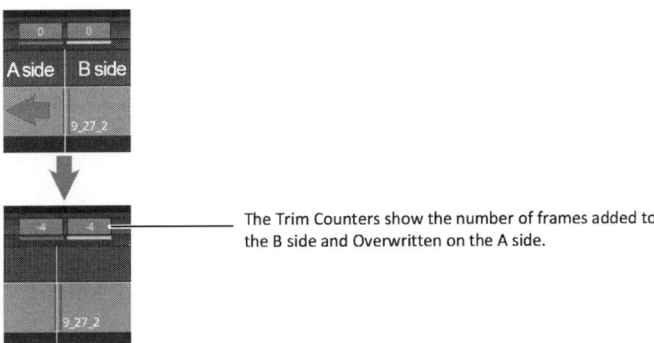

Figure 12.10 A 4-frame trim to the left adds 4 frames to the B side and Overwrites 4 frames on the A side.

Ripple Trim

When you are in Ripple Trim mode, there will be a yellow roller on either the A side or the B side of the edit in the timeline. Ripple Trim combines Extract and Splice-In functions.

- When the roller is on the A side:
    - A trim to the left **Extracts** frames from the tail of the segment on the A side and the following segments in the timeline move to the left to fill the gap.

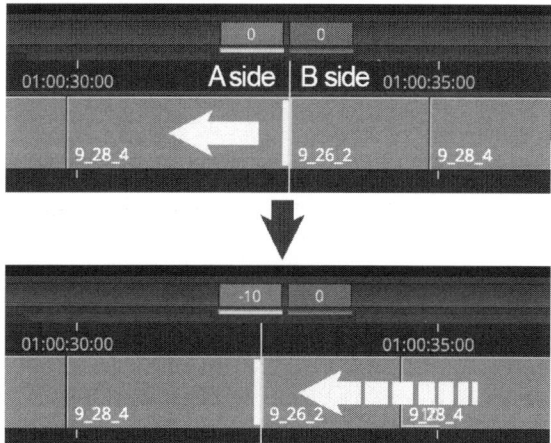

Figure 12.11 A 10-frame trim to the left Extracts 10 frames from the A side and following segments move to fill the gap.

- A trim to the right **Splices-In** frames to the end of the segment on the A side and the following segments move to the right to make room for the extra frames.

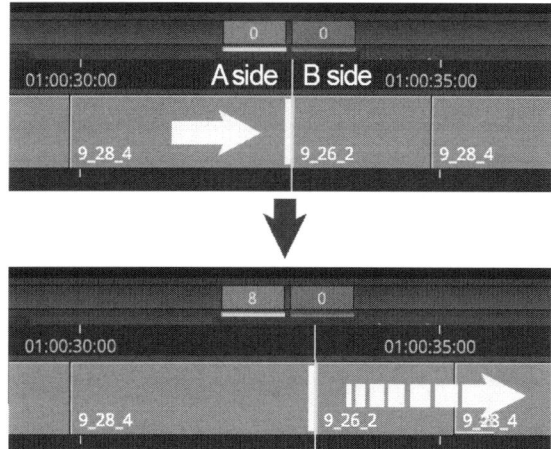

Figure 12.12 An 8-frame trim to the right Splices-In 8 frames to the A side and following segments move down the timeline to make room.

- When the roller is on the B side:
  - A trim to the left **Splices-In** frames to the head of the segment on the B side and the following segments in the timeline move to the right to make room for the extra frames.

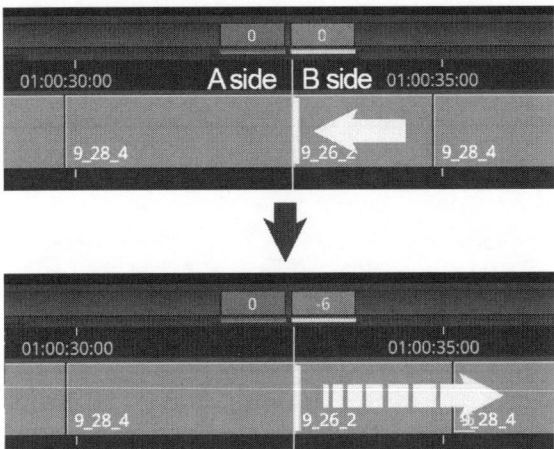

Figure 12.13 A 6-frame trim to the left Splices-In 6 frames to the head of the B side and following segments move down the timeline to make room.

  - A trim to the right **Extracts** frames from the head of the B side and the following segments move to the left to close the gap.

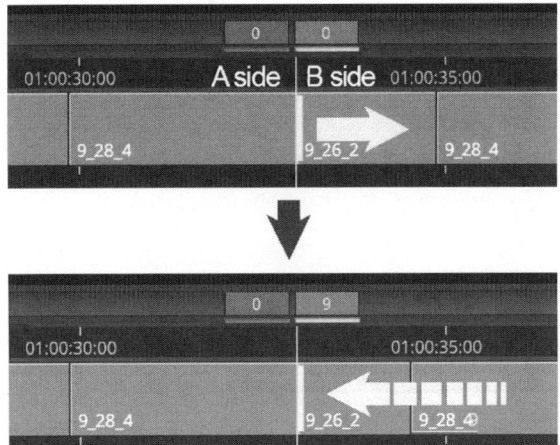

Figure 12.14 A 9-frame trim to the right Extracts 9 frames from the head of the B side and following segments move up the timeline to fill the gap.

Using Overwrite Trim to Clean up Audio

Sometimes a visual cut between shots works well but the audio at the cut needs cleaning up. For instance, the outgoing shot has some extraneous sound just before the edit. The Overwrite Trim tool is an effective way of cleaning out extraneous audio without changing the timing of the cut.

Perform an Overwrite Trim

In the **Jacuzzi** project, open the duplicate of the sequence **Scene 9 Rough Cut**. (The name of the duplicate sequence should be appended with *.Copy.01*.) About half way through the sequence, Leeroy calls out to Ivan, *'Boss, let's go. Want to pick up some frothies.'* (*Frothies* is a colloquial term for beer.) Before the cut to Ivan, we catch the start of his response, *'We are….'*. After the cut, Ivan repeats those words and continues on, *'We are talking here.'*

To clean up the audio on the A side of the edit:

1. Turn off the **Link Selection** toggle.

2. Move the mouse pointer close to the **A side** of the edit on **A1** and hover it over the top half of the segment. **Click** when the mouse changes to the red **Overwrite Trim** icon. A red roller should appear on the **A side** of the edit on the **A1** track.

3. The Composer window will change to display the Trim Mode Interface.

4. Click the **Play Loop** button.

5. Use the keyboard key - comma (,), to trim to the left one frame at a time. Each time Play Loop updates you will hear the change as frames are Lifted from the segment. Keep trimming until you can no longer hear Ivan. If you trim too far, press the period (.) key to trim back to the right and reinstate frames.

6. When the trim is complete you will have Lifted frames of audio and replaced them with Filler. But now you can hear the background sound has disappeared where you trimmed out the frames.

7. To replace the Filler with natural sound, place a red Overwrite Trim roller on the **B side** of the edit on **A1**.

8. Enter **Play Loop** and use the keyboard keys to trim to the left and Overwrite the Filler with audio from the incoming segment.

9. When the edit is clean, stop the Play Loop and exit Trim mode.

You could have done the trim in one step by starting the Overwrite trim on the B side of the edit. By trimming to the left you would have been simultaneously Lifting frames from the A side and Overwriting frames from the B side. Alternatively, a Dual-roller trim would have achieved the same result.

Using Ripple Trim to Adjust Pacing

The Ripple Trim tool is a very effective way to adjust the pacing of a scene and improve the matching of action between shots. This is done in two ways:

- **A-side (Outgoing shot)** – This trim adjusts the timing as you leave one shot and move on to the next. It adjusts how long you want to stay focused on that shot before cutting to the next. In the context of cutting a dialogue scene, this typically refers to how quickly you cut away from an actor after he or she finishes speaking.

- **B-side (Incoming shot)** – This trim adjusts the timing of the shot you cut to. This often refers to how long it takes an actor to start speaking after you cut to him or her.

As a general rule, dialogue scenes are cut tight, meaning there are very few additional frames after a character finishes speaking. A shot shouldn't hold on to an actor any longer than is necessary to deliver the line or to react. Trimming away the extra frames will increase the pace of the scene.

On the other hand, if there is reason for the pause, hold the shot. Allowing a pause in the scene can be a powerful technique. Most of us know from experience what it is like to be in a tense conversation. That awkward silence between one person's statement and the other person's response is telling of the emotion. But it's not just the pause that creates the tension; it is a character's body language. As an editor, you may even be able to create that too, by manipulating when and where the audience sees a certain reaction.

Perform a Ripple Trim

It is obvious when you play the sequence **Scene 9 Rough Cut.Copy.01** and watch the edit between the first two shots that some trimming needs to occur. There is a repetition of action and dialogue at the edit point. Pacing also needs to be improved, so Ripple Trim is the right tool for the job.

1. To clean up the cut, consider which side of the edit you should trim first. Since the head of the second shot is a repetition of the end of the first shot, perhaps placing the trim rollers on the **B side** of the edit is a good place to start. You can always swap to the other side of the edit if you change your mind.

2. Make sure the **Link Selection Toggle** at the top of the Timeline window is turned **on** so the edits on all associated tracks will be selected. This will maintain sync between the video and audio as you trim.

3. A little further down the timeline there is a cutaway shot on **V2** that you also want to keep in sync with the other tracks as you trim, so in the Track Panel turn on **Sync Locks** `TC1` for all tracks.

4. With the **Trim Mode** button enabled and automatic selection between trim modes active, roll the mouse close to the edit and over the lower half of the **B side** segment.

5. When the mouse changes to the yellow Ripple Trim icon, click so yellow rollers appear on the **B side** of the edit on both tracks **V1** and **A1** of the timeline.

6. The Composer window changes to show you the **Trim Mode Interface**. Look at the **A side** monitor and note the position of the actors in the last frame of the outgoing shot.

7. Use the **trim buttons** in the Trim Mode Interface or the **keyboard shortcuts** to perform single-frame trims to the **right**. Keep removing frames from the head of the **B side** shot until it looks like the actors are in similar positions in both the outgoing and incoming frames.

8. You could exit Trim Mode to play and check the edit, but instead, stay in Trim Mode. Press the **Play Loop** button under the B-side Monitor and the Trim Mode Interface changes to a single monitor. The sequence plays in a repeating loop around the edit so you can decide how well the trim works at play speed.

9. While in **Play Loop** mode, use the keyboard shortcuts to add or remove frames by trimming to the right or left. Each time the edit jumps back to the start of the loop, the sequence will update, and you can see how effective the trims have been. A trim of approximately 40 frames or so to the right

will just about achieve an acceptable cut. But you can experiment with trimming frames on either side of the cut to see if you can produce a result you like better. (During the exercise you might like to try trimming both sides so the cut occurs right on the hand shake between the two boys.)

10. Exit trim mode by clicking in the **Time Bar** or **Timecode track** of the timeline.

11. The edit between shots 2 and 3 can also benefit from a trim to improve the pace and remove some repetition of action. Use the yellow **Ripple Trim** to adjust either side, or each side in turn. Keep an eye on both foreground and background action. **Play Loop** will help here as well.

Finish trimming the sequence for pace and action before coming back to further fine tune the scene.

Creating Split Edits

There is another technique that contributes to achieving seamless, invisible edits. If the video and audio always change at the same time – commonly referred to a straight cut - the edits may become obvious to the viewer. Instead, by having the audio and video change at different moments, called a split edit, you effectively interweave the audio and video into a cohesive whole.

 Split edits are also commonly referred to as L-cuts or J-cuts.

There are two keys to creating split edits:

- Use dual-roller trim.
- Disable Link Selection Toggle.

Remember, dual-roller trimming affects both sides of a transition by adding frames to one side while subtracting the same number of frames from the adjacent side.

If you only trim the video edit and leave the audio alone, you will effectively move the video transition point earlier or later in the sequence. Because both sides of the transition are equally affected, the trim does not change the position of any segments in the track and sync is maintained.

Figure 12.15 shows what happens when you use dual-roller trim to move an edit point later in the sequence.

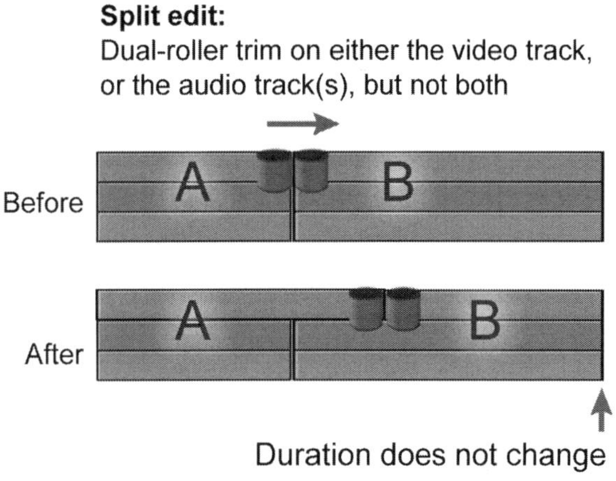

Figure 12.15 A dual-roller trim on either the video track or the audio track(s) but not both (here, on the V1 track) creates a split edit.

Perform a Split Edit

In the sequence:

1. Turn off the **Link Selection Toggle**.

2. Move the mouse pointer over the edit on **V1** in which Ivan responds to Leeroy's calling out. This is the same moment in the scene where you earlier cleaned up the audio edit.

3. Click when the pointer changes to the white **Dual-roller Trim** icon. Pink rollers will appear on both sides of the video edit.

4. Drag the transition point or use the trim buttons/keyboard keys to move the transition point earlier, i.e. to the left. Again, **Play Loop** can help you trim to the best point in the performance. Trim the video edit to the left so you see Ivan reacting to Leeroy saying, *'want to pick up some frothies.'* At the end of Leeroy's line, the shot of Ivan continues as he responds with, *'We are talking here.'*

 You could also achieve the same split edit by using the red Overwrite Trim. You would place a red roller on the B side of the video edit and trim to the left.

Maintaining Sync

Media Composer | First provides a number of tools for editing clips, trimming them and moving them in a sequence. The color coding of the tools is an indication of how they function. Red tools add or remove frames from the timeline without moving segments either side of them. Yellow tools add or remove frames with the result that 'downstream' segments move in the timeline to accommodate the changes. As a result, the yellow tools are the most likely to cause a break in sync as you edit.

There are several ways that you might break sync. Likewise, there are several easy ways to avoid breaking sync. Here's a quick review.

Common ways to break sync include:

- Trimming only one side of a transition, without selecting all tracks
- Extracting frames from only the video or audio track
- Splicing in only audio or video
- Moving only audio or video when in Segment mode

It follows then, that you can prevent breaking sync by:

- When trimming a single track, always use either dual-roller, or the Overwrite Trim.
- Whenever you add frames or subtract frames from an audio or video track, also add or subtract the same number of frames from all the other tracks. It is especially helpful to remember this rule when using any of the yellow tools, for example: trimming, splicing, or extracting.

- Whenever you want to add frames or subtract frames from only one track, use Lift or Overwrite instead of Extract or Splice-In.
- Work with Sync Locks turned on.

Recognizing and Repairing Broken Sync

By default, the Timeline displays sync breaks whenever they occur during editing. These appear at break points as positive or negative numbers indicating the number of frames out of sync. Sync-break indicators appear only in the affected track(s), as shown in figure 12.16.

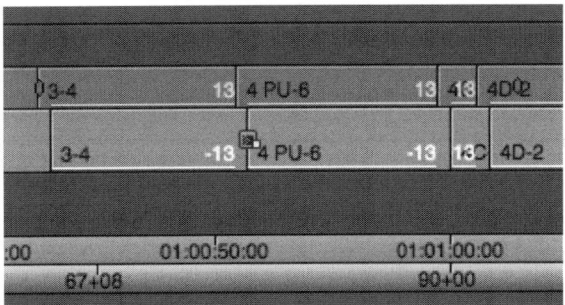

Figure 12.16 These segments are out of sync by 13 frames.

 Sync break information is not displayed if the audio and video tracks come from different sources.

Using Trim Mode to Correct Sync

In Trim mode, you can restore sync by performing one or more single-roller trims on the out-of-sync track(s). To reverse the sync break, you trim the exact number of sync-break frames displayed in the Timeline. Dual-roller trims or Overwrite trims do not remove sync breaks.

Open the sequence Scene 9 Sync Breaks. The Editor was doing a good job of trimming the sequence to improve the pacing and remove repetitions but made the mistake of not trimming all tracks when performing yellow Ripple Trims. The shot where Ivan says, *'We are talking here'*, is now obviously out of sync. The small numbers in the timeline indicate it is out of sync by 5 frames. All following segments are also out of sync but by different amounts.

To fix broken sync:

1. Begin the resyncing process at the first edit point where broken sync appears.

    By using the yellow Ripple Trim to make the correction, the segments ripples downstream, to the right.

2. Enter **Ripple Trim** mode at the head of the first video segment that displays a sync break number.

3. Add the yellow trim roller to only one of the **tracks** that is out of sync. If you know which one caused the issue, then select that one. If you're unsure, it can often be easiest to simply select the edit on the video track. Make sure only that track has trim rollers on the edit.

4. Apply the roller to the **A side** of the edit.

   You could instead choose the **B side**, but it's much easier to choose the A side since it's a bit easier to visualize what is happening in the Timeline.

5. Use the **trim buttons** or **keys** to add or subtract the appropriate number of **frames**.

   - It is often difficult to know which way to trim but there is a simple way to find out. Just start trimming in either direction – to the left or to the right. If the sync break number increases (either as an increasingly negative or increasingly positive number), you are trimming in the wrong direction. Simply trim in the opposite direction. When the sync break number disappears, you have reinstated sync at that point in the timeline.

6. Work your way down the timeline and perform Ripple Trims on all following edits where sync breaks appear in the segments. Continue down the timeline until all sync breaks have been rectified.

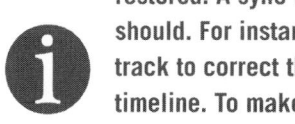

Simply removing the white numbers does not mean the original edit has been restored. A sync break may be fixed but the video edit may not work as well as it should. For instance, you may extend the end of a shot by adding frames to the video track to correct the sync but in so doing effectively move the cut point to later in the timeline. To make sure that your sequence works well, play it back and carefully review the repaired sections. After fixing sync you may then need to use Overwrite trim or Dual-roller trim to reposition the video edits the way you intended.

Review/Discussion Questions

1. What 3 trim modes can be automatically selected by hovering the mouse near, or on, an edit point in the timeline?

2. When you enter any of these automatically selectable trim modes the Composer window reconfigures as the Trim Mode Interface. What does the left monitor display and what does the right monitor display?

3. Which keys in the keyboard allow you to trim to the left or trim to the right?

4. In Trim mode, what function is associated with the Play button?

5. What do the Trim Counters display in the Trim Mode Interface?

6. What is a split edit? What is the benefit of creating split edits in the sequence?

7. What trim tool would you use to create a split edit?

8. How can you ensure that you maintain sync while using Ripple Trim?

9. Describe the process to restore broken sync.

EXERCISE 12

Exercise Break 12.1
Pause here to practice what you've learned.

GOALS

- Use trim tools to refine Scene 7 of Jacuzzi.
- Adjust audio levels
- Publish to YouTube

Refine the Edit of Scene 7 of 'Jacuzzi'

1. From the Jacuzzi project, locate your **Scene 7 Rough Cut** and make a duplicate of it. Rename the duplicate **Scene 7 Fine Cut**.

2. Open the duplicate sequence in the Record/Timeline windows.

3. If you have clips edited onto **V2** of the timeline, move them onto **V1** so they overwrite the shots already there. To do this, hover the mouse over a segment on **V2** until the mouse changes to the red Segment mode. Select the segment with the segment mode tool. To avoid slipping the segment sideways, hold down **Ctrl+Shift (Windows)/Command+Shift(Mac)** and drag the segment from **V2** to **V1**. The segment will only move vertically as you shift it from one track to the other.

4. Your timeline should now only have video on track V1.

5. Review the sequence and use the yellow Ripple trim tool to adjust the pacing of the scene. If necessary, also adjust the edits to match the action from one shot to the next.

6. Use Dual-roller trim to create a split edit.

7. If appropriate, use red Overwrite Trim to clean up any audio edits.

8. Adjust audio levels and add crossfades to smooth out the sound track as necessary.

9. Publish your finished sequence to YouTube.

LESSON 13

Introduction to Segment Effects

In Lesson 7, you learned how to apply transition effects between video and audio segments in the timeline. In this lesson you will learn about effects that you apply only to individual video segments. Visual effects can add interest and drama to a story and also allow Editors to fix shots that are less than perfect. The shots could be poorly exposed or there might be excessive camera shake that distracts the audience. This lesson covers some of the common tools used to improve a variety of those imperfect shots.

Media: Rock Climber & Jacuzzi

Duration: 40 minutes

GOALS

- Learn to work with segment effects, a.k.a. Filters
- Flop a shot to reverse screen direction
- Stabilize a shot
- Apply Color Correction
- Hide jump cuts with Fluid Morph
- Resize clips
- Set standard keyframes

Adding Segment Effects

In Media Composer | First, visual effects can be classified into three different types:

- Transition effects: As you've learned, these are applied at the transition point between two clips, often to emphasize a change of time, location or theme. Transition effects include dissolves, dip-to-color effects, wipes, pushes, squeezes, spins, etc.

- **Segment effects**: These are applied to an entire segment within a sequence to change the look of a shot. Segment effects include color effects, masks, resizes and more.

- **Motion effects**: These are applied to entire clips within a sequence or to source clips to vary the frame rate or motion of the footage. Motion effects are covered in Lesson 15.

1. Get started by opening the **Rock Climber Demo** project and loading the short **Rock Climbing** sequence.

2. Open the **Effect Palette** from the **Tools** drop-down menu. Segment effects are accessed through the **Filters** button in the Effect Palette, as shown in figure 13.1.

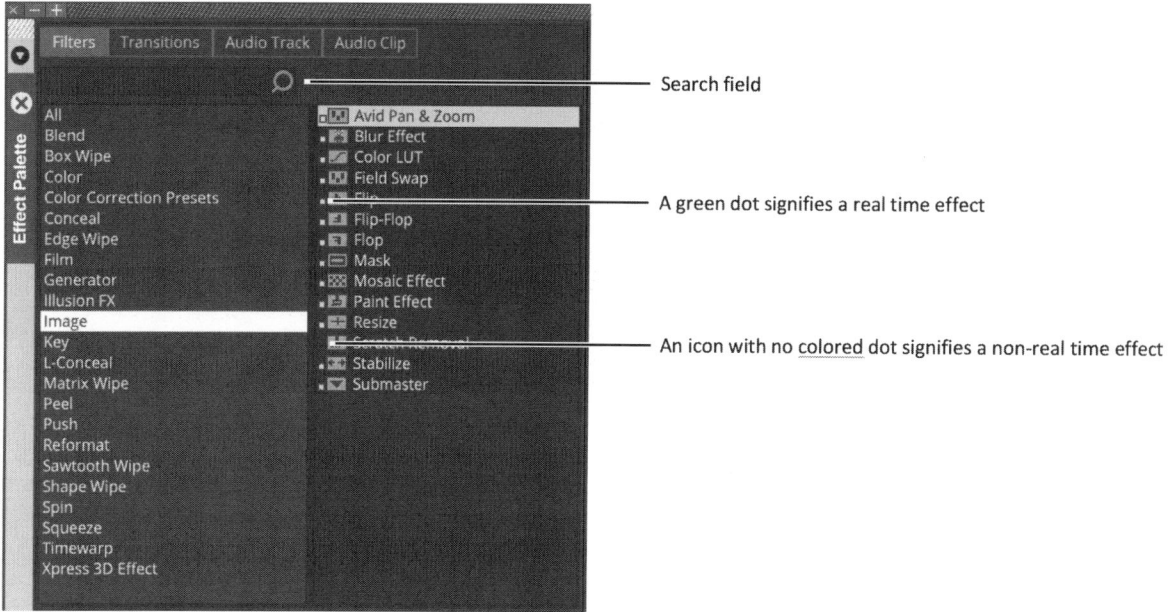

Figure 13.1 Displaying effects in the Image category

The Effect Palette has a series of buttons across the top – Filters, Transitions, Audio Track, and Audio Clip – which organize the effects by type. Each type of effects is further organized into categories listed in the left column, with individual effects appearing in the right column. Arguably, many of the most commonly used segment effects are found in the Image category.

Because the Effect Palette contains so many effects, you can also look for a specific effect through a search field at the top of the Effect Palette.

To search for the Flop effect:

1. Type the name in the Search field. For the purposes of this lesson, type "**Flop**".

2. When you start typing, Media Composer | First dynamically filters the effects displayed in the Effect Palette as you type, as seen in Figure 13.2. Even before you finish typing the full word, the list of effects becomes significantly shorter.

Figure 13.2 Search results update dynamically as you type. The category in which the effect resides is shown in parenthesis.

Once you find the effect you want to add, there are a couple ways you can quickly add it to the first segment in the Rock Climbing sequence.

To add the Flop segment effect, do one of the following:

- Drag the **flop** icon from the Effect Palette on to the video segment in the Timeline.

- Enter **Effect Mode**, select the **segment** in the Timeline to which you want to add the segment effect, and then double-click the **flop** icon in the Effect Palette.

- Select the segment using either a red or yellow **Segment Mode**, then double-click the **Flop** segment effect in the Effect Palette.

  When you add the Flop segment effect, the frame in the Composer window immediately shows the clip reversed from left to right. (Not all effects display an immediate result. For some, you need to modify parameters before you see any change in the image.) The timeline also displays a segment effect icon on the segment (see Figure 13.3). Each effect icon in the timeline is designed to symbolize the effect that you have applied. The Effect Editor also opens but in the case of the Flop effect, there are no parameters that you can adjust.

Figure 13.3 Timeline segment effect icon

Of course, the question is why you might want to use the Flop effect? In the example shown in figure 13.3, where the effect has been applied to the R04_160 Matt Climbing Top clip, the climbers left and right hands have been effectively switched. This may help solve a continuity issue in which the right hand needs to be the one performing the action in both shots. Another common problem that the Flop effect can help solve is when two people in conversation have mistakenly been filmed facing in the same screen direction. Applying the Flop effect to one of the shots can reverse the screen direction and make it seem as if they are now facing each other.

Removing an Effect

Similar to removing transitions, the **Effect** button can be used to remove segment effects.

To remove the segment effect:

1. Make sure the **track** is selected in the Track Selector panel.
2. Place the **position indicator** over the effect icon on the segment in the timeline.
3. Click the **Remove Effect** button.

Realtime vs Non-Realtime Effects

Regardless of whether media has been linked or imported into a Media Composer | First project, no media file is changed when Realtime effects are applied to a clip. Realtime effects non-destructively process the video or audio content. These types of effects can be removed, and the media file remains exactly as it originally was.

When an effect icon has a green dot beside it in the Effect Palette (see Figure 13.1) or on the effect icon in the timeline (see Figure 13.3), Media Composer | First has determined that it can process that effect in real time as the clip to which it is applied is playing.

Any effect that Media Composer | First cannot process in real time will not have a colored dot beside the effect icon in the Effect Palette but will have a blue dot on the icon in the timeline. A non-real time effect must be rendered before you can play the effect in the timeline. A rendered effect is a new media file that is a modified copy of the original file with the effect permanently 'baked in'.

When an effect has been rendered, the effect icon in the timeline losses its colored dot, regardless of whether it was a real time or non-real time effect.

> ### Working with the Effect Editor
>
> Because the Effect Editor is only active when you need it, there are times when you might unintentionally close it or the parameters disappear from the Effect Editor interface. This is most likely to happen if you try to review an effect by scrubbing the timecode track / time bar in the Timeline. When working with the Effect Editor you need to scrub the position bar at the bottom of the Effects monitor to review the effect.
>
> You can access the Effect Editor in a couple of ways:
>
> 1.) Use the Effects Editing Workspace. To open the Effects Editing workspace, select **Windows > Workspaces > Effects** or click on the **Effects** button in the sidebar on the right-hand side of the user interface. The Effects Editing workspace is an arrangement of tools and windows specifically for working with effects. This includes opening the Effect Editor and positioning it on the main display right next to the Composer window, which also changes to a single large Effects monitor.
>
> 2.) Use the **Effect Mode** button located in the tool bar at the top of the Timeline window or select **Tools>Effect Editor**. The Effect Editor opens next to the Composer window that remains in a two-monitor configuration. The right-hand monitor has reconfigured to be the Effects monitor.

Stabilizing Shaky Footage

A common problem you will encounter as an editor is unstable camera work. In a documentary, it's not always possible to use a tripod. And sometimes, you want the look and energy of a handheld shot, but just want it toned down. Media Composer has a flexible stabilization effect that can either lock down an unstable shot, removing all camera motion, or just eliminate the erratic bumps and jitters but keep the general camera movement. The beauty of the Stabilize effect is that is practically "auto-magical."

To smooth out a bumpy, shaky shot:

1. From the Image category in the Effect Palette, drag the Stabilize effect onto the <u>third</u> segment of the **Rock Climbing** sequence in the Timeline.

Almost immediately, the Tracking Window opens (see Figure 13.4), and the process of stabilization begins automatically. You will see green dots appear and disappear over the image as Media Composer | First uses its advanced 3D tracking engine to automatically identify and track reference points in the image, and then use that information to stabilize the shot.

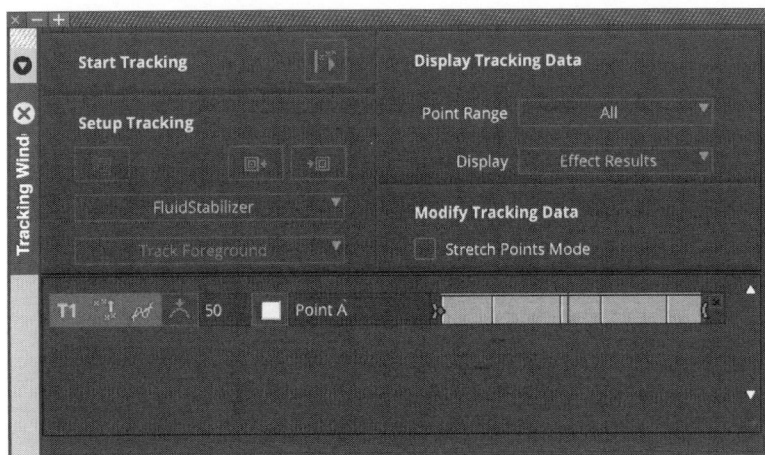

Figure 13.4 The Tracking Window

The effect quickly steps through the segment one frame at a time, analyzing and comparing the frames to extract the motion data of the camera. Once the entire segment is analyzed, the Stabilize effect inverts the motion data and applies it to the clip, leaving only the smooth movement of the camera. For instance, if the camera suddenly jerks down to the left, the motion data offsets it by repositioning the frame up to the right. The amount the frame has to be offset determines how much it also has to be scaled up in size so the image still fills the frame. The end result is a clip that appears much smoother because it repositions each frame by the same amount but in the opposite direction to the detected movement.

2. Close the Tracking window and play the clip to view the results.

To compare the smoothed segment to the original, you need a way to enable and disable parameter groups within the effect. The Effect Editor includes highlighted "enable" buttons for active parameters, as shown in Figure 13.5. You can disable the Stabilize effect by turning off the active parameters in the Effect Editor. The Parameter group's settings are still retained, so they can be enabled again at any time.

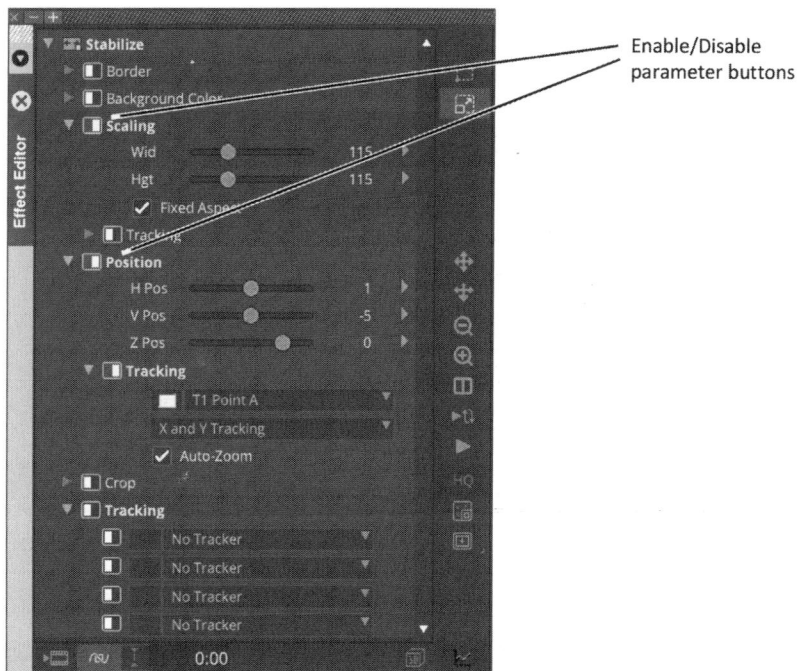

Figure 13.5 The Effect Editor's enable/disable buttons

 If you disable the Scaling parameter on a stabilized segment, you can see how the motion data is applied to the clip. When you play the effect, the frame moves around within the Effect Preview monitor. This is the motion data, offsetting the camera movement.

Locking Down a Shot

That covers just one method of stabilizing, the smoothing method. A more traditional type of stabilization technique aims to create a locked-down shot. All camera movement is removed, and the clip appears as if the camera were on a tripod. The Stabilize effect can be used quite effectively for this, with one slight modification.

By default, the Stabilize effect utilizes the SteadyGlide feature. SteadyGlide is designed to allow movement on one axis – up/down, left/right – while eliminating movement on the other. For example, it will allow for a horizontal pan, but eliminate any vertical wobbles introduced by the camera operator. If you disable SteadyGlide, in many instances, it can produce a result that looks tripod-steady.

To lock down a shot with Stabilize:

1. From the **Image** category in the Effect Palette, again drag the **Stabilize** effect onto the third segment in the Timeline. This will replace the original Stabilize effect.

2. Allow the effect to process as normal, but do not close the **Tracking Tool** window.

3. In the Tracking Tool window, toggle off the **Steadyglide** button, as shown in Figure 13.6.

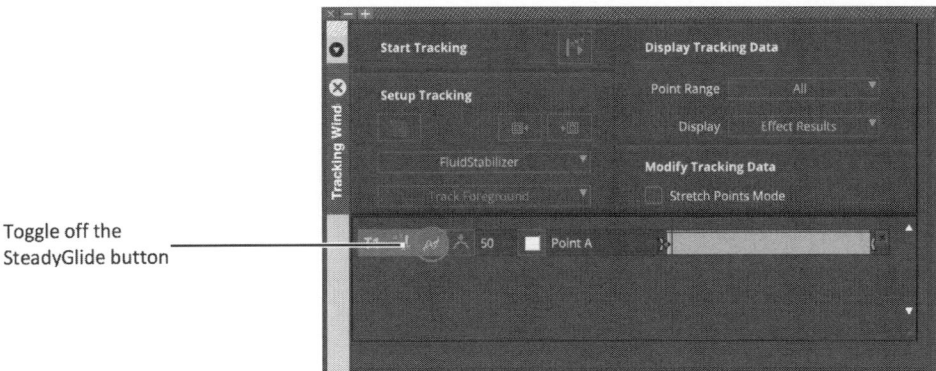

Toggle off the SteadyGlide button

Figure 13.6 Disable the SteadyGlide button to eliminate most camera movement

Using Color Correction to Improve the Footage

There are many times that you will work with footage that is poorly exposed, has low contrast, or color balance problems. Color correction can do a lot to solve these common problems and improve the look of your program. Figure 13.7 shows a before and after example of a shot with corrections applied.

Figure 13.7 A before and after look at how color correction can improve your shots

There are usually three goals associated with using the color tools in Media Composer | First.

- Firstly, you need to fix any exposure or color related problems in each segment of a sequence. This is the correction stage.
- Secondly, you want one shot to look the same as the next in terms of brightness and color when the shots are all from the same location and time of day. This is the matching stage.
- Finally, you may want to stylize a series of related shots to give a certain 'look' to a scene. For example, give the scene an overall warm appearance.

The Color Correction Tool

Media Composer | First has a color correction tool that is based on adjusting three basic properties of an image - the Hue, Saturation and Luminance.

- **Hue** refers to the actual colors reproduced in an image. The overall hue of an image can be described as its color balance.

- **Saturation** refers to the colorfulness or intensity of the colors in an image.

- **Luminance** refers to how light or bright the image is. This can often be described in terms of the exposure of the image.

The color correction tool in Media Composer | First is therefore described as an HSL Color Corrector.

Setting Up the Color Correction Effect

There are two ways in which you can apply color correction to a segment in the timeline. Either you can apply the **Color Correction** effect from the **Color** category in the **Effect Palette** or you can open the **Color Workspace**. Both have similar controls to adjust parameters, but the Color Workspace has a dedicated interface that offers some real advantages. One advantage is the ability to apply some automatic adjustments that make correcting image brightness and color balance much quicker.

In the Rock Climbing sequence, park the Position indicator near the middle of the <u>second</u> segment.

To open the Color Workspace (Figure 13.8), do one of the following:

- Select the **Windows > Workspaces > Color**.

- Click the **Color** workspace button in the sidebar at the right of the user interface.

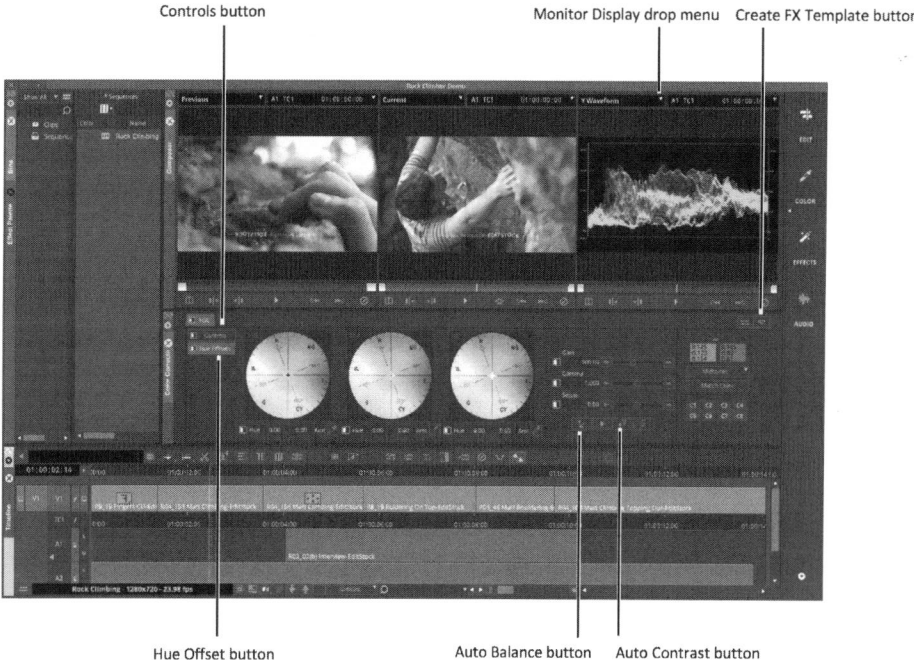

Figure 13.8 The Color workspace

The Color Workspace has a three-monitor display in which the middle monitor shows the segment on which the blue Position indicator is parked in the timeline. This is the image to which corrections will be applied. The shot preceding it in the timeline is displayed in the left-hand monitor. This allows you to visually compare the segment you are working on with the previous segment.

The right-hand monitor normally displays the next segment in the timeline, again so you can make a visual comparison. But it can also provide another very useful display.

- Click the **Monitor Display** drop-down menu above the right-hand monitor (which currently reads "**Next**") and select the **Y Waveform** from the list.

The graphical display shows you the brightness values from left to right across the image you are going to correct. The brightness range of the image is more correctly called the 'luma range'. The brightest areas of the picture should not extend above the **100** mark in the scale on the right-hand side of the Y Waveform display while the darkest areas should not fall below the **0** mark. If any luma value falls outside the 0 – 100 range, the waveform for that area of the picture changes color from green to white.

Drag the **Position indicator** under the middle monitor or in the timeline to see how the waveform changes from one frame to the next as the visual information in the segment changes while the rock climber moves.

Using the HSL Hue Offsets Controls

1. Move your **Position indicator** to the point in the timeline that intersects with the segment that you want to modify. For the purposes of this lesson, park the indicator over the second segment.

2. Click the **Hue Offsets** button to display the auto correction tools. (The **Controls** button also provides a number of complementary parameters you can adjust. More on that in a moment.)

3. Click the **Auto Contrast** button and the luma range is automatically corrected for the frame on which you are parked. Either side of the Auto Contrast button are the **Auto Black** and **Auto White** buttons, which are indicated in Figure 13.9. They produce a similar result to Auto Contrast but they adjust the brightest and darkest areas independently.

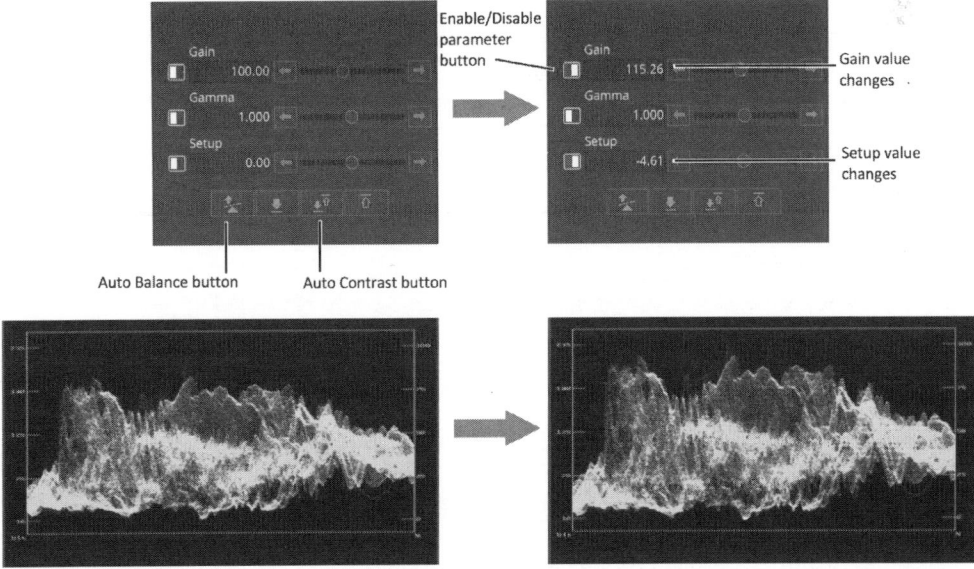

Figure 13.9 Auto Contrast

In this example, the **Gain,** affecting the brightest areas, has increased to a value of approximately 115 and the **Setup,** affecting the darkest areas, has been lowered by a value of approximately -5. The waveform has increased in vertical size to visualize the changes in values. You can toggle the **Enable/Disable** buttons for each parameter to see the before-and-after of the changes. Also, notice that as soon as you apply some correction to the image, an effect icon appears on the segment in the timeline.

Now click the **Auto Balance** button so the color balance of the image is automatically corrected to remove any unnatural color hue. White areas of the picture should look white on screen and black areas should remain neutral in color.

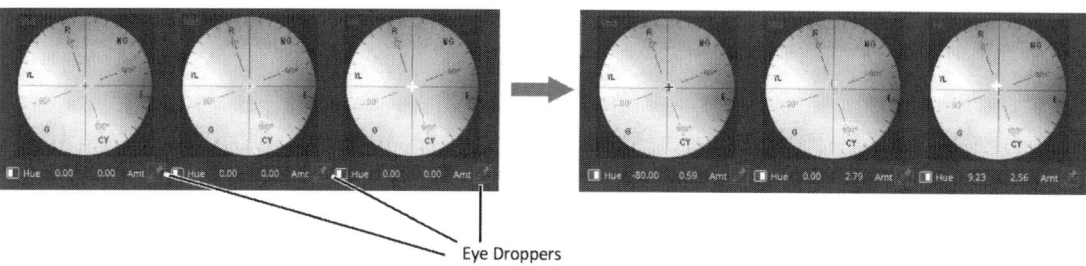

Figure 13.10 Auto Balance

Notice how the white crosshairs in the middle of the color wheels have shifted by small amounts to remove any detected color casts in the **Shadows, Mid-tones** and **Highlights** (as shown in Figure 13.10). These three areas of the picture correspond to the three brightness areas controlled by the **Setup, Gamma** and **Gain** adjustments of the luma range.

Auto Contrast and **Auto Balance** have returned the image to standard luma and color setups, but each parameter can also be adjusted manually to make fine adjustments if necessary. You can click and drag the **Gain** and **Setup** sliders or click the **left** or **right** arrows to make incremental changes to the luma values.

Each color wheel also has an **eye dropper** that allows you to manually select a shadow, mid-tone or highlight area in the picture. Figure 13.10. For instance, if there is an object within the highlight region that should be white, use the eye dropper to select that object in the image. The color corrector will sample the color values of that object and automatically adjust the position of the cross hairs to compensate for any detected variance from pure white.

You can also click and drag the small white crosshairs in the color wheels to manually make adjustments to the color balance in the highlight, mid-tone and shadow regions of the image.

Adjusting Gamma

Gamma is the one luma parameter that Auto Contrast has not adjusted. **Gamma** adjusts the mid-tone brightness areas of the picture.

While in the Color Workspace, move the **Position indicator** down to the fifth segment in the timeline.

1. Scrub through the segment and notice in the waveform monitor that the brightest and darkest areas already fall within the full luma range. However, the rock face is much darker than in the preceding image in the left-hand monitor. The Gamma control will help fix this.

2. Click and drag the **Gamma** slider to the right until the rock face looks similar in brightness to the rock face in the left-hand monitor. A Gamma value of approximately 1.6 looks about right.

3. Because there is some interaction between the three luma areas of the image, notice that the darkest areas of the picture no longer sit around 0 in the waveform monitor. Use the **Setup** slider and/or left and right arrows to readjust the Setup value until the darkest areas are back around 0. As you adjust the parameters you may find that Gain also needs some fine tuning.

4. You can also click the **Auto Balance** button to correct for any color casts in the image but note that the luma values may need some further adjustments as a result.

Using Color Match

Another consequence of making these adjustments may be that the color of the rock face now looks slightly different to the color of the rock face in the preceding segment. In the wider shot, the rocks may look predominantly grey while in the closer shot their color is more brown.

Within the Hue Offsets window is the **Color Match** control area, as shown in figure 13.11.

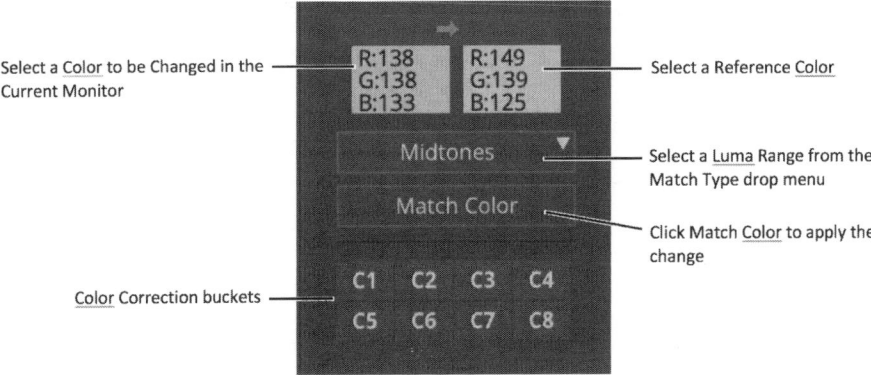

Figure 13.11 Color Match control

This section of the Color Correction window allows you to select a reference color from any image and apply that color setting to a nominated color in the middle monitor of the Color Workspace.

To match the color of the rock face in the fifth segment to the color of the rock face in the preceding segment:

1. Click in the **left-side color section of the Color Match section** to activate the eyedropper tool then select a color to be changed in the current monitor. Note that when you choose a color, the field around the values changes to indicate that particular hue.

2. Click in the **right-side color section of the Color Match section** to activate the eyedropper tool then select the reference color from the image in the left-hand monitor. Note that when you choose a color, the field around the values changes to indicate that particular hue.

3. From the **Match Type** drop menu, select **Midtones** as the luma area to which the color change is to be applied.

4. Click the **Match Color** button to apply the color change. Notice that the crosshair in the 'Mid' color wheel changes position as a result.

If you don't like the result you can select a different reference color and try again or manually adjust the crosshair in the color wheel for the mid-range luma values.

Using HSL Controls

By clicking on the **Controls** button in the Color Workspace, an alternative set of color correction tools opens. Unlike the Hue Offsets that can be applied to different luma bands, these are coarser controls that are more universal in how they modify the picture. However, they can produce similar results to the Gain and Setup parameters if used cautiously.

Move your **Position indicator** to the middle of the sixth segment in the timeline.

1. Look at the center monitor and compare the waveform display. The overall image looks under exposed.

2. Adjust the **Brightness** slider to a value of approximately 24 and adjust the **Contrast** slider to a value of approximately 13. The image is a fairly close match to the preceding shot.

These setting don't work for the entire clip however—when you scrub down to the end of the segment you see that the camera tilts up and the sky appears in the top of frame. The area of bright sky now exceeds the maximum acceptable luma range as seen in the waveform monitor.

3. To compensate for this without reducing the overall expose of the picture, turn on the limiter that will clip the over-bright areas to the maximum luma value.

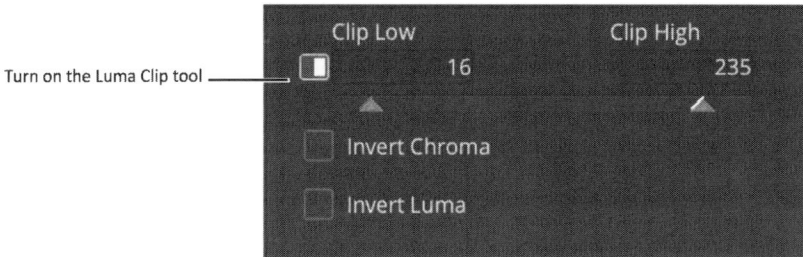

Figure 13.12 Luma clip tool

Like the Hue Offsets window, the Controls window has a Color Match area, but the Controls window uses a different set of options in the Match Type drop menu. These options are based on the parameters available in the Controls window.

Using both HLS Controls and Hue Offsets

As mentioned above, the Controls and Hue Offsets are complementary ways of adjusting the color of a segment in the timeline. You can use both of them in combination to achieve a desired result.

To see how they work together, do the following:

1. Park the **Position indicator** on the first frame of the second segment in the timeline. Notice that there is a highly reflective metal carabiner anchored to the rock face. The image has been color

corrected using the parameters in the Hue Offsets window, and although the overall picture falls within the luma range, the brightness of the carabiner exceeds the maximum limit. You can see this as a small spike in the waveform.

2. Switch to the **Controls** window and turn on the limiter to clip the brightness of the carabiner to the maximum luma level.

3. Now park somewhere in the middle of the fifth segment in the timeline. You used the Gamma parameter in the Hue Offsets window to increase the brightness of the rock face. But sometimes, increasing the Gamma can noticeably reduce the saturation of the colors in the picture.

In the same way that there are upper and lower limits to the luma range, there are also limits to the color saturation.

4. In the right-hand monitor of the Color Workspace, click on the **Monitor Display** drop-down menu and select the **Vectorscope** (see Figure 13.13). Like the waveform view, the vectorscope is a graphical display of the visual information in the image, but instead of luma levels it shows color hue and saturation.

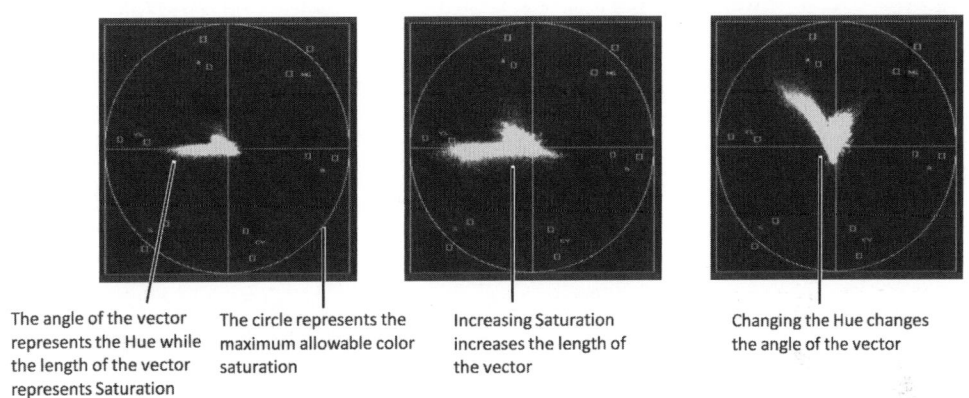

Figure 13.13 The Vectorscope display

5. From the **Controls** window, adjust the **Saturation** slider to increase the overall color saturation of the image. A slider value of approximately 130 should help improve the colors in the picture. Notice how the length of the vector changes as you move the Saturation slider. By dragging the slider all the way to the left, you will remove all color saturation and the image will become monochrome, i.e. black and white.

6. The **Hue** slider can produce very pronounced changes in the colors of the image, so use it sparingly. However, a slight adjustment can correct for some overall color balance issues. Notice how the angle of the vector changes as you adjust the Hue slider.

FX Templates

If you have a series of segments that all suffer from similar problems, you can create an FX template that you can reuse without the need to adjust the parameters every time.

To create a template:

1. Park the **Position indicator** on the color effect icon on the <u>second</u> segment of the timeline. The parameters in the Color Workspace will show the adjustments applied to that color effect.

2. Click and drag the **Create FX Template** button from the Color Workspace (see Figure 13.8) into an open bin. The color affect has now been saved. (It is often a good work practice to create a bin specifically for holding any FX templates that you create.)

You can now apply the color effect while working in any workspace of Media Composer | First. To apply the template to the <u>fourth</u> segment in the timeline:

3. From the bin, drag the effect icon onto the segment in the timeline.

To modify the parameters for any color effect, you can open the effect in the normal **Effect Editor** or return to the **Color Workspace**.

The Color Correction Buckets

In both the Controls and Hue Offsets windows there is a group of 8 buttons below the Color Match area. (shown in Figure 13.11). These buttons are common to both windows and are called the **Color Correction Buckets**. They are available for temporarily saving correction settings as FX templates. Unlike bins that can permanently save effects templates, these **Color Correction Buckets** will only hold settings during the current editing session. When Media Composer | First is closed and relaunched, the buckets will be clear of any color correction settings you saved in them during the previous session. Although temporary in nature, they can be a convenient way to store and access multiple correction settings while in the Color Workspace.

To save a color correction effect in a bucket, do the following:

4. Park the **Position indicator** on the <u>sixth</u> segment in the timeline that has the color effect you want to save.

5. **Alt+click (Win)** or **Option+click (Mac)** the bucket in which you want to save the effect. A color effect icon appears in the bucket, indicating that the settings have been temporarily stored in that bucket.

To apply the color correction from the bucket:

6. Park on the <u>first</u> segment in the timeline.

7. Click the bucket that holds the effect you want to apply.

The color correction is applied to the clip in the timeline and a color effect icon appears on the segment. It's worth nothing at this point that any previously applied effects will still be active. This is a unique property of the buckets – let's take a look at an alternative workflow: Earlier you created a color FX template and saved it in a bin. You then applied that FX template to the fourth segment in the timeline. Applying it to a clip from the bin will yield a different result.

8. Drag the color FX template from the bin and drop it on the <u>third</u> segment in the timeline (the clip that you previously applied the Stabilize effect to).

9. Notice that although the color correction has been applied and a color effect icon is now on the segment, you have lost the stabilize effect. You can tell because the text at the bottom of frame is no longer moving around as it did when the clip was stabilized.

10. Undo the last action to restore the Stabilize effect. Now use the Color Correction bucket to apply the saved effect to the third clip. Now both the Stabilize effect and Color Correction effect are active.

In general terms, this demonstrates that when you apply color correction from the Color Workspace you can directly combine color correction with an effect already applied to the segment. In contrast, applying a color effect from either a template in a bin or from the Effect Palette will replace an effect already applied to a segment. You'll learn more about applying multiple effects in the next lesson.

Limitations of Automatic Color Correction

Automatic color correction is a useful tool to solve basic image problems very quickly. Like any fully automatic function, it won't produce a perfect result in every situation.

The weakness of automatic color corrections is that the system cannot see what's in the scene. It doesn't see a landscape or faces; it can't differentiate between foreground and background; it only knows that there is some white, yellow, blue, and so on. It will make assumptions about the colors in the frame—assumptions that may or may not be correct. Also, automatic corrections do not compare one shot to another.

There are many color-correction problems that are not appropriate for automatic correction. These include:

Extreme light conditions: If a significant area of an image is deliberately overexposed or underexposed, automatic color corrections may misunderstand the intent and produce an undesired result.

Extreme color-balance problems: Automatic color corrections might not provide the expected result on images that show extreme white-balance issues or in mixed-lighting conditions where part of the image is white balanced while other parts of the image are not. A night club scene with deep and multi-colored lighting is a typical example.

Images lacking the appropriate distinct white or black regions: Automatic color corrections are effective only with images that have the appropriate content for calculating either white, black, or both, such as areas of strong highlight (white or close to white) and areas of strong shadow (black or close to black).

Stylizing a Scene Using Color Presets

After you have adjusted individual shots in the timeline for correct color balance and exposure, then matched shots for consistency throughout the sequence, you might want to introduce a specific look to enhance the emotional impact of the scene. Media Composer | First has a large selection of preset color effects that can quickly and easily stylize or colorize a group of shots.

While it is possible to apply the preset color effect to each segment in turn, it is much easier to apply it to an entire group of segments in one go. It also makes trying different looks much easier.

To apply a preset color effect to a group of segments:

1. From the menus at the top of the screen, select **Timeline>New>Video Track**. A new V2 track will be created in the timeline.

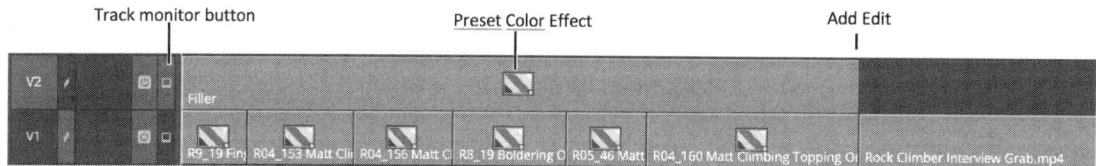

Figure 13.14 A preset Color Effect applied to Filler

2. Turn off all the Record **Track Selectors** except for the V2 track.

3. Park the **Position indicator** on the first frame of the first interview Grab segment in the timeline and click the **Add Edit** button. Remember that a 'blank' video track actually contains Filler, so the Add Edit has created an edit in the Filler.

4. Open the **Effect Palette** and in the left-hand column select the **Color Correction Presets**.

5. Perhaps you want to dramatically suggest the climber is climbing in very low light conditions. From the right-hand column, click and drag the **Dark Winter** preset onto the Filler at the start of the V2 track.

6. To make sure you can see the effect, switch the track monitor to the V2 track.

7. To try a different preset, simply drag and drop the alternative effect onto the V2 track. The new effect will replace the original.

Hiding Jump Cuts with FluidMorph

Although most corrective effects are segment effects, Media Composer | First does have a unique transition effect that can also be used to hide problems in a sequence. FluidMorph, located in the Illusion FX category (see Figure 13.15), specifically helps solve the problem of jump cuts, where two shots of the same subject are edited back to back with only slight differences between them. It's a jarring cut because elements within the frame suddenly change position on screen. FluidMorph can warp the two images to better align with each other, so they perform a more seamless transition. The effect is well suited to disguising jump cuts in interviews.

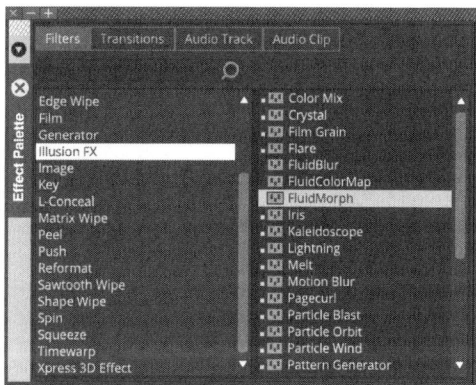

Figure 13.15 Fluid Morph is located in the IllusionFX category of the Effect Palette.

In the **Rock Climbing** sequence, after the opening series of rock climbing shots, is a group of three interview grabs that have been edited together. Play the grabs and see the two jump cuts at the edit points.

To hide the jump cuts using a FluidMorph effect:

1. From the **Illusion FX** category, drag the **FluidMorph** effect onto the first cut point.
2. In the FluidMorph Effect Editor window, choose **Still > Still**.
3. Click the **Render Effect** button at the bottom left of the Effect Editor. The **Render Effect** window will appear, prompting you to choose a location for the rendered file.

Don't be disappointed at the first result from applying the effect. While Fluid Morph does not require any user input to work, there are a few options in the Effect Editor that may produce a more invisible transition.

By default, FluidMorph warps both images based on the luminance of the images. **Feature Match** may improve the warping by aligning feature patterns as it warps from one image to the other (see Figure 13.16).

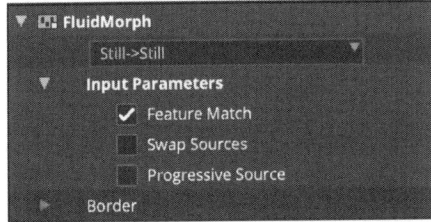

Figure 13.16 The Fluid Morph Feature Match option in the Effect Editor

 Fluid Morph works best when the majority of the image is the same and the difference in the object that moves is not too severe.

The next level of assistance for improving FluidMorph's results is to try different combinations of outgoing and incoming frames at the edit point. You can select the options through the drop menu at the top of the Effect Editor window, as shown in figure 13.17.

By default, FluidMorph takes the safest approach and uses **Still>Still**. It uses freeze frames on the outgoing and incoming sides of the edit in place of moving video during the morph transition. The simplicity involved in warping two freeze frames to create the morph produces more reliable results but doesn't always look the most realistic.

An alternative is to set the drop menu to warp each side of the transition frame by frame. This is the **Stream > Stream** setting. It is the most complicated of the settings but will produce the most realistic results if—and this is a big if—the movement doesn't vary all that much. This setting is more likely to result in artifacts because you have two images moving that must be aligned.

Setting one side or the other of the transition to **Still** instead of **Stream** splits the difference; these half-and-half settings lower the complexity by creating a freeze frame for one of the shots but produces a more realistic result because one shot still has normal motion.

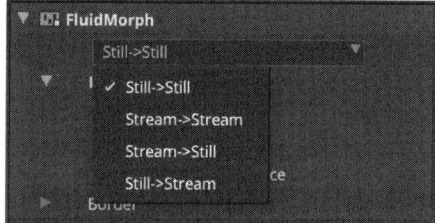

Figure 13.17 The FluidMorph drop menu options in the Effect Editor

A further consideration is the duration and alignment of the transition. Often a shorter duration of 3 to 10 frames will produce a better result than one of 25 frames.

After you have chosen all your settings, you can use the **Effect Preview** monitor's position bar to click through the various stages of the effect, but the subtlety of this effect can really only be judged by playing it in real time, which requires rendering.

The final recommendation with FluidMorph is to try various combinations of:

- Transition duration
- Transition alignment
- Source outgoing and incoming frames

In the case of the first jump cut between the interview grabs the following settings produce a good result:

4. Source drop menu – **Still>Stream**
5. Feature Match – **On**
6. Transition alignment – **Starting at Cut**
7. Duration – **6 frames**
8. For the second jump cut try these settings:
9. Source drop menu – **Stream>Stream**
10. Feature Match – **On**
11. Transition alignment – **Centered on Cut**
12. Duration – **6 frames**

Resizing a Shot

If you've ever have taken a photo and used a crop tool to cut out unwanted scenery around the edges, you'll understand the value of resizing clips in Media Composer | First. The difference here is that instead of cropping down a photo, you scale up the shot to focus the viewer's attention on a specific area. The result is the same: Unwanted material around the edges of a shot can be removed, and the attention of the viewer can be focused on the important area.

Park the **Position indicator** on the last segment in the Rock Climbing sequence.

To use the Resize effect:

1. Select the **Image** category in the Effect Palette.

2. Drag the **Resize** effect (which you'll find in the **Image** category of your **Color Palette** window) onto the segment in the Timeline.

3. With the **Effect Editor** open, use the parameters to resize and reposition the image to crop out the man standing at the bottom of the rock wall. (If you cannot see any parameters displayed in the Effect Editor, check that the Track Selector for V1 is turned on. Park on the effect icon in the segment then reopen the Effect Editor.)

4. To avoid distorting the image while you resize it, check the box next to **Fixed Aspect**. This ensures the width and height are adjusted in proportion when using the parameter sliders. It also means you only need to change either the **X** or **Y Scaling** parameter as the other parameter will follow. A value of 135 is just about right.

5. Now use the **Y Position** parameter to move the image down until the top of the image sits at the top of the frame in the Effect Preview monitor. A value of 156 should do it.

Unlike many other effects, the Resize effect can be manipulated directly in the Effect Preview monitor when the Effect Editor is open. You can reduce the size of the viewing area in the Effect Preview monitor by using the **Reduce** button (see Figure 13.18), making it easier to work outside the boundaries of the visible frame (to increase the size of the viewing area, click on the **Enlarge** button). The degree of enlargement or reduction of the viewing area relative to the normal display size is shown as a percentage in the top right corner of the Effect Preview monitor.

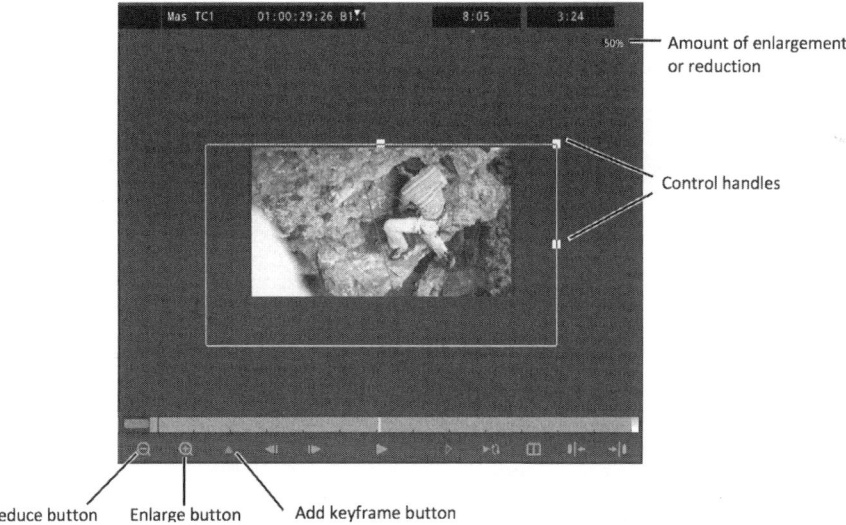

Figure 13.18 Use the Reduce button to zoom out on the Effect Preview monitor

A white outline surrounds the frame in the Effect Preview monitor. The outline allows you to directly manipulate the Resize effect from within the monitor. Resize changes are made by dragging the white handles. The handle in the upper right allows you to maintain the image aspect ratio as you resize the frame.

Additionally, by dragging within the white outline, you can reposition the scaled image to re-center the shot or eliminate unwanted parts around the edges of the frame.

 Any time you directly manipulate the image from within the Effect Preview monitor, Media Composer | First adds a keyframe where the Position indicator is parked. If you don't want the keyframe, select the keyframe and hit Delete on your keyboard to remove it.

The only parameters within the Resize effect that do not have controls in the Effect Preview monitor are the crop parameters. The crop parameters in the Effect Editor enable you to cut out unwanted areas around the edges of the frame without scaling. Since Resize is not a compositing (blending) effect, when you crop it does not create a transparent area. Instead a colored background is revealed. You can adjust the background color using the background parameters similar to the parameters you use when adjusting the Dip to Color effect.

When you resize, reposition, or crop the image, the effect is set for the entire segment's length. This is true if you change the parameters using the Effect Editor or if you change them from the Effect Preview monitor. The difference is that the Effect Editor does not automatically create a keyframe whereas the Effect Preview monitor does. Provided there is only one keyframe in the effect, the parameters will not change over time.

When you start using more than one keyframe, you have the ability to change parameters over time. For instance, you may want to start the segment with the image in its unresized position and by the end of the segment it has zoomed in to part of the frame.

Using Standard Keyframes

Under the Effect Preview monitor is a position bar that represents the duration of the segment. **Keyframes** are added at the location of the blue Position Indicator. Selected keyframes are displayed in purple, while unselected keyframes are gray (see Figure 13.19).

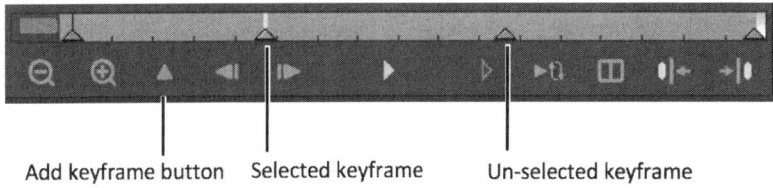

Figure 13.19 Keyframes located under the Effect Preview monitor

Once a keyframe is added, selecting it and then changing any parameter sets the parameter value for that frame. Selecting another keyframe and changing the same parameter causes an interpolation (transition) between the different parameter values on the keyframes. This interpolation creates the dynamic change of the parameters over time. So, creating animation is the process of selecting keyframes at various points in time and adjusting parameter values differently for each keyframe.

There are three ways to add keyframes:

- Direct manipulation of the image in the Effect Preview monitor.
- Clicking the **Add Keyframe** button under the Effect Preview monitor.

- Pressing the **Keyframe** button on your keyboard (semicolon).

    By using the **Add Keyframe** button under the Effect Preview monitor as shown in Figure 13.19 (or the **Keyframe** button on the keyboard), you can add as many keyframes as required anywhere within the position bar.

To use keyframing to do a zoom and tilt of the last segment in the sequence:

1. Open the Effect Editor for the Resize effect.
2. Park the **Position indicator** at the beginning of the effect.
3. Add a keyframe by clicking on the **Add Keyframe** button. A keyframe appears in the position bar.
4. Do not change any of the parameters for this keyframe as the starting size and position will be as setup previously i.e.
    - X & Y Scaling = 135
    - Y Position = 156
5. Still in the Effect Preview monitor, move to the last frame of the segment and add another keyframe.
6. Change the values of the same parameters listed in step 4, i.e.
    - X & Y Scaling = 155
    - Y Position = 262
7. Use the **Play Loop** button under the Effect Preview monitor to view the resulting animation.

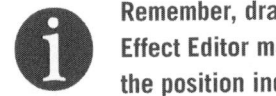

Remember, dragging the position indicator in the Timeline will cause you to exit Effect Editor mode. Use the position bar beneath the Effect Preview monitor to move the position indicator within the effect and stay in Effect Editor mode.

You can add any number of keyframes to animate different parameters, but if you want a parameter adjustment to be applied across the entire effect, you must select all the keyframes in the position bar before making the parameter change.

To select all keyframes, click in the Effect Preview monitor to activate it then either:

- Press **Ctrl+A (Windows)** or **Command+A (Mac)**
- Choose **Select All** from the **Edit** menu.

Alternatively, if there are no keyframes added to the effect then any parameter adjustments will be applied to the entire effect.

Another point to note is that the more you scale up a video frame in size the poorer will be the image quality. So, it is worthwhile keeping the amount of scaling to a minimum.

Review/Discussion Questions

1. There are 3 ways you can apply a segment effect to a segment in the timeline. What is one of those ways?

2. How do you remove a segment effect from the timeline?

3. What does a green dot on an effect icon mean?

4. What does a blue dot on an effect icon mean?

5. What does it mean when an effect icon does not have either a green or a blue dot?

6. Although there is a Color Correction effect in the Effect Palette, what is the best way to work with adjusting exposure and color balance of segments in the timeline?

7. What is the FluidMorph effect able to do?

8. What do the Enlarge and Reduce buttons do in the Effect Preview monitor?

9. When using a Resize effect, where are you able to change the scale and position parameters?

10. What do keyframes allow you to do in the Resize segment effect?

EXERCISE 13

 Exercise Break 13.1
Pause here to practice what you've learned.

GOALS

- Apply effects to fix issues with shots
- Color correct to adjust color balance and luma levels and match shots within a sequence
- Publish the sequences

Finishing Scene 7 of the Jacuzzi Project

Picture Lock is the term commonly used to describe the stage in editing when all editorial decisions have been made and approved. The film is then handed over to the finishing processes such as on-line editing, color grading and audio mixing.

By this stage you will have completed editing Scene 7 of the Jacuzzi project (in the form of the Scene 7 Fine Cut sequence, which you should open now). What remains is color correction and some effects work to fix up any problems with the footage.

Start by applying the Resize effect to solve an issue with one segment, then use the Color Workspace to adjust exposure and color balance.

At one point in the scene, Leeroy says, *'We'll have to go all the way back to the warehouse.'* During that take, the microphone bobs up into shot from bottom of frame.

1. Park on the frame in which the microphone is most visible in the shot.
2. From the Image category of the Effect Palette, drag and drop the Resize effect onto the segment in the timeline.
3. Enlarge the shot to eliminate the microphone from the frame by either using the Scaling and Position parameters in the Effect Editor or by manipulating the image in the Effect Preview monitor. Try to keep the size increase to a minimum so as much of the picture quality is preserved as possible.

When you play the sequence, it is obvious that there are exposure differences between the shots of the boys unloading the truck and Don and Ivan in the shade of the front porch of the house.

4. Open the Color Workspace and use the Hue Offsets window to adjust the luma levels so all shots fall within the maximum and minimum values.

5. Use the Gamma slider to adjust the mid-tones of the shots of Don and Ivan so there is a better match with the shots of Leeroy and Moose.

6. Publish the sequence to YouTube.

Fix Jump Cuts in the Rock Climber Story

The *Rock Climber* story is also nearly complete. It too needs some adjustments during the finishing stage of postproduction.

1. Open the Rock Climber Version 6 sequence from your My Second Project_(Student ID) project.

2. There are several jump cuts in the interview where *'ums'* and *'ahs'* have been removed. Use the FluidMorph effect (from the Illusion FX category) to disguise those transitions.

3. If a FluidMorp effect just doesn't seem to work well enough, an alternative technique to disguise a jump cut is to use the Resize effect. By rescaling the shot on one side of the edit, the change in shot size can effectively mask the jump cut. You can try different amounts of resizing to see what degree of change between shots works the best.

There is more work yet to do in the Rock Climber story, so you will revisit it again before final color correction is applied.

LESSON 14

Combining Multiple Effects

In Lesson 13 you learned that with segment effects, when you drag an effect on top of another in the timeline (from the Effects Palette), the new effect replaces the existing one. The exception has been the special case of the Color Workspace where a color correction can be applied to segments that already have effects applied to them. More generally however, there are times when more than one segment effect is required. For example, perhaps you want to apply a mask to an image that you have resized. The process of combining effects is called *nesting* effects.

Media: Rock Climber & Jacuzzi

Duration: 40 minutes

GOALS

- Apply more than one effect to a clip
- Change the order of nested effects

Nesting Effects

In this lesson you will learn how to apply multiple effects to a single segment via the *nesting* process. A good analogy to describe nesting effects is the Russian babushka or nesting dolls. When you open one, there's another inside, and another inside that, and so on. At the most basic level, a nest can contain any number of effects on a single video segment. This can be very beneficial, especially in advanced effects operations where you need to apply multiple treatments to a clip.

Nests, however, can be much more complex, with multiple tracks of video all nested within a single segment.

Autonesting

If you need to apply more than one effect to a clip, the easiest approach is to use a technique known as *Autonesting*. This technique allows you to add a new effect on top of an existing effect.

1. Open the **Rock Climber Demo** project and once again load the **Rock Climbing** sequence.

In the last lesson you applied a Resize to the last segment in the timeline. Initially this was to hide the man at the bottom of frame. You then used keyframes to scale the segment over time, producing a slow zoom in on the image. As mentioned, the possible problem with scaling up an image is an obvious loss of picture resolution. There is an alternative solution to solving the issue without producing any loss of picture resolution. It still requires using the Resize effect but to it is added a Mask.

To Autonest one effect on top of another:

2. Place the position indicator over the last segment in the timeline. It should already have the Resize effect applied from the previous lesson. Make sure the **Track Selector** for **V1** is active. Use the **Remove Effect** button to delete the effect from the segment.

3. From the **Effect Palette** select the **Image** category and again apply the **Resize** effect to the segment. Do not modify any parameters yet.

4. Hold down the **Alt key (Windows)** or **Option key (Mac)** and from the **Image** category, drag the **Mask** effect on top of the segment in the timeline.

The effect icon changes. Instead of the original Resize segment effect icon, you now see the newly applied Mask effect icon. The second effect has been Autonested on top of the original effect with the Resize effect still there underneath the Mask. At this stage, because you have not adjusted any parameters, you can't see the result of applying either the Resize or Mask effects, but you can use the Effect Editor to see that both effects have been applied, as shown in figure 14.1.

 There are a few effects that cannot be used with nesting. If you attempt to create a nest with one of these, Media Composer I First will alert you with an error message.

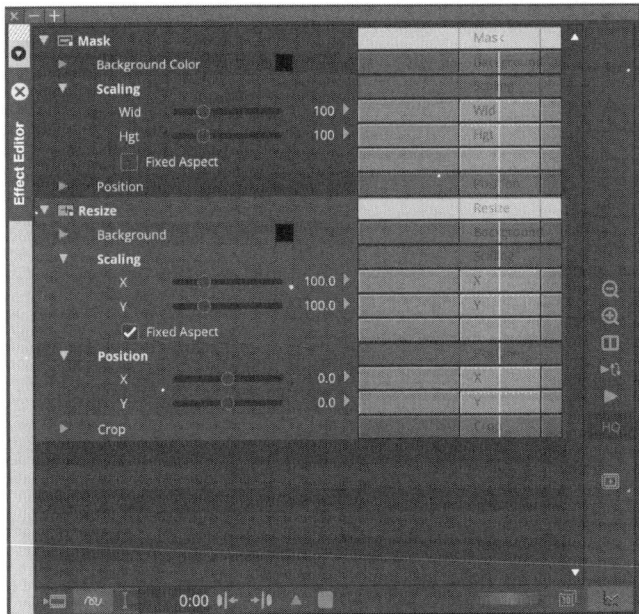

Figure 14.1 The Effect Editor with two effects displayed

Seeing Multiple Effects in the Effect Editor

With multiple effects applied to a single segment, the parameters for each effect are available in the Effect Editor.

The bottom-most effect in the Effect Editor is at the bottom of the nest – that is, closest to the video segment. Effects are always processed from the bottom of the nest first. All other effects are listed, traveling upward, in the order they reside on the segment and therefore the order in which they are processed. The top effect in the Effect Editor is the effect icon that you see on the segment in the Timeline and is the last effect to be processed.

This order of processing can have a significant impact on the final appearance of the clip. As you will see later in this lesson, it is easy to change the order of processing if you decide the combined result is not as expected.

Modifying the Effect Parameters

Since parameters for all nested effects are displayed in the Effect Editor, you can adjust each effect to see how they interact with each other. And you don't need to modify parameters in the order in which the effects are applied. You can adjust any parameter for any effect as needed and you will immediately see the combined result on screen.

To modify the nested effects, start with the **Mask** effect.

1. In the **Scaling** parameter group, make sure the **Fixed Aspect** box is unchecked. Adjust the **Hgt** (height) parameter to crop the top and bottom of frame. A slider value of **75** should be sufficient. (See Figure 14.2) With the control point on the slider selected, you can either:

    - Drag the slider to the left or right to adjust the value.
    - Type a value on the keyboard, then press **Enter**.
    - Click the left/right arrows on the keyboard to make incremental adjustments.

Scrub the **Position indicator** under the Effect Preview monitor and see that throughout the clip the top of the climber's head has been cropped while the man at bottom of frame is also still visible. The Mask by itself has not achieved a satisfactory result.

This is where the Resize effect comes into play. But before adjusting the parameters for the Resize, it will be helpful to add a background color to the Mask effect so you can see exactly what is going on.

2. Open the group of parameters for the **Background Color** in the **Mask** effect. Adjust the sliders for **Hue, Sat** (saturation) and **Lum** (luminance) until you achieve a background color you like. Alternatively, you can use the **Color Picker**, the small box at the top of the **Background Color** group of parameters, shown in figure 14.2.

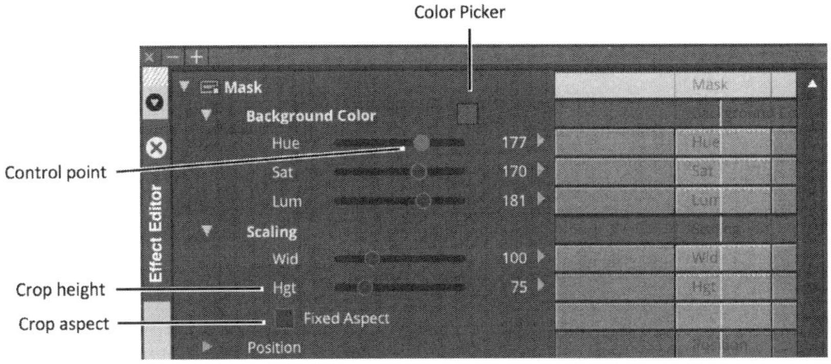

Figure 14.2 The Mask effect parameters

To use the Color Picker:

1. Roll the mouse over the box and the pointer will change into an **eye dropper**. Click to activate the color picker.

2. Now move the mouse pointer over the image in the **Effect Preview** monitor. The Color Picker will sample the color of the target area you roll the mouse over and display that color in the box.

3. To select the sampled color you want, click the mouse. The background color of the masked region of the image will now change to the selected color.

Now adjust the **Resize** effect to reposition the image behind the masked area. Use the **Y Position** parameter to slide the image down in frame. A value of **110** should suffice.

Notice how the position of the mask remains unchanged. This is because, in order of application, the Resize processes the image first then the Mask processes it second (see Figure 14.3).

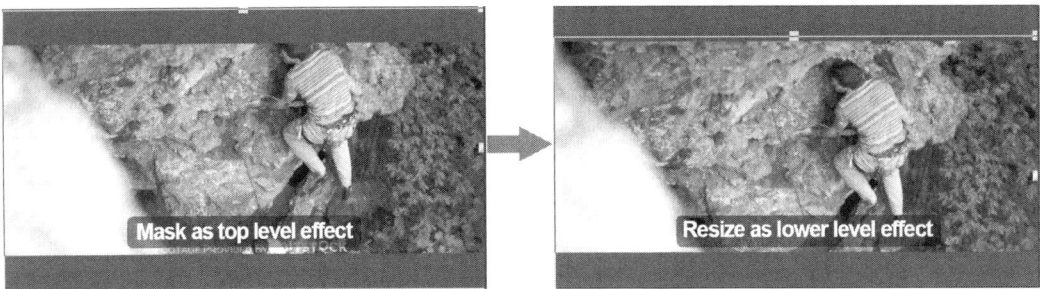

Figure 14.3 The image repositioned behind the mask

Changing the Order of Nested Effects

The example above demonstrates that you can modify parameters in any order. What is important is the order in which nested effects are processed. It is the order in which effects are applied that determines how the combined result will appear on screen. Sometimes you might need to change the priority of the effects in the nest because you made a mistake and applied them in the wrong order. To see just what applying effects in the wrong order can look like, you can rearrange the order of the Mask and Resize effects that you have already applied to the segment.

The Effect Editor makes re-ordering the nested effects very simple.

- Within the Effect Editor, click the icon of the **Mask** effect and drag it down below the **Resize** effect. The order in which the effects are processed has now been reversed, as shown in figure 14.4. Look in the timeline and notice that the Resize effect icon is now visible on the segment instead of the Mask icon.

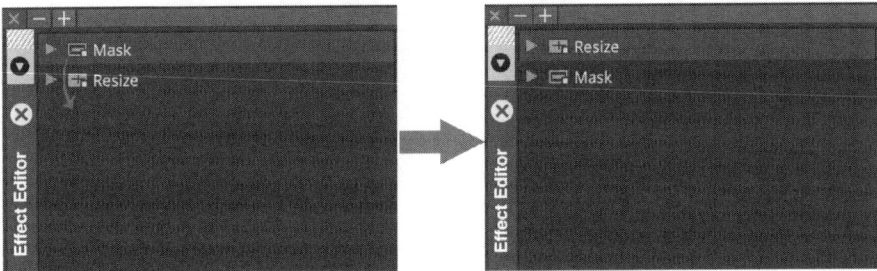

Figure 14.4 The effect priority is changed by clicking and dragging the effect icons to rearrange the order.

Although none of the parameters of the effects have been modified, the result on screen is quite different.

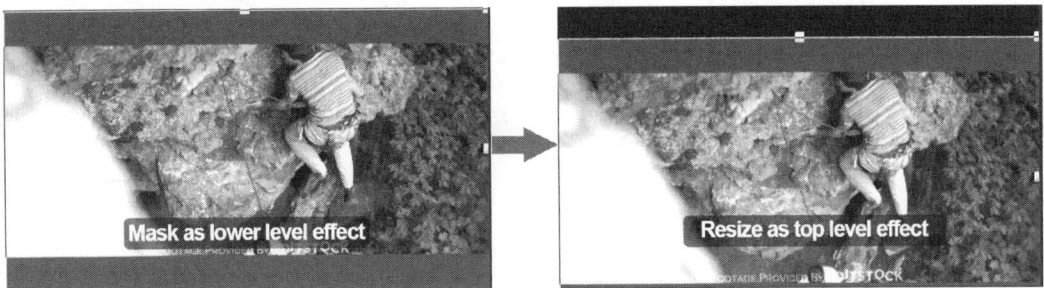

Figure 14.5 The result on screen is different because the processing order of the effects has changed.

Because the Mask effect has been processed first and then the **Y position** of the Resize effect has been processed second, the combined result is that the mask + image have moved lower in frame.

To return the nested effects to their original order, click and drag the Mask effect icon back above the Resize icon in the Effect Editor.

Displaying a Nest in the Timeline

In addition to the Effect Editor, there are two other ways in which you can view effects within a nest. These two methods are called *Simple Nesting* and *Expanded Nesting*, and both are viewed in the Timeline window.

Method One: Simple Nesting View

In this method, you travel down inside a nest, and the video Track monitor travels with you, allowing you to view the lower effects in isolation from the effects above them. This is a very useful technique, especially for complex nests with numerous effects and/or video tracks, because it enables you to "dive underneath" higher effects so that you can focus on the effects beneath. To move down through each effect and back up to the top effect, you use the Step In/Step Out buttons located at the bottom of the Timeline window, shown in figure 14.6.

Figure 14.6 The Step In/Step Out buttons

To step into an effect nest using Simple Nesting View:

1. Park the **Position indicator** on a segment with nested effects.
2. Make sure the **Track Selector** is active.
3. Click the **Step In** button (the down-pointing arrow) at the bottom of the Timeline window.

When you step into a nest, three things happen. Firstly, the Timeline view changes, and only the content of the nest (that is, what's beneath the top effect) is visible, as shown in Figure 14.7. In the case of our nested Mask and Resize effects, you have stepped in under the Mask effect and you can now only see the Resize effect applied to the segment. The timeline shows nothing else.

Figure 14.7 Simple Nesting reveals the lower level effect in the timeline.

The second change is the Effect Preview monitor only shows the result of the lower level effect (see figure 14.8). You cannot see the result of any higher-level effects (in this case, the Mask) applied to the segment.

Figure 14.8 The Effect Preview monitor only shows the result of the lower level effect.

And thirdly, the Effect Editor only shows you the parameters for the lower level effect (in this case the Resize). You cannot adjust the parameters for the upper level Mask effect.

The overall result is that Simple Nesting completely restricts your view to that of various levels of effects of a segment. In the timeline, not only are the clips before and after the effect you stepped into not accessible, but neither are the audio tracks.

You can continue to step downward as long as there are effects to step into. To tell how deep you are in a nested effect, you can look at the Track Panel. Beneath the video tracks appears a nest depth indicator, shown in Figure 14.9.

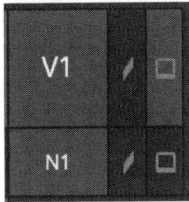

Figure 14.9 The N1 on the Nest depth indicator shows that you have stepped downward by 1 effect.

Adding Effects while in Simple Nesting

You can use the **Step In** button as many times as necessary until you reach the level at which no effects are applied to the segment. At this level you can open the Effects Palette and apply a new effect to the segment. This new effect will now be at the lower level and will be the first effect processed in the nest. All other effects will shift up one level in the nest.

To apply an effect below the Resize effect in our example:

1. **Step In** under the Mask effect then **Step In** under the Resize effect. The segment will be displayed in the timeline and the original un-effected clip will be displayed in the Effect Preview monitor.

2. From the **Effects Palette**, select the **Color** category and locate the **Color Effect**. Be careful not to choose the Color Correction effect by mistake. The **Color Effect** is a simple way to alter the color balance of a clip, which is ideal for this exercise. Drag the **Color Effect** onto the segment in the timeline.

3. The **Effect Editor** should automatically open, showing the parameters for the **Color Effect**.

4. Go to the group of **Color Gain** parameters and make slight adjusts to the **Red**, **Green** and **Blue** sliders until you are satisfied with the result. (A word of warning though. This effect is not a color corrector and can easily push the color values outside the limits you were introduced to in the previous lesson on color correction. So, don't make excessive adjustments to the color sliders. Just apply a slight color tint to the segment.)

5. Use the **Step Out** button to return to the normal view of the timeline. Each time you step out you will see the progressive result as each higher level of effect processes the image in turn.

Method Two: Expanded Nesting View

Compared to Simple Nesting, *Expanded Nesting* lets you see the entire sequence and the nest contents simultaneously. It also allows you to listen to audio and access all material in the sequence before and after the nested effects that you are working with.

In addition, unlike Simple Nesting, the video monitor button in the timeline tracks is always positioned at the top of the nest and cannot travel into the nest. As a result, with Expanded Nesting, you can edit the contents of a nest and still see the composite result of all effects within the nest.

To expand an effect nest:

1. Park on a segment that is Autonested with effects.
2. Make sure that the **Track Selector** is active.
3. **Alt+click (Windows)** or **Option+click (Mac)** the **Step In** button.

The Timeline displays the tracks inside and outside the nest, with the tracks inside the nest appearing directly above the track that contains the nest, as shown in Figure 14.10. This can be somewhat confusing at first. With the Expanded Nesting view, Media Composer slides the underlying layers up from behind. In Figure 14.10, the Resize is actually underneath the Mask effect in terms of compositing order. However, in the Expanding Nesting view it has been raised from behind the mask, so we can see it.

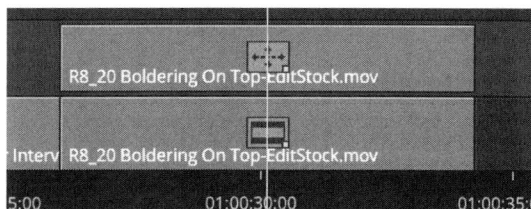

Figure 14.10 Expanded Nesting

 You can also enter and exit Expanded Nesting by double-clicking a segment with an effect on it. This can be disabled via the Timeline setting.

As with simple nesting, the Track Panel indicates the nest level for each element within the nest, this time using two numbers separated by a period instead of just one.

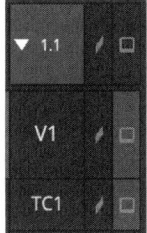

Figure 14.11 Expanded Nesting track indicators

The first number indicates the nest level of the track. In this case, the number 1 indicates that you have stepped into the first nested level (i.e. the Resize under the Mask). The number 1 after the period indicates that there is one track within this nested level.

When you select the **V1 Track Selector**, all the effects and their parameters will be accessible from the Effect Editor when you enter effects editing mode.

If you had selected the **1.1 Track Selector** only the effect on that nested level and any effects below it will be accessible in the Effect Editor.

To exit Expanded Nesting either:

- **Alt+click (Windows)** or **Option+click (Mac)** the **Step Out** button.
- **Double click the segment.**

Review/Discussion Questions

1. How do you add an effect to a clip in the Timeline on top of an existing effect?

2. What is the process of adding an effect to a clip in the timeline on top of an existing effect called?

3. What are the two different methods you can use to view the effects inside of a nest in the timeline?

4. What is an advantage of simple nesting?

5. What is an advantage of expanded nesting?

6. How can you change the order of effects within a nest?

7. In which order are effects processed in a nest?

EXERCISE 14

 Exercise Break 14.1
Pause here to practice what you've learned.

Media: Jacuzzi

GOALS

- Apply nested effects
- Reorder effects in a nest

Apply Finishing Effects to Scene 9 of Jacuzzi

In one of the clips in Scene 7 of **Jacuzzi** you used the Resize effect to remove the boom microphone from the bottom of frame.

In Scene 9 there is another clip where the microphone is very obvious at the top of frame. The resize effect would not be appropriate to use with this shot as the degree of enlargement would reduce the picture quality to an unacceptable degree. Fortunately, the Mask effect will be ideal for fixing this clip because the Producer wants the entire sequence to have a more 'filmic' aspect ratio.

Television screens have a fixed relationship between their width and their height. This is referred to as the picture aspect ratio, and for widescreen television that ratio is expressed as 16:9, i.e. the picture width is close to 1.78 times the height. Cinema, on the other hand, often exhibits films with a picture width considerably wider compared to the height. An aspect ratio of 2.39:1 is typical.

For the wider 2.39:1 aspect ratio film to be displayed on a television screen, the image must be scaled back to 75% of its full size so the entire picture width can be seen. This in turn means the vertical height of the picture is also reduced, resulting in black bars at the top and bottom of frame where there is no picture information, as shown in figure 14.12.

The Producer of Jacuzzi wants to simulate the wider cinema aspect ratio of film, so the solution is to apply a Mask effect on all the clips in the sequence. This will crop the top and bottom of frame without rescaling the images. The result will give the appearance of a wide aspect ratio film reformatted to fit the television screen's aspect ratio. If necessary, some clips may also need a Resize effect applied to reposition the action within the masked area of the frame.

Figure 14.12 A wide aspect ratio film must be scaled down in size to fit within the television screen's aspect ratio

1. Open the **Jacuzzi** project and load the **Scene 9 Rough Cut.Copy.01** sequence.

2. In the sequence, park the **Position indicator** on the shot in which the microphone is visible at top of frame.

3. From the **Effect Palette** locate the **Mask** effect in the **Image** category.

4. Drag the **Mask** effect icon onto the segment in the timeline. The **Effect Editor** will automatically open.

5. Adjust the **Hgt** parameter of the **Scaling** group to a value of **75**. This will achieve the desired simulation of the wide screen cinema aspect ratio and crop out the microphone at the same time.

6. Before closing the Effect Editor, drag the **effect icon** from the top of the Effect Editor window into an open bin. This will create an effect template of the Mask effect.

7. Now apply the effect template to each segment in the timeline to create the mask effect on every shot.

8. Now play the sequence and decide whether any clips need to have a resize effect applied below the Mask to reposition the action within the masked area.

While this has successfully achieved the desired result, a problem becomes apparent when you now try to color correct the sequence. If you select the Color Workspace and begin grading each shot to achieve correct levels and color balance you discover that you are also affecting the black bars top and bottom of frame. Can you explain why this is occurring?

In the previous lesson you learned that you could use filler on a higher-level track in the timeline to simultaneously apply an effect across a number of segments.

See if you can devise a solution whereby you can:

- Individually apply a Resize effect to clips as necessary.
- Apply color correction to all segments to achieve correct levels and color balance.
- Mask all segments to achieve a uniform filmic aspect ratio to the sequence.

9. Publish your final result.

LESSON 15

Freeze Frames and Motion Effects

When putting a scene together, sometimes the original timing of the shot needs to be adjusted. For example, you may need a shot to last longer than what was actually shot. This lesson introduces you to motion effects that enable you to vary the playback speed of a clip or freeze the clip entirely.

In the exercise you will apply motion effects to some of the shots in your Rock Climber project and in the process discover some more new techniques.

Media Used: Rock Climber

Duration: 40 minutes

GOALS

- Explore the different types of motion effects
- Create a freeze frame
- Create a motion effect

Types of Motion Effects

Motion effects vary the speed at which frames from clips play. Avid editing systems can create three different types of motion effects:

- **Freeze frames:** These are created using a master clip or subclip in the Source monitor and create a new clip containing only the desired frame.

- **Motion effects:** These are also created using a master clip or subclip in the Source monitor. In these types of effects, you can speed up or slow down the video. The new clip that is created plays faster or slower than the original, but still at a constant speed.

- **Timewarp effects:** These are applied to a segment in the Timeline in the same way you have applied other segment effects, like a Mask or Resize. The rate of motion can be keyframed and varied over time within a single clip. This means you can create motion effects where, for example, a shot of a person running can ramp from normal speed into slow motion to add drama or tension.

The key difference between the three effect types is that two of them—freeze frames and motion effects—are created from the source side of the Composer window, while Timewarp effects are created from footage that already exists in your Timeline. Depending on the stage of your edit, one may be more convenient to use than the other.

Progressive vs Interlaced Frames

There is an important consideration when creating a motion effect. If your original source media is either Standard Definition or High Definition, the camera footage will be generated using either Progressive or Interlaced frames. A progressive frame is generated from the output of the camera sensor by reading a single stream of data from top to bottom of frame. An interlaced frame is generated by reading the output of the camera sensor as two streams of data, one after the other. The first stream of data reads the sensor from top to bottom but skips every alternate line of information in the frame. The following second stream also reads from top to bottom of frame but reads the lines of information skipped by the first scan. Each scan in an interlaced frame is called a 'Field'. When you create a freeze frame or motion effect you need to know if the camera generated the video footage as Progressive or Interlaced frames. Fortunately, Media Composer | First provides that information.

In the bin, right-mouse click on a clip. From the menu that appears, select **Get_Info**. The **Info window** opens. In the Video information area, look at the Field Motion row. Figure 15.1. It will indicate whether the frames are Progressive or Interlaced.

```
▼ Video
                    FPS   23.98
                  Raster  1280x720p
      Image Aspect Ratio  16:9
              Image Size  1920 x 1080
             Color Space  Rec.709 [video levels]
      Chroma Subsampling  4:2:2
            Field Motion  Progressive
      Pixel Aspect Ratio  1.000
                Reformat  Stretch
```

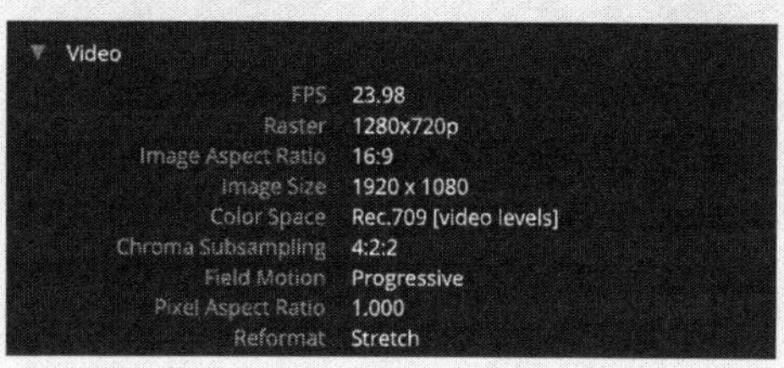

Figure 15.1 Video information area shows the Field Motion of a clip

There is also another significant difference: Applying a motion effect to a clip in the Source monitor changes the duration of the new motion effect clip compared to the original. For instance, if the duration of the original clip in the Source monitor is 5 seconds and you apply a 50% slow motion effect, the new motion effect clip will be twice as long i.e. 10 seconds. On the other hand, if you apply a 50% speed Timewarp effect to a clip of 5 seconds duration in the timeline, the motion effect clip in the timeline still runs for 5 seconds. The difference is you only see half of the action in the motion effect clip compared to what you saw in the original. This distinction will become clearer as you proceed through this lesson.

Creating Freeze Frames

A freeze frame displays a single frame from a clip on the screen for a duration you choose and are generated from a master clip or subclip in the Source monitor and creates a new clip in the bin. Then, as with all other types of clips, a portion of the freeze frame clip is edited into your sequence.

Open the **Rock Climber Demo** project and once again load the **Rock Climbing** sequence.

1. From the Rushes bin open the master clip **R05_46 Matt Bouldering-EditStock** in the Source monitor. **Mark In** at the beginning of the clip and **Mark Out** at timecode 19:16, just as the climber's legs swing under the rock face after he falls.

2. Edit the marked section of the clip to the end of the sequence in the timeline.

You are now going to create a freeze frame of the last frame of that segment and edit the freeze frame to the end of the sequence in the timeline. You create the freeze frame from the master clip still loaded in the Source monitor.

3. Park on the **Mark Out** point in the Position bar of the Source monitor. The easiest way to make sure you are parked on that frame is to press the **W key** on the keyboard. The Position indicator will snap to the OUT point.

4. With the Source monitor as the active window, from the menu bar at the top of the user interface, select **Composer > Freeze Frame**, as shown in figure 15.2.

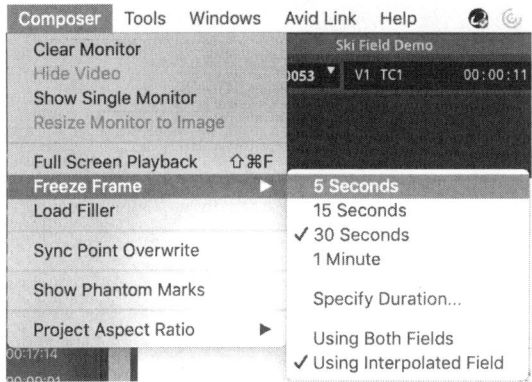

Figure 15.2 Freeze frame

5. The first decision is whether to choose **Using Both Fields** or **Using Interpolated Field**. If the clip was created using Progressive frames, then you can ignore this setting. If the clip was created using Interlaced frames, then you need to decide between the options. The easiest way to decide is to play the clip in the Source monitor. If there is a lot of movement in the clip at the point where you want to create the freeze frame, then the best option is **Using Interpolated Field**. On the other hand, if there is little or no movement occurring in the clip then **Using Both Fields** will probably be OK. Why is this choice important? If there is a lot of movement occurring in the clip, then a freeze frame using Both Fields may produce unacceptable jitter between fields when you play the effect clip. Using Interpolated Field is a clever way of solving a jitter problem. It mathematically creates a new field that removes any jitter between fields. If ever in doubt, use the interpolated field option.

6. In this case, the original clip uses progressive frames so you need not interact with the setting, but if you click to choose a field option other than the one already selected, the Freeze Frame window will close. To nominate a duration and create the new effect clip, reopen the **Composer** menu and reselect **Freeze Frame**.

7. Select one of the preset durations or click on **Specify Duration...** to type in a custom duration for the effect (for the purposes of this lesson, choose **5 Seconds**). Creating a freeze frame creates a small media file, so Media Composer | First displays a dialog box asking where to store the media.

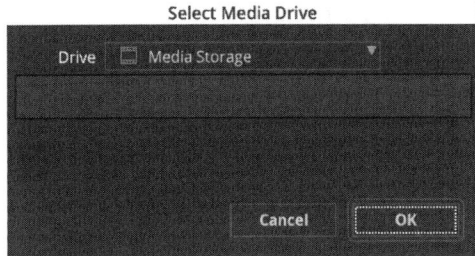

Figure 15.3 Render drive selection

It is generally a good idea to store the rendered media on the same drive as the rest of your media. It is also worthwhile reminding you that the Media Creation setting is a useful tool to ensure the resolution and destination drive for the rendered file is correct.

 You can also access the Freeze Frame menu by right-clicking on the image in the Source monitor.

8. If you have at least one bin open, Media Composer | First next asks where to store the freeze frame clip. Figure 15.4. You also have the option at the bottom of the window to create a new bin. If you have room in your project for one more bin, it is a good idea to create a dedicated FX bin in which to store your Freeze Frames, Motion Effect clips and other effect templates. It helps you keep the project organized.

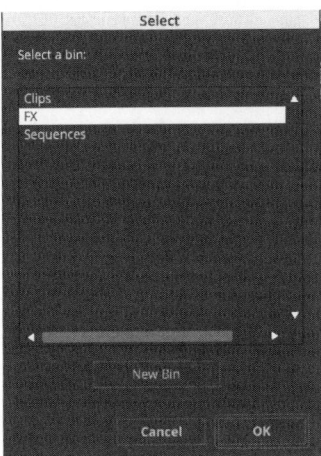

Figure 15.4 Bin selection

After you save the Freeze Frame, it is automatically loaded into the Source monitor and appears in the bin. Freeze Frames can be easily distinguished from other clips in the bin by their unique icon (shown in figure 15.5). Also note that after the name of the clip, Media Composer | First has added "FF" to indicate that it is a freeze frame.

Figure 15.5 Freeze frame in bin

9. Now edit the freeze frame to the end of the segment in the timeline. Notice that the freeze frame in the timeline has an effect icon on the segment. Figure 15.6.

Figure 15.6 The effect icon on the clip indicates it is a rendered effect

The effect has neither a green or blue dot on the icon, indicating it is a rendered effect and a media file has been created and saved in the Avid MediaFiles folder. Play the two clips and see how the movement of the climber instantly freezes at the edit point.

It is worthwhile knowing what has actually happened when the freeze frame was created. The new rendered clip is 5 seconds in duration and the frame rate of the clip is nearly 24 frames per second (23.976fps to be precise). That means there are 120 (5 x 24) frames in the new clip, each of which is a copy of that one single frame. When you play the clip, you are not viewing a static image but a series of identical frames being shown at the project frame rate, just like any normal clip. This becomes helpful in understanding what happens when you create a slow motion or fast motion effect.

Creating Motion Effects

With motion effects, you control the frame rate at which a clip plays, resulting in fast or slow motion. It's even possible to purposefully add a stuttered look to the video, called *strobing*. When creating motion effects, the more noticeable the motion is in a clip, the more careful you should be when you choose a frame rate or render method. For example, if someone is running quickly through the frame, not all frame rates and render methods will create acceptable results.

As with freeze frames, motion effects are generated from clips in the Source monitor using the Motion Effect tool.

1. Once again load the original clip R05_46 Matt Bouldering-EditStock into the Source monitor. It still has the In and Out marks you added earlier. You can reuse these to designate which part of the clip you want to apply a motion effect to. With the Source monitor as the active window, from the menu bar at the top of the user interface, select **Tools > Motion effect editor**. The Motion Effect tool opens, as shown in figure 15.7.

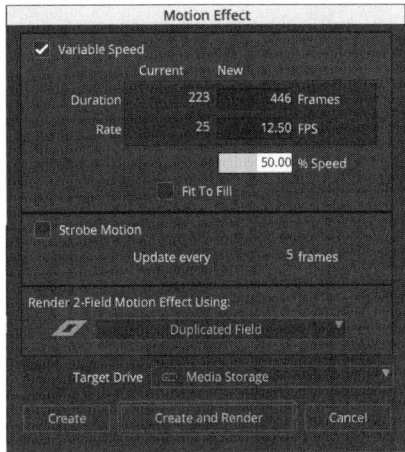

Figure 15.7 Motion Effect dialogue box

The Motion Effect Editor can actually open two different tools, depending on which monitor is active when you select it. If the Source monitor is active, then the "Motion Effect" window opens, as shown in Figure 15.7. If the Record monitor or Timeline is active, then the "Motion Effect Editor" window opens, used with Timewarp effects (we will explore the Timewarp effect in a moment).

 You cannot use the Motion Effect Editor button in the tool bar, at the top of the Timeline window, to create a motion effect. This button is used only to modify a motion effect that has already been created in the sequence.

2. You have the option in the Motion Effect dialog box to change the playback speed in a few ways. You can enter in a new duration, a new frame rate, or a percentage of the actual playback speed, as shown in Figure 15.8. You can also nominate how interlaced footage should handle the two fields of each frame. On this occasion, leave the default value of **50% Speed**.

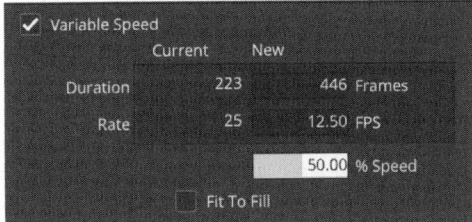

Figure 15.8 Enter the speed change by changing the number of frames, the frame rate, or the percentage of speed

In the Motion effect tool, you can compare the values you enter in the Frames field and FPS fields with the current value for each. Entering a larger number in the Frames field will create a slower motion; and entering a smaller number will create faster motion.

The percentage of speed works similarly: A number lower than 100% will create slow motion and a number greater than 100% will create fast motion. Entering a negative value in either the Rate or the % Speed field will create reverse motion.

With the exception of reverse motion effects and very high-speed motion effects, it is not typically necessary to render motion effects if you are editing on modern computer hardware and drives. If you are slowing down a clip or speeding it up by a factor of three or five, you will not have to render the clip; you can just click the **Create** button.

3. When you click **Create** or **Create and Render** at the bottom of the Motion Effect tool, the Bin Selection dialog box will be displayed, allowing you to choose the bin in which to store the newly created motion effect. In the bin, motion effect clips have the same clip icon as a freeze frame but are named to indicate the change in frame rate applied to the clip (see figure 15.9). As with freeze frames, the newly created clip is automatically loaded into the Source monitor.

Figure 15.9 Motion effect in bin

Notice that when you play the motion effect clip in the Source monitor that the entire clip plays at half speed. The part before he falls tends to be tedious to watch but the fall in slow motion is quite interesting. As you will see, the Timewarp effect allows you to play the first part at normal speed but slow down the second part.

So, what has happened when you created the 50% speed slow-motion effect? The duration between the Mark In and Mark Out on the original clip was close to 5 seconds. Therefore, the duration of the new motion effect clip will be 10 seconds. To double the duration of the effect, you have doubled the number of frames in the clip. Applying a 50% speed variation has duplicated every frame. For example, frame #1 is now shown twice in the clip, followed by frame #2 shown twice, etc. If you had applied a 25% speed variation, there would be 4 copies of each frame in the clip. If you slow the motion down excessively, then the effect appears to stutter when it plays. This is because you begin to see the effect as groups of freeze frames being played one after another. Alternatively, if you had created a fast-motion effect by speeding up the clip by 200% you would have removed every second frame so the effect clip duration will be half that of the original.

Creating Motion Effects Using Fit to Fill

Another useful option when creating a motion effect is the **Fit to Fill** check box. Use this option when you have a specific part of a source clip that you want to fit to a specific duration in your sequence.

Unlike a typical three-point edit, using Fit to Fill requires that you have four marks set: two in the Source and two in the Timeline. The four marks define two different durations. Media Composer | First calculates the difference and will speed up or slow down the source material so that the new clip that is generated fits exactly into the marked region of the sequence.

Here's a simple example: If the duration marked in the Source were 1 second, and the duration marked in the Timeline were 2 seconds, the resulting rate would be 50%. Or, if the duration marked in the Source were 1 second, and the duration marked in the Timeline were ½ second, the resulting rate would be 200%.

Real examples are never so precise, so be aware that creating motion effects in this way can cause fractional frame rates that may not produce as good a result as even frame rates. Despite this, they can still be an efficient way to generate things like a very high-speed version of a long, slow shot.

To create a Fit to Fill motion effect:

1. **Mark In** and **Mark Out** in the sequence where you want to place the motion effect clip.
2. Load a clip in the Source monitor.
3. **Mark In** and **Mark Out** on the source clip.
4. With the Source monitor selected, open the Motion Effect Editor from the Tools menu.
5. Enable the **Fit to Fill** check box in the Motion Effect dialog box.
6. Press the Return or Enter key (or click the **Create** or **Create and Render button)**.

Media Composer | First creates the new Motion Effect clip, places it in the bin you have selected and also automatically loads it into the Source monitor for you.

Since the new motion effect clip's duration exactly matches the duration marked in the sequence, and because the blue position indicator is placed at the beginning of the clip by default, all you have to do now is use the Overwrite function to edit it into the Timeline.

7. Press the **B key** on the keyboard (or click the Overwrite button in the Composer window).

How a Camera Records Motion

Early in the development of motion pictures it was determined that smooth motion could be represented by filming a scene at 24 frames per second. Provided the film was projected at the same frame rate, the eye and brain interpreted the rapid succession of images as a convincing representation of motion.

It quickly became apparent that a slow-motion effect could be created by filming at a higher frame rate but still project at 24 fps. For example, if the camera records at 48 fps and the frames are displayed at 24 fps then what took 1 second to occur in real time lasts 2 seconds on screen. This technique produces high-quality slow-motion effects because each of the 48 frames is unique and shows the subtle variations of motion over time. At even higher frame rates motion can be recorded that is imperceptible to the human eye. The path of a bullet slicing through an apple is a classic example of ultra-slow-motion photography.

Creating Motion Effects from Segments in the Source Monitor

As discussed above, a limitation of creating motion effects from clips filmed at standard frame rates is that speed variations are typically generated through the duplication or removal of frames from the original clip. Especially with slow-motion effects, it can become obvious to viewers that they are seeing slow motion as a series of still images rather than a smooth reproduction of actual motion. This is an inferior alternative to the high-speed camera that can film at 4 times the normal frame rate.

Creating Motion Effects from Segments Already Edited into the Timeline

The Timewarp effect overcomes the limitation of creating motion effects of fixed frame rates. The Timewarp effect uses sophisticated techniques to work out how to represent motion when action is sped up, slowed down and stopped – all in a clip that was filmed at a standard frame rate.

To apply the Timewarp effect:

1. Load the original clip R05_46 Matt Bouldering-EditStock into the Source monitor. Press the T key on the keyboard and the entire clip will be marked from In to Out. The duration between marks will be 5:20.

2. Edit the clip to the end of the sequence in the timeline.

3. Open the **Effect Palette** and from the **Timewarp** category drag the **Timewarp** effect onto the segment in the timeline.

4. The **Motion Effect Editor** opens, as shown in figure 15.10. The Motion Effect Editor can display two graphs, Speed and Position. They provide complementary visual ways of manipulating the frame rate of the original clip. If not already visible, open the graphs by clicking on their respective buttons.

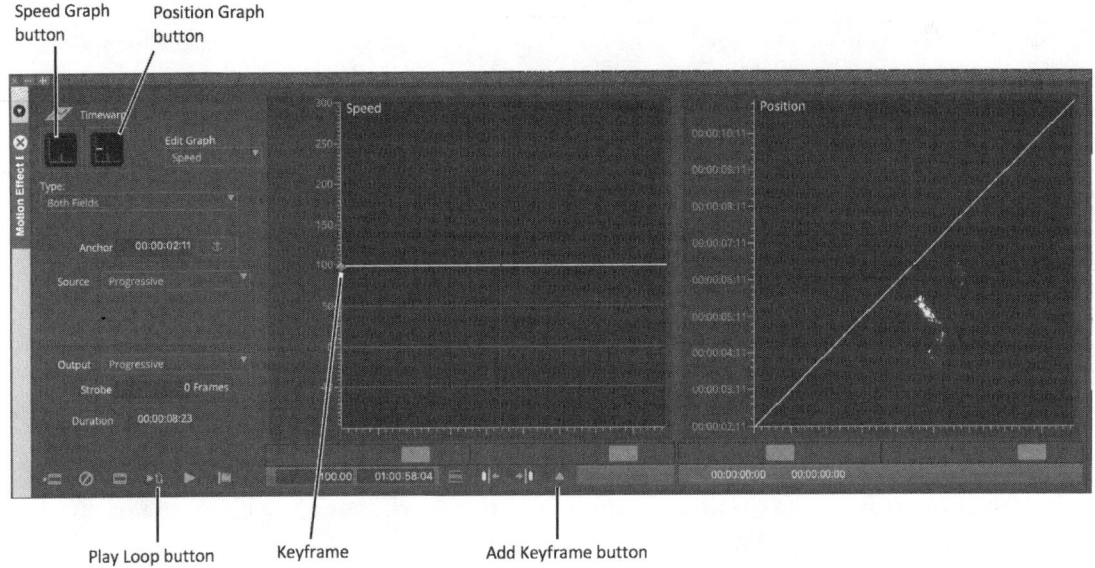

Figure 15.10 Motion Effect Editor

The Speed graph is perhaps the easiest way of understanding how you can vary the frame rate of the clip over time.

Notice that by default the Speed graph shows a green horizontal line at the 100 mark on the vertical scale on the left-hand side. The vertical axis represents the speed and direction of motion. A positive value means the motion is forward while a negative value means the motion is in reverse. The horizontal scale represents the duration of the segment. At the default start position, the green line indicates that for the duration of the segment in the timeline, the action plays at normal or 100% speed.

Also, by default there is a keyframe at the start of the green horizontal line. By clicking and dragging the keyframe up or down you can reposition the green horizontal line against a faster, slower, forward or backwards motion.

To vary the replay speed of the segment in the timeline:

1. Click and drag the keyframe so the green horizontal line sits at the **50** mark on the vertical scale. As you drag the keyframe down you will see a green number displayed at the top of the graph showing you the corresponding value of the horizontal line as you move it.

2. Click the **Play Loop** button at the bottom of the Motion Effect editor and watch the slow-motion replay in the Record monitor. The replay is equivalent to how a 50% speed variation was created from the clip loaded into the Source monitor.

3. To take advantage of the Timewarp's ability to create speed and direction changes over time, drag the keyframe back to the 100 mark. Now move the blue **Position indicator** in the speed graph window to just before the climber begins to fall. Click the **Add Keyframe** button.

4. Move the Position indicator a few more frames so you see the fingers slipped off the rock. Add another **keyframe**.

5. Drag the new keyframe down to approximately the **50** mark on the vertical scale.

6. Click the **Play Loop** button and watch the action. The climber ascends the rock at normal speed but falls at 50% slow motion. This is where you see how Timewarp does not change the duration of the segment in the timeline. The play loop ends before the climber's legs swing under the rock face. The clip in the timeline is still 5:20 in duration.

7. Use the yellow **Ripple Trim** tool to extend the end of the clip in the timeline, adding the frames that the Timewarp effect has removed in order to maintain the same duration of the segment in the timeline.

8. Click the **Play Loop** button again in the Motion Effect Editor and see now that the climber's legs swing under the rock face and swing out again but at 50% speed.

9. Now move the blue **Position indicator** to the frame just as his legs complete their swing under the rock face. Add a new **keyframe**.

10. Move a few more frames down the timeline and add another **keyframe**. Drag this keyframe down to the 0 value in the Speed Graph.

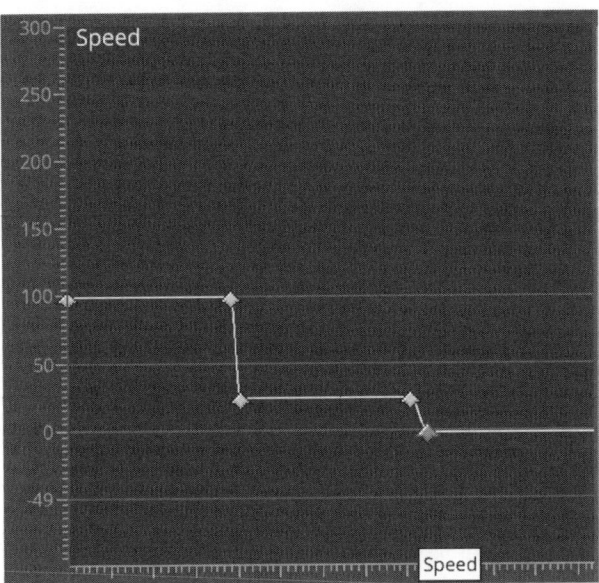

Figure 15.11 Motion Effect Editor Speed Graph

11. Click the **Play Loop** button. The motion stops just as his legs swing under the rock face. You can modify the speed and direction value for any keyframe by dragging the keyframe vertically. You can move a keyframe's position in time by holding down the **Alt(Windows)** or **Option(Mac)** key and dragging the keyframe left or right.

Review/Discussion Questions

1. What are the three types of motion effects?

2. How can you create a freeze frame?

3. What are the two different ways a video frame can be generated?

4. Why is it important to set the freeze frame render type?

5. How are motion effects created?

6. How many marks in total are required to create a Fit to Fill motion effect?

7. Describe two ways in which creating a motion effect from a clip in the Timeline is different to creating a motion effect from a clip in the Source monitor.

EXERCISE 15

 Exercise Break: Exercise 15.1
Pause here to practice what you've learned.

Media: Rock Climber

GOALS

- Use motion effects to change the speed of clips

Apply Motion Effects to the Rock Climber Sequence

1. Open your **My Second Project_(Student ID)** project.

2. Duplicate your latest sequence and open the duplicate in the Record/Timeline windows.

The opening three segments in the sequence are all slow-motion shots created in-camera by filming at twice the project frame rate. You need to apply motion effects to make the action play at normal speed. If possible, you want the re-timed shots to have the same duration as the segments already in the timeline. There are a couple of ways in which you can approach this.

3. The first segment is the close-up shot of the hand running along the side of the rocks. From the **Effect Palette** locate the **Timewarp** category and apply the **Timewarp** effect to the first segment.

4. The **Motion Effect Editor** should open automatically and by default the **Speed Graph** will be the active tool to modify the speed of the clip. Instead of dragging the first keyframe to change the speed of the clip, click in the **Percent Speed** window (Figure 15.12) at the bottom of the graph and type 200.

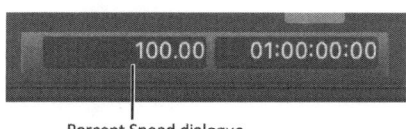
Percent Speed dialogue

Figure 15.12 Change speed via the Percent Speed window

5. Click the **Play Loop** button and notice how the climber's hand now moves off the wall at the end of the shot. You can adjust the start frame of the segment from within the Motion Effect Editor.

6. From the **Edit Graph** drop menu, select **Position** instead of Speed, as shown in figure 15.13. The Position Graph is now the active graph.

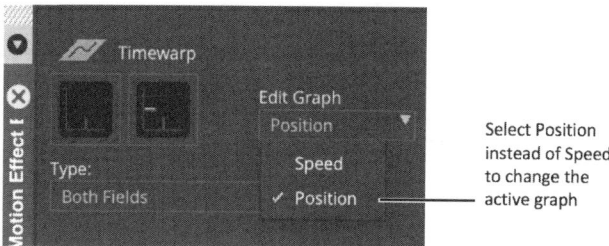

Figure 15.13 Select the Position Graph as the active tool

7. The Position Graph now shows a keyframe at the bottom left corner of the graph and indicates the timecode for the first frame of the source clip in the timeline, as shown in figure 15.14.

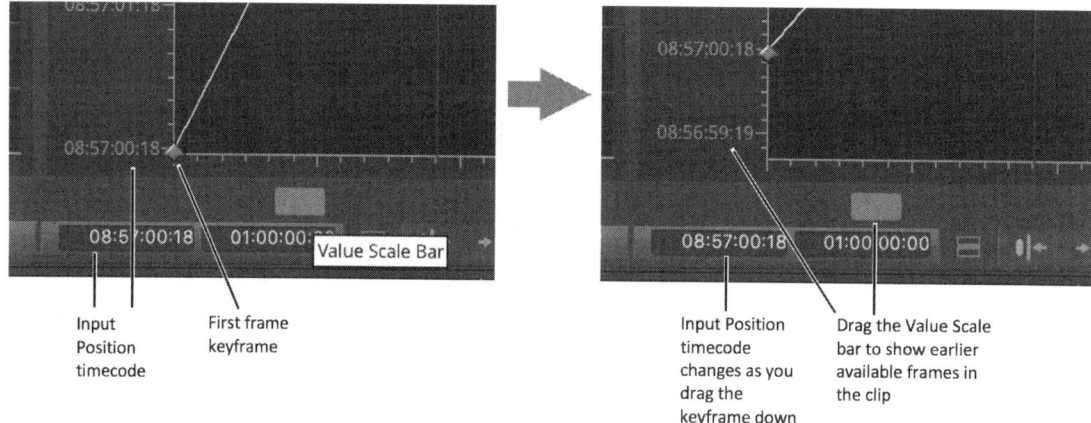

Figure 15.14 Adjust the Value Scale Bar to show any available frames earlier in the clip

8. Now click and drag the keyframe down so an earlier frame in the source clip becomes the start frame in the timeline. Watch the Preview monitor as you move the keyframe, so you see the earlier frames revealed. A timecode value for the earlier keyframe will be displayed in the **Input Position** window under the Position Graph. A new **Input Position** timecode of around 08:56:58:22 should be about right.

9. Switch the **Edit Graph** drop menu back to activate the **Speed Graph** and click the **Play Loop** button. The clip should now play at normal speed and the hand should remain on the wall for the full duration of the segment in the timeline.

10. Now employ the same technique to adjust the speed and start frame for the second clip in the timeline. To maintain continuity, you are wanting the hand to be on the wall when you cut from the close-up of the hand to the wider shot from behind the climber.

11. Repeat the steps for the third clip in the sequence, increasing the speed to 200%.

The third clip poses a problem. By adjusting the speed and start frame, you are able to maintain the continuity of the hand on the wall at the cut point, but the end of the shot now doesn't work very well. The camera pans off before the cut to the next shot (you could've adjusted the speed to 150% to make the action fit the duration, but the speed variation will be noticeable). A better solution is to use the Extract tool you learned how to use in an earlier lesson.

12. Park the blue **Position indicator** on the frame just before the camera begins to pan away from the climber. Notice that the Position indicator may also be parked on the voice over clip on track A3 of the timeline. If it looks like extracting part of the timeline at this point will also remove part of the voice over, you may need to slide the voice over clips out of the way. To do so, use the red **Segment tool (Lift/Overwrite)** to move the voice over clips to the left until they are clear of where the Position indicator is parked.

13. **Mark In** just before the camera pans away and **Mark Out** at the end of the segment. Turn on all **Record Track Selectors** and press the **X** key to extract the marked section. If you previously moved audio clips out of the way, now would be a good time to reposition them so that the voiceover sounds natural.

Later in the sequence there is also another slow-motion clip **R8_81 SLOW Chalk Bag-EditStock** (if it isn't in your session, please edit it on the end of your timeline now). You could also use the Timewarp effect to change the speed of this clip, but it is worthwhile using the alternative technique of creating a motion effect from the Source monitor.

14. Park the **Position indicator** on the clip in the timeline. It should be the shot before the close-up of the hand slapping onto the rock. This is just before the music starts. Turn off all **Record Track Selectors** except for **V1**. Press the **T** key on the keyboard to mark the segment from In to Out. Only the segment on the V1 track should be highlighted.

15. You could go to the Clips bin and find the original clip, but there is a more direct way of finding the clip and opening it in the Source monitor. In the timeline, park on the first frame of the clip you are going to replace. Hold down the **Shift key** and press the **M** key on the keyboard. Media Composer | First performs a **Match Frame**. It automatically locates the original clip, opens it in the Source monitor, parks it on the same frame as you are parked on in the timeline and places a **Mark In** on that same frame of the source clip.

16. In the Source monitor go to the end of the clip and add a **Mark Out**. It will not matter if the motion effect clip you create is longer than the marked section of the timeline.

17. With the Source monitor as the active window, go to the menus at the top of the screen and select **Tools>Motion Effect Editor.**

18. In the Motion Effect tool, change the **% Speed** to 200 and click create. The motion effect clip automatically opens in the Source monitor.

19. Press the **B** key on the keyboard to **Overwrite** the motion effect clip into the timeline, replacing the original slow-motion clip.

20. Check the new shot to make sure it works as a replacement in the timeline.

21. If you are happy with the result, publish your work.

LESSON 16

Combining Layers and Creating Titles

In Lessons 13 and 14 you learned how to apply effects to segments in the timeline and how to nest multiple effects on a single segment. In this lesson you will be introduced to how clips can be combined in the timeline to create composite images. A common example of this is a title superimposed over a background image.

Your exercise will be to create an opening title for the *Rock Climber* sequence plus a 'lower-thirds' graphic to superimpose the name of the rock climber over one of the interview grabs.

Media: Jacuzzi and Rock Climber

Duration: 40 Minutes

GOALS

- Understanding and applying Vertical Effects
- The Avid Titler+ tool
- Using the Avid Titler+ as a segment effect on a clip in the timeline
- Using the Avid Titler+ as a vertical effect
- Applying fades to Avid Titler+

Vertical Effects

In Lesson 10 you learned how to create new video tracks and patch source tracks so clips can be edited onto them. The ability to combine or 'composite' images relies on the use of multiple video tracks to 'stack' segments on top of each other in the timeline. In Figure 16.1, track V1 is the background layer over which is composited the foreground segment on V2. A special type of segment effect is applied to the foreground layer to achieve the composite image. In this case the segment effect is a Picture-in-Picture. Any effect that combines segments on video tracks is referred to as a Vertical Effect. As the viewer, your point of view is always looking from the top most layer down through the layers below.

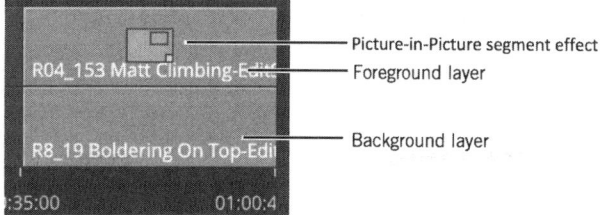

Figure 16.1 Multiple Tracks used to create composite images

To create a picture-in-picture effect:

1. Open the **Rock Climber_Demo** project and from the Sequences bin load the **Rock Climbing** sequence into the Record/Timeline windows.

2. If there is not already a V2 track in the timeline, create one by selecting **Timeline>New>Video Track**.

3. From the Clips bin, locate and load the **R8_19 Boldering On Top-EditStock** clip into the Source monitor. **Mark In** and **Mark Out** around the best 5 seconds of the clip. At the end of the timeline, edit the clip onto track **V1**. Notice that the action is happening on the right side of frame and the climber is facing from right to left.

4. Now locate and load the R04_153 Matt Climbing-EditStock clip into the Source monitor. Add **In** and **Out Marks** around the best 5 seconds.

5. With only the **Record V1 Track Selector** active, press the **T key** on the keyboard to mark the clip from **In** to **Out**. Now turn off the Record Track Selector for **V1** and turn on the **Record Track Selector** for **V2**. The **V1 Track Selector** for the source clip will **Auto-Patch** against **V2** of the timeline.

6. **Overwrite** edit the source clip into **V2** of the timeline. Because the new clip on V2 is above V1, you will not be able to see the original clip underneath the V2 layer. Notice that the new clip has the action occurring on the left side of frame and the climber is facing from left to right.

7. Open the **Effect Palette**, click the **Filters** button and from the **Blend** category drag the **Picture-in-Picture** effect icon onto the segment on **V2** of the timeline. The **Effect Editor** automatically opens so you can modify the effect parameters.

The Picture-in-Picture effect has a default set of parameters that reduces the foreground image to ¼ frame size and positions it in the center of the Preview monitor, revealing the background image behind it on V1. However, it is important to remember that your ability to see the composite image depends on the position of the track monitor switch at the head of the video tracks in the Track Panel. Figure 16.2.

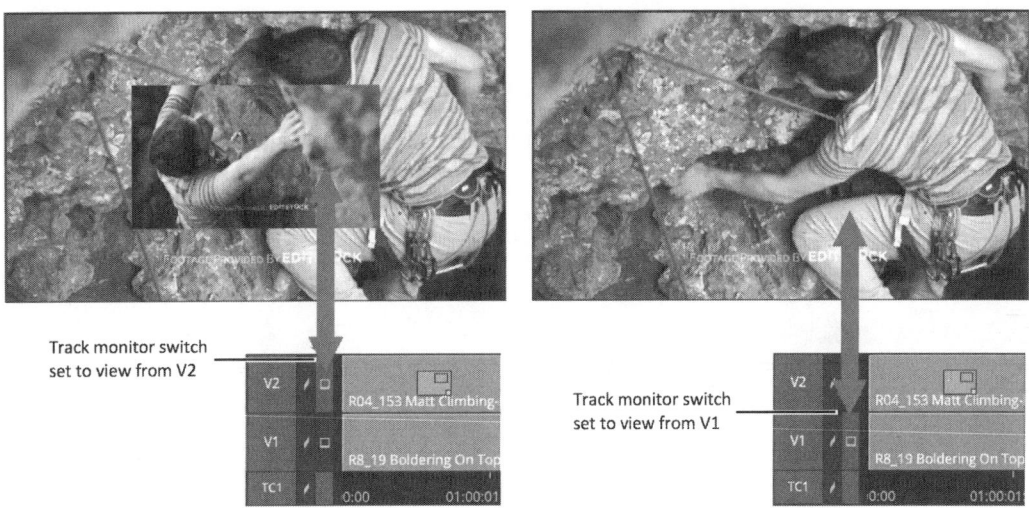

Figure 16.2 Track monitor button

8. Here is a suggestion to capitalize on the contrasting screen directions of the action occurring in the two images. Use the **Rgt** (Right) slider in the **Crop** section to remove the right side of the frame. A value of approximately **-500** is about right. **Scale** up the image to a value of about 90 and use the **X Position** to move the Picture-in-Picture to the left. A slider value of **-35** looks OK. Use the **Play Loop** button to preview the composite image.

9. From within the Effect Editor you are also able to modify parameters over time using keyframes. For instance, you can animate the foreground layer so it resizes and moves across screen.

Your ability to produce a complex multilayered composite is only limited by the four video tracks available in Media Composer | First.

Creating Titles Using Avid Titler+

One vertical effect that you will regularly use is a title. A title can be created in a graphics program such as Photoshop and input into Media Composer | First in the same way you access any media file. However, Media Composer | First is also able to generate its own titles.

There are in fact two graphics tools available in Media Composer | First – the Title Tool and the Avid Titler+ tool. We will use the Avid Titler+ because in some circumstances it is able to superimpose a graphic over a background segment without needing to use a second video track. In other circumstances you do need to create a second video track. But in either case the title is effectively a vertical effect that automatically superimposes the graphic over the background image. The big advantage of generating titles within Media Composer | First is that they are immediately editable. If there is a change of detail or a spelling correction required, then it can be easily updated in a way similar to editing any segment effect.

Applying a title to an entire segment in the timeline

1. Close the **Rock Climber Demo** project and open the **Jacuzzi** project. Load your **Scene 9 Rough Cut.Copy.01** sequence. The first segment on Track V1 will provide a good background image for a title.

2. If you want to superimpose a title on the entire segment, select the segment in V1 by clicking on it in the timeline, then either:

   - Click the **Avid Titler+** button in the tool bar at the top of the Timeline window, as shown in figure 16.3.
     - Select **Tools > T+Avid Titler+** from the menu at the top of the screen.

Figure 16.3 Avid Titler+ button

Four things occur when the title is applied to the segment:

- A title effect icon appears on the segment in the timeline.
- The Avid Titler+ tool opens.
- The Effect Editor opens.
- The Preview monitor has a white rectangular box superimposed over it to guide you with the placement of the title you are about to create. Titles should always remain within this Safe Title area.

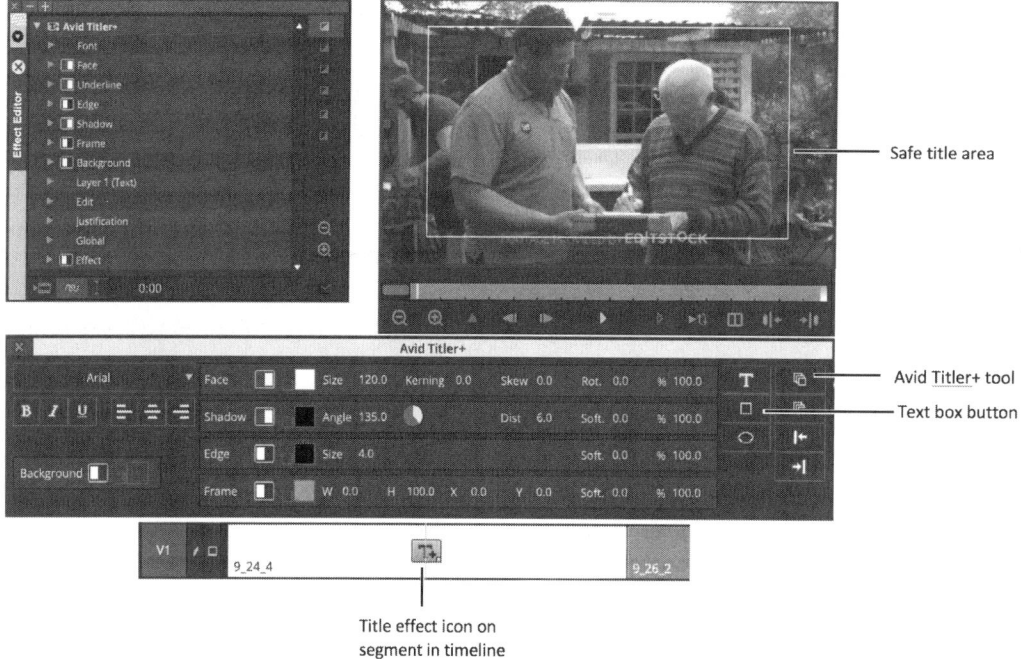

Figure 16.4 Avid Titler+ tool

The Avid Titler+ has a set of basic text and shape creation tools. In conjunction with the Effect Editor, a number of parameters can be modified and animated over time using keyframes.

To start creating a title:

1. Click on the **Text box** button in the Avid Titler+ tool. A text box of a default size appears in the Preview monitor.

2. Without being too concerned about font type, size, and other attributes, begin typing the title. The text will appear inside the text box (see figure 16.5).

Figure 16.5 Text typed inside the text box

3. With the text box as the active element in the Preview monitor, you can begin modifying the basic text attributes in the Avid Titler+. You will probably be familiar with the text attributes of Font selection, Bold, Italic, Underline, Shadow and Justification as they are common to many text editing programs such as Microsoft Word. With control handles visible around the text box, you can also reposition and resize the text from within the Preview monitor.

Figure 16.6 Text attributes can be modified from this area

4. Other more advanced parameters can also be modified and animated from within the Effect Editor. Many of these parameters are replicated in both the Effect Editor and the Avid Titler+ tool so you can use either to modify the title.

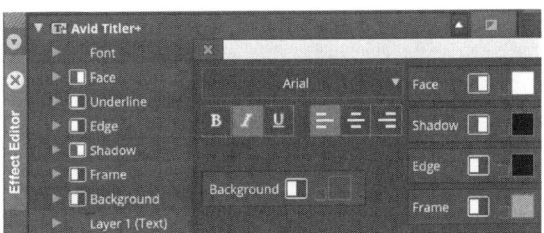

Figure 16.7 Parameters such as Face, Shadow and Edge are replicated in both editing tools.

5. Sometimes the background image is too bright compared to the title, so the creation of an additional background element within the title may help with legibility. To create a background shape, select either the rectangular or circular shape tool. A default shape is created and is visible in the Preview monitor.

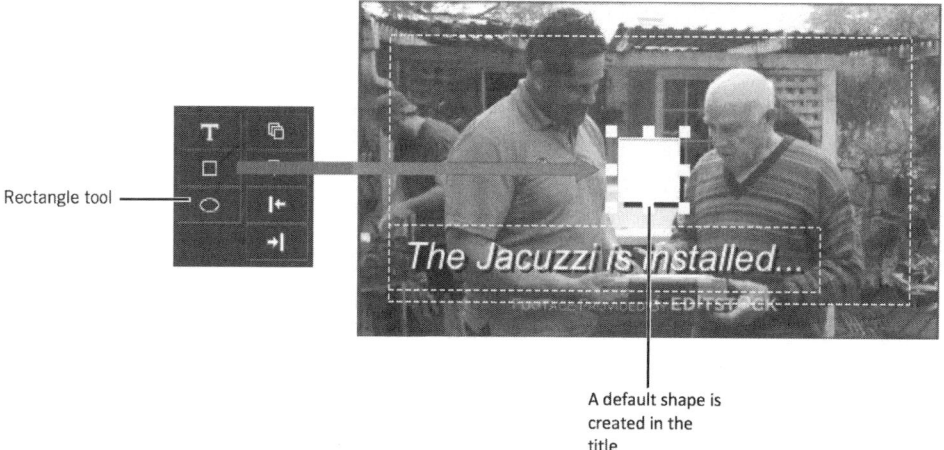

Figure 16.8 Click on the rectangle tool and a default shape is created in the title

6. You can resize and position the shape using the control handles.

7. The layer priority tool can send the background shape behind the text (see figure 16.9).

Figure 16.9 Click on the layer priority tool and the shape is sent behind the text

8. The color and transparency of the background shape can be modified from within the **Face** parameter group in the Effect Editor.

9. Even though the title is behaving like a segment effect, and as a result is applied to the entire segment, you can use keyframes to control when to see the title and when to lose the title within the segment. To dissolve the title up, in the **Preview monitor** park the **Position indicator** where to begin dissolving up the title. Add a keyframe by clicking on the **keyframe** button under the Preview monitor, as shown in figure 16.10.

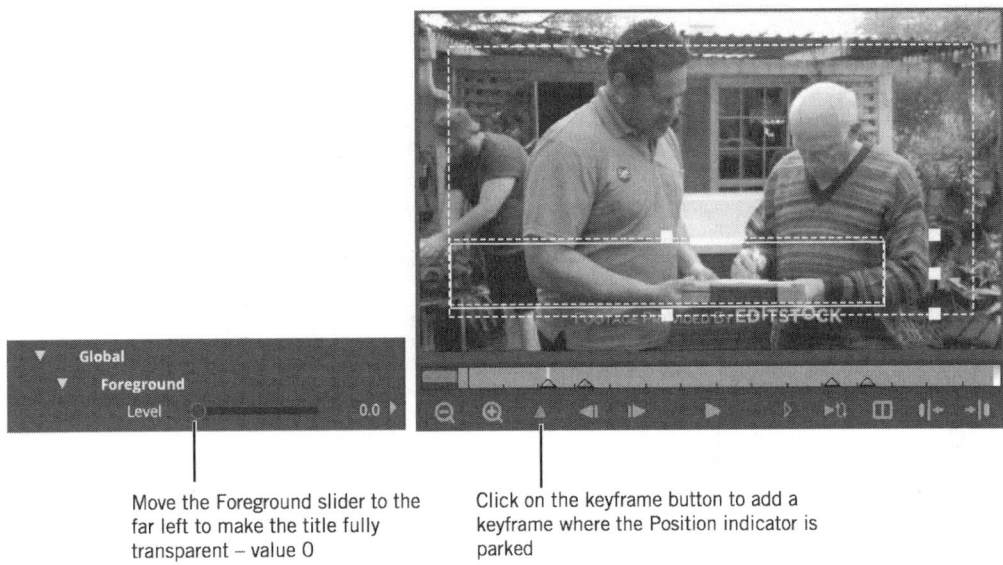

Figure 16.10 Use the Foreground slider in the Global group to make the title fully transparent.

10. In the **Effect Editor**, open the **Global** group of parameters and give the **Foreground** parameter a value of **0**.

11. Add another keyframe where you want the title to be fully faded up and adjust the **Foreground** parameter to a value of 100.

12. Add another pair of keyframes where you want the title to fade out and give the keyframes values of 100 and 0 respectively.

To save the title as a template in a bin, click and drag the **effect icon** out of the Effect Editor window and into the desired destination bin.

To modify an existing title in the timeline, select the segment in the timeline and reopen the Avid Titler+.

To apply a title from a bin to a segment in the timeline, select the segment and double-click the title effect icon in the bin or simply drag and drop the title icon onto a segment in the timeline.

To remove a title from a segment, either:

- Turn on the **Track Selector** for the track the effect is on, park on the effect icon and click the **Remove Effect** button.

- Select the segment in the timeline and press the **Delete key** on the keyboard.

Applying a Title Over More Than One Segment in the Timeline

As seen above, when adding a title to an entire segment the effect behaves like a typical segment effect. However, there are many occasions when you want the title to span across two or more segments. To achieve this, the title behaves more like a Vertical Effect because you apply it to a video track above the background layer.

Before you proceed, make sure you have saved a copy of the title effect as a template in a bin. Then delete the title effect from the segment in the timeline.

To apply a title over more than one segment:

1. If necessary, create a **V2** video track by selecting **Timeline > New > Video Track** from the menu at the top of the screen. (The same menu is available by doing a right-mouse click in the Timeline window.)

2. Turn on the **Track Selector** for **V2** and turn off the track selectors for all other record tracks.

3. Switch the **Track monitor** to the **V2** track.

4. In the timeline, park the blue **Position indicator** where you want to fade up the title and click the **Add Edit** button located in the tool bar at the top of the Timeline window.

5. Move down over the second segment in the timeline and apply another **Add Edit** to the V2 track where you want to fade out the title. Depending on the brightness of your user interface, you should be able to see the two add edits even when there is no clip edited into the V2 track. Even without a clip on a video track, the track is occupied by 'Filler'.

6. Drag and drop the Title template from the bin onto the Filler between the Add Edits (see figure 16.11).

Figure 16.11 Title template applied to Filler on track V2

7. When you play the timeline, you will see the title fade in and fade out over the background image on track V1 but probably not where you expected it to occur. You will need to modify the position of the keyframes in the Effect Editor.

8. Open the Effect Editor and notice that the keyframes are in the same relative positions to each other as they were in the original title. Hold down the **Shift key** and select the first 2 keyframes. Both of them will be highlighted pink.

9. To move the keyframes, hold down the **Alt (Win)** or **Option (Mac)** key and drag the pair of keyframes to the head of the position bar under the Preview monitor (see figure 16.12).

10. Now select the second pair of keyframes and drag them to the end of the position bar under the Preview monitor. Click the **Play Loop** button to check the title fades up and down at the beginning and end of the title on V2.

Figure 16.12 With the first pair of keyframes selected, they can be moved to the start of the title effect.

Review/Discussion Questions

1. A Vertical effect is a special type of Segment effect. What does it allow you to do?

2. How do you control which video track is being monitored when you are compositing multiple layers in the timeline?

3. How does an Avid Titler+ effect behave when it is applied to an entire segment in the Timeline?

4. How does an Avid Titler+ effect behave when it is applied to Filler on a higher-level track than the background layer?

5. How can you save a title as a template?

6. How do you define what part of a Filler track you add an Avid Titler+ effect to?

7. What does adding a title to a Filler track allow you to do compared to adding it to a segment?

EXERCISE 16

 Exercise Break: Exercise 16.1
Pause here to practice what you've learned.

Media: Rock Climber

GOALS

- Add titles to a sequence

Add Titles to Your Rock Climber Sequence

1. Open your **My Second Project_(Student ID)** project and load your latest **Rock Climber** sequence.

2. If you don't already have one, create a V2 video track or a video track higher than the track on which your opening shots are edited.

3. Apply **Add Edits** to the Filler on the higher-level video track so a title will span across two shots at the beginning of the sequence. The duration between the **Add Edits** should be approximately 5 seconds so try to add the last **Add Edit** before of the cut to the front shot of the climber.

4. Apply an Avid Titler+ effect to the Filler, making sure you are monitoring from the higher video track.

5. In **Avid Titler+** select the text box tool and type a suitable title for you Rock Climber story. Use the available text attributes to give your title a style appropriate for the program content.

6. Using keyframes, add fades up and down to the title. The fades should be about ½ second in duration.

7. Now locate the first interview grab where the rock climber is on camera. Remember, there may be a jump cut at the start of the interview grab that you disguised with a FluidMorph effect, so add the title to the longer second segment of the interview.

8. This time, apply the **Avid Titler+** effect directly to the interview clip. The title will last the full duration of the segment.

9. Create a lower-thirds super for the interviewee. His name is *Matt Rodgers*. A lower-thirds super usually has two lines of text. The first line for the interviewee's name and the second line to identify their relationship to the story, or their position if they work for a company, or what they do. In Matt's case, the second line would probably describe him as *Professional Rock Climber*. Create a background shape to sit behind the text.

10. Remember to keep the lower-thirds within the safe title area of the Avid Titler+ window. You would usually sit it in either the bottom left or bottom right corner of the safe title area.

11. Use keyframes to fade the title up and down so it has an on-screen duration of 5 seconds. This is probably shorter than the duration of the segment, so add the keyframes later in the effect, not at the start of the effect.

12. Publish your sequence.

LESSON 17

Exporting Your Video

Media Composer | First provides a simple and direct way of publishing your work to a few popular social media sites. You are already familiar with exporting to YouTube - more broadly though, there are a multitude of formats and a multitude of platforms for which a sequence can be exported from a timeline. For instance, a major motion picture will have one or more versions produced for cinema release, there will be multiple versions for broadcast and online streaming plus DVD, Blu-ray and Ultra HD Blu-ray. Learning how to export your video is a steppingstone to understanding the variety of digital formats and how they impact the size of the file and the quality of the video.

In this lesson you will also explore the process of exporting to a local drive attached to your computer.

Media Used: Jaccuzzi & The Rock Climber

Duration: 20 minutes

GOALS

- Configure the Publish settings for export to a hard drive
- Publish a sequence to YouTube

Exporting Your Video

Apart from the broadcast and feature film industries, exporting a file for the Web is one of the most common types of delivery today. Whether you are posting to YouTube, Vimeo, Facebook or a company Web site, you will first need to export the finished program as a file out of Media Composer | First and then upload it to an internet site. Media Composer | First simplifies the two-step process by combining both in a single tool.

As well as providing the ability to export a sequence and upload it directly to a social media site, Media Composer | First allows you to export a sequence and save the file to a local drive attached to your computer.

Exporting a Sequence to a Local Hard Drive

To export a sequence to a local drive:

1. From the **Jacuzzi** project, load one of the finished sequences into the timeline – either **Scene 7** or **Scene 9**.

2. From the menu bar at the top of the user interface select **File > Publish to > Local Drive ....** Alternatively, right-click on the **Record monitor** and select **Publish to > Local Drive ....**

   The Publish dialog box opens, as shown in figure 17.1. Some settings are greyed out, meaning these options are not available.

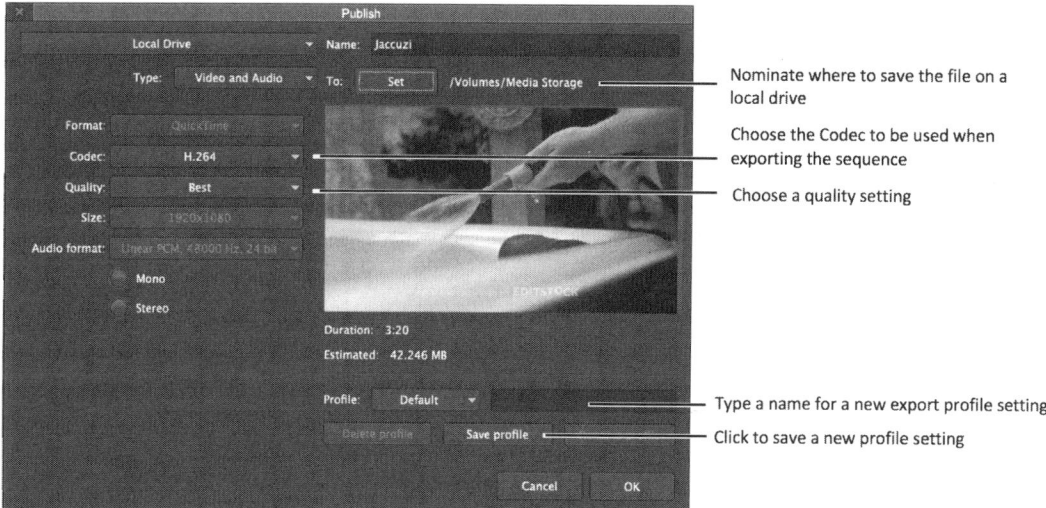

Figure 17.1 Publish dialogue box

3. From the **Type** drop menu select what you want to export from the timeline.

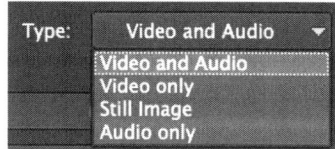

Figure 17.2 Type drop menu

4. Click the **Set** button to navigate to the destination drive and folder.

5. From the **Codec** drop menu select the type of compression you want to apply to the exported file. In this first instance, choose the **H.264** codec.

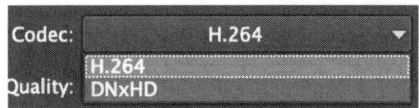

Figure 17.3 Codec drop menu

6. From the **Quality** drop menu, select **Best**. This setting is only available when exporting using the H.264 codec.

Figure 17.4 Quality drop menu

7. Select the **Stereo** radio button. Audio will be exported as a stereo track with left and right channels. The mono option will export the audio as a single channel of audio.

These settings can be saved as a Profile that you can recall whenever you want to export another sequence using the same settings. Type a name for the Profile in the dialogue box and click **Save Profile**. The profile can be recalled from the **Profile** drop menu.

8. Click **OK** and a progress bar will appear indicating how long the export is taking, as shown in figure 17.5.

Figure 17.5 Export progress bar

 While Media Composer I First is exporting, you will not be able to use the application.

9. Once the export is complete, locate the exported file on the destination drive you nominated and play it on the computer desktop. It should be as you expect – the full duration of the sequence, with video and audio and no missing shots.

Re-export the Sequence

Now export the sequence again to the local drive, but this time choose the **DNxHD** codec from the **Codec** drop menu.

When the export is complete, compare the file size of the H.264 version with the file size of the DNxHD version. The DNxHD file size will be considerably larger than the H.264 file but when you play both files there should be no observable difference in video quality.

So, what is the difference? The H.264 codec heavily compresses the file while maintaining a high-quality image. It is an excellent codec when you want to publish a video to the internet. The smaller the file, the easier it is for it to stream over the internet without interruption.

The DNxHD codec is a 'softer' codec that retains more data, and therefore more information, in the exported file than the H.264 codec does. While the larger file size is generally unsuited to playing over the internet, it is ideal as a master format from which other versions can be produced. For instance, it could be used to author a high-quality DVD or Blu-ray disc. DVD and Blu-ray also use heavy compression but recompressing an already heavily compressed H.264 file risks losing more visual information and therefore degrading the picture quality compared to a disc produced from the better DNxHD file. It ultimately comes down to choosing an export file format that suits the intended purpose. Producing a DVD or Blu-ray disc is a publishing step that is not directly available in Media Composer | First.

Exporting to YouTube, Vimeo or Facebook

If instead of choosing the local drive as the destination, you select YouTube, Vimeo or Facebook, Media Composer | First will compress the file using the H.264 codec and upload it directly to your social media account - the two steps in one.

To publish to YouTube (for instance):

1. Load the sequence into the Timeline.

2. From the menu bar at the top of the user interface select **File > Publish to > YouTube** Alternatively, right-click on the **Record monitor** and select **Publish to > YouTube**.

3. When the **Publish** dialogue box appears, notice that you can no longer navigate to a local destination drive or select a codec other than H.264.

4. The dialogue box now includes a **Login** button at the bottom left.

    Figure 17.6 Login button

5. Click **Login** and you will be taken to the YouTube login web page. Once logged in, you may need to provide authorization for Avid to publish to YouTube on your behalf. A message will appear beside the **Login** button indicating that you have successfully logged in to YouTube.

6. Click **OK** and you will be taken to a page in which you can enter details about the movie you are about to export and upload.

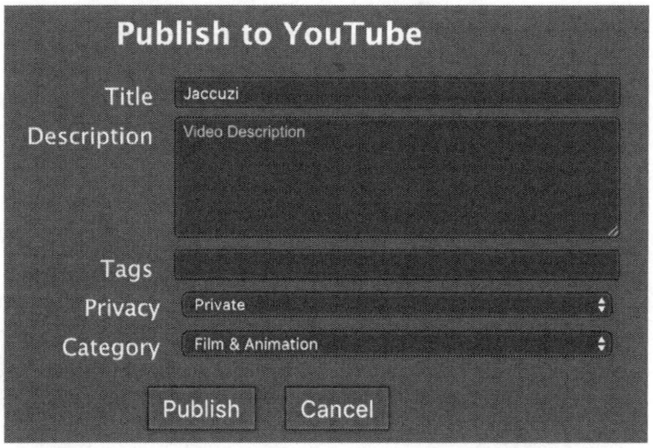

Figure 17.7 Publish to YouTube dialogue box

7. Click **Publish** and the export progress bar will pop up.

Figure 17.8 Export progress bar

8. When the export is complete a Publish Progress window will appear showing you what percentage of the file has been uploaded to YouTube.

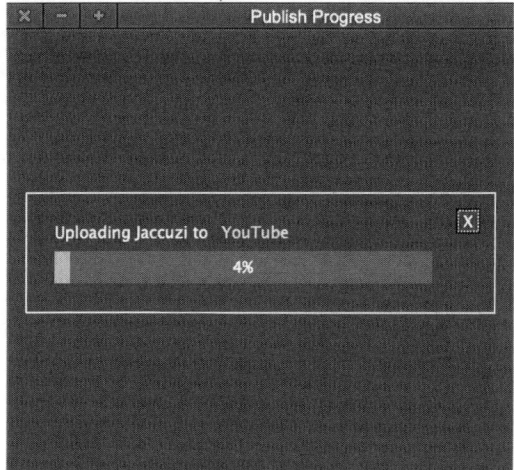

Figure 17.9 Publish Progress window

Understanding the Quicktime Movie Format

When comparing the two files that you earlier exported to the local drive, you may have noticed that both were in the form of Quicktime movies even though they had been compressed using different codecs. QuickTime is still the most common delivery format when exporting to YouTube, Vimeo or Facetime, but as you have seen, not all QuickTime movies are the same. The QuickTime format is nothing more than a container file (often referred to as a "wrapper") that can hold many types of media. To use a metaphor, telling someone that you will give them a QuickTime movie is no more descriptive than telling them you will give them a sandwich. Sure, they know it's not pizza, but there are still many questions you haven't answered. What kind of bread? What's inside? Is it hot or cold?

So, while each social media platform accepts a Quicktime movie, compressed using the H.264 codec, there are subtle differences between those platforms that dictate that each Quicktime movie is created with slightly different parameters to meet the delivery requirements of each platform. Media Composer | First automatically adjusts for those differences when you choose the social media platform you are going to publish to.

Review/Discussion Questions

1. In which menu can you find the **Publish To** command?

2. What publishing destination allows you to change the codec used to export the video?

3. What codec is used to create a file published to YouTube, Vimeo or Facebook?

4. What is one of the obvious differences between a Quicktime movie created using the DNxHD codec compared to one created using the H.264 codec?

5. What advantage would a larger exported file size have?

6. If you had exported your sequence but the exported file contained no audio, what Publish setting would have caused that to happen?

EXERCISE 17

 Exercise Break: Exercise 17.1
Pause here to practice what you've learned.

Media: Rock Climber

GOALS

- Export and Publish to YouTube

Publish Your Rock Climber Story

By now you should have finished editing your Rock Climber story (in your second project), applied segment motion and transition effects, mixed the sound track, created titles and color graded. The final stage is to publish the film.

While you can share your work by publishing directly to a social media platform, it is also advisable that you export a high-quality version to a local drive attached to your computer. This provides a master copy that you can archive for future reference should you ever need to produce a different version for a different publishing platform.

1. Open your **My Second Project** project and load the final sequence into the Record/Timeline windows.

2. Publish the sequence two times – firstly to the social media platform of choice and then to a local hard drive using the highest quality codec.